NORMA FIELD'S

IN THE REALM OF A DYING EMPEROR

"Powerful . . . a searing, persuasive indictment."
—Elisabeth Bumiller, *Washington Post Book World*

"In a style packed with poignant details, important facts and vivid historical description, Field analyzes issues of class, ethnicity and gender, further exploring the murky separation of church and state in contemporary Japan . . . One of the most original and insightful discussions to emerge from recent Japan scholarship."
—*San Francisco Chronicle*

"Brilliant . . . At a time when America and Japan administer nasty bashings to each other on a daily basis, the deeper understanding of Japanese society provided by Norma Field . . . is vital. She bridges the two cultures and dramatizes as few writers could the pitiless price exacted from those ordinary Japanese . . . who made 'high growth economics' possible."   —*Chicago Tribune*

"Rich and complex."   —*The Economist*

"In this remarkable book, Norma Field returns to the land of her birth . . . and examines it through the lens of its own taboos by portraying stories of people who have transgressed them. *In the Realm of a Dying Emperor* is the most insightful book about modern Japanese society that has come along in a decade. Field's ironic yet sympathetic style is both engaging and compelling."
—*Far Eastern Economic Review*

NORMA FIELD

IN THE REALM OF A DYING EMPEROR

Norma Field was born to a Japanese mother and an American father in Occupation Japan. She currently teaches Japanese literature as an associate professor at the University of Chicago. She is the author of *The Splendor of Longing in the Tale of Genji*, and the translator of *And Then* by Natsume Sōseki.

IN THE

REALM OF A

DYING EMPEROR

NORMA FIELD

VINTAGE BOOKS
A DIVISION OF RANDOM HOUSE, INC.
NEW YORK

FIRST VINTAGE BOOKS EDITION, FEBRUARY 1993

Library of Congress Cataloging-in-Publication Data
Field Norma, 1947–
    In the realm of a dying emperor : a portrait of Japan at
century's end / Norma Field.—1st Vintage Books ed.
        p.   cm.
    ISBN 0-679-74189-5
    1. Japan—Politics and government—1945–
2. Nationalism—Japan. 3. Japan—Social life and
customs—1945–   4. Hirohito, Emperor of Japan, 1901–1989.   I. Title.
DS889.15.F54   1993
952.04—dc20   91-51190
                        CIP

Book design by Fearn Cutler
Map by Ikumi Kaminishi
Author photo courtesy of the University of Chicago

Manufactured in the United States of America

6789B

*For Maia and Matty
and the children with whom
they must make a world*

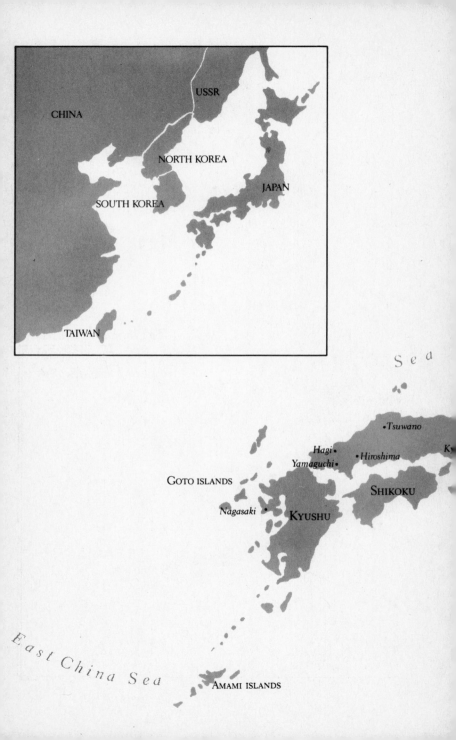

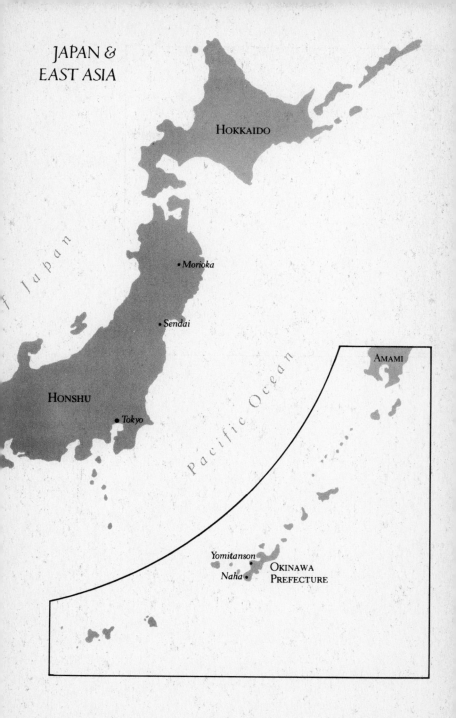

JAPAN &
EAST ASIA

HOKKAIDO

• Morioka

• Sendai

HONSHU

• Tokyo

Pacific Ocean

AMAMI

Yomitanson
Naha •

OKINAWA
PREFECTURE

CONTENTS

PREFACE

EMPEROR HIROHITO of Japan, posthumously known as Emperor Showa, collapsed on September 19, 1988, and died on January 7, 1989. His state funeral, evidently attended by more foreign dignitaries than any other funeral in world history, took place on February 24. Those five-and-a-half months were lived with particular intensity by most Japanese. For the first time since the nation had been transformed by economic prosperity, there was an attempt to reflect on World War II and its legacy, especially on the role of Japan as aggressor as well as victim. At the same time, such newly critical reflection was truncated or repressed altogether by a spectacular exercise in self-censorship.

This book is a meditation on the death of Hirohito, the deaths in the Pacific War (the Fifteen Year War), and the death-in-life quality of daily routine in the world's most successful economy. It is also an act of paying homage to those who resist the comforts of amnesia and the lure of fabulous consumption, who insist on thinking of the past and the present against each other.

More literally than many books, this book depends on others for its existence. My heartfelt thanks to all who appear in it for the generosity of time and spirit they extended to a stranger. My profound debt to family members who are part of this book can only be acknowledged, never discharged. This book is a modest tribute to them, too, especially the womenfolk who raised me with grace at such cost to themselves.

In Okinawa I was guided materially and conversationally by Hiyane Miyoko and Teruo, Kakazu Katsuko, Miyagi Harumi, Shimabukuro Toshiko, Shimojima Tetsurō, Takara Ben, and Terukina Kei. I am also grateful to Kamiyama Shigemi, Muratsubaki Yoshinobu, and Yoneda Masaatsu of Siglo, Ltd.

In Yamaguchi, Urabe Yoriko and Yabuki Kazuo were generous with their insights and hospitality. Hayashi Kenji, Imamura Tsuguo, and Tanaka Nobumasa helped me understand the Christian struggle in modern Japan.

Brian and Michiko Burke-Gaffney, Iwamatsu Shigetoshi, Tsuchida Teiko, and Harada Naō, together with all those drawn to his two-room publishing house, had a hand in the Nagasaki chapter.

The poets Chong Chuwol and Michiura Motoko have a special place in the journey underlying this book.

Kuriyama Masako generously advised and facilitated.

Old and new friends sustained the actual writing by reading the pieces I thrust upon them. I wish I could thank each of them with the particularity they deserve. René Arcilla, Bill Brown, Celia Homans, and Richard Rand expressed unrequired enthusiasm that proved essential through fainthearted periods.

Leslie Pincus and Miriam Silverberg grubbed through the manuscript. Their comments became steadfast companions, prodding me through my self-doubting revisions.

Finally, there is Maria Laghi, who was there in the beginning to make it all possible.

Following Japanese custom, I have cited Japanese names surname first. I have also adopted the forms of reference and address prevailing in their communities for Chibana Shōichi, Nakaya Yasuko, and Motoshima Hitoshi: thus, Shōichi, Mrs. Nakaya, and Mayor Motoshima or simply, the mayor. Titles of Japanese works are given in English translation in brackets. Subsequent references will be to an abbreviated version of the translated title. Except for citations from the official translations of the Imperial Rescript on Education of 1890 and the postwar Constitution, all translations from Japanese-language sources are my own.

IN THE REALM OF A DYING EMPEROR

THE PARADOX OF LAMENTATION

I open the box of paradoxes: "My lord,
we regret the passing of your time as a flame
before the wind. Truly, truly, we
cannot bear this grief. Aigō!
Cries of aigō swirl forth.
At this instant, when you are still of this world,
even as life regrettably exhausts its span
at this instant when you, symbol
of abstraction, neither Great Deity
nor human, are at last, oh at last
    realized as individual
and we rejoice for your sake
at your return to human being:
it is autumn in the era's leftover year
when sympathy dances over the proud profusion
of chrysanthemums in the fields.
My lord, thou needst not die—just yet.
Because the blood of the Great Deity, the source
of common ancestry of the Japanese and Korean peoples—
    your blood—
flowed through his veins, he was conscripted, my father,
    as your own babe, to become
a miner at the Chikuhō coalfields. My father
who, through the regimen of suffering, said he would,
    he was, he had to, if he didn't—
become an upstanding citizen, who said he
memorized the subject's pledge to the Empire:
my father, dispersed as an element
in a clod of archipelago soil

to nourish your reign, your land.
Ah, my lord, thou needst not die.
You, too, because you were not a citizen, had no rights,
so said my father (who changed his ancestral name
    to Boss of the Rice Paddies,
who crowned himself with the title,
    Keeper of Dog-Shit Food)—
words he bequeathed as a shriek before the end,
or as the whisper of an insect breathing its last.

  My lord
thou needst not die just yet.
Live and hear my father's last testament:
I am you! and you are me! hear his lamentation,
and concentrate your forces, your remaining strength,
that the good fortune of
praying from afar, in your shadow,
for your deliverance from the privilege of sovereign immunity
    into freedom,
might be sustained, from yesterday to today, and then
    till tomorrow; ah, my lord
thou needst not die—not as thou art
aigō!

                                        Chong Chuwol*

---

*"Ai no Paradokkusu." *Asahi Jānaru*, October 14, 1988, p. 21.

PROLOGUE

AUGUST IN JAPAN. The skies are brilliant, the air is heavy with the souls of the dead. The New Tokyo International Airport heaves with its own ghostly hordes straining for the beaches of Guam and Waikiki and the shops of San Francisco, Los Angeles, and New York, where everything is cheap, from paper napkins to Vuitton bags. Those who cannot participate in this rite of self-confirmation as members of the newly internationalized breed of Japanese may still join the exodus to the countryside that leaves Tokyo in a sun-blasted silence four or five days of the year. For this is O-bon: time to welcome the souls of ancestors, feast, and then encourage them to return whence they came so that the living can proceed with the business of the living. Less refreshed than their forebears, families struggle home, laden with gifts received in exchange for offerings dragged from Tokyo but a few days earlier. Increased efficiency in the dissemination and satisfaction of taste means that the goods traveling to and from the ancestral home are increasingly indistinguishable. Nature, for its part, gallops in flight from this meeting of city and countryside.

It isn't only folk custom that makes August the haunted month. First the sixth, then the ninth, and finally the fifteenth: Hiroshima, Nagasaki, and surrender. So many souls to be appeased. Television coverage of memorial rites in the two cities has declined precipitously since I was a child. In fact, second city Nagasaki barely makes it to the morning and evening news. Every year, however, in both cities there are still the black-clad representatives of the bereaved, the white-gloved officials, speeches, wreaths, and doves. A scant minority insist on calling August 15 the Anniversary of Defeat rather than, more reassuringly, the Anniversary of the End of the War. (Just across the Japan Sea, in Korea, August 15 is the Return of Light Day, marking the joyous dissolution of the Japanese Empire.) In 1988 a dying Hirohito officiated as usual in the ceremonies held at the giant hall for martial arts constructed for the Tokyo Olympics. He was flown in by helicopter from his summer villa to alight as a frail embodiment of the war, still nullifying all possibility of its discussion. The era closed with his life; does changing a name guarantee the obliteration of memory?

In 1989 it was the new emperor, nasal-voiced and distinctly uncharismatic, and doubtless the more useful for it. He was too long the diligent son waiting in the wings. I don't know how he did on the fifteenth. Since boldly announcing his resolve to protect the Constitution "together with all of you" on his first public appearance after the death of his father—a statement noteworthy not only for its sentiment but for its startling and eloquent use of the second person—he has receded into a predictable cautiousness.

Blistering August has its geographical and temporal role in my own perpetual calendar: birthday month for a biracial child ("one of them war babies!" as the father of a prospective student put it when I guided him and his daughter around the college of my choice in California) bused to school on an American base far from home. Which meant, of course, that there were no school-mates around to celebrate with me. It would have been reckless anyway to invite those delicate sensibilities into a Japanese house-hold. Ephemerally transplanted, pampered by the novel services of maids and chauffeurs, the American children of the Occu-pation and its aftermath were singularly respectful of such dictates as don't drink their water, don't eat their candy. It was better to leave my classmates out, even if my mother could and did pro-duce birthday cakes from *Betty Crocker* or the *Joy of Cooking*, volumes worn with the effort to please her American husband. She invited her second cousins from across the street—three brothers who were closer to me in age—and the girl next door, my best and only friend until our families feuded over six inches of land. That was comfortable enough as long as my father wasn't around to scare them off.

August was also the last month of endless summer vacations, when I reread the same dozen books (especially a bilingual edition of *Little Women* and a battered Modern Library *Jane Eyre*), because I couldn't read enough Japanese, because it was too much trouble for the adults to take me to the school library, and because there was no money to take me anywhere else. Since my father's departure from the family, whether by choice or under duress, my grandparents' business of making and selling black-and-white postcard-sized pictures of American and European movie stars was faltering under the pressures of television and the growing popularity of color posters.

It was the August sun that saw me off when I finally left Japan after high school. It was hot in Los Angeles, too, where my father had been living for some years with his Scottish-immigrant mother under the barbarous palm trees. I met my American relatives for the first time: what d'you want to see first—Disneyland, college, or Forest Lawn? Eager to please, I went to them all, cemetery first and college last.

Since then, August has been the time for leave-taking. After a crammed yet timeless stay in my grandmother's house, the morning comes for the silent ride to the airport, followed by that endless flight over the Pacific and the Alaskan peaks to the American metropolises that have become my home. Then the walled skies of Manhattan or the vastness of Lake Michigan recover their cold unreality, and I am suspended between worlds equally remote.

In August of 1988, I reversed tracks and arrived, daughter and son in tow with husband to follow, to take over the two upstairs rooms of my grandparents' house for a year. The house stands on the plot of land where I was born, delivered by the same midwife who had delivered my mother. This one was built with savings my grandmother had managed from the successes in the 1960s of Robert Fuller and Eric Fleming (of "Laramie" and "Rawhide," respectively, television and my grandparents' business having reconciled themselves by then) and above all, of Zeffirelli's *Romeo and Juliet*. It is the house to which my mother and grandmother had hoped to welcome me upon my graduation from college, until they learned that their worst fears had come true: letting me go off to America had meant, inevitably, the emergence of an American son-in-law.

The house strains to accommodate the four of us with our mostly American bodies. The three of them—mother, grandmother, and grandfather, whose combined ages exceed 230, as my mother is fond of pointing out—help by shrinking their already modest selves into a yet more concentrated diminution. We settle in.

I remind myself that this is necessarily an artificial homecoming. I must become, again, daughter, granddaughter, and even niece, a process akin to regenerating amputated limbs. I know that I will have to shed these same limbs at the end of the year, when my resuscitated capacity to lunch with family while con-

versing amiably about the noonday women's show and reporting
on the obligatory reception attended the previous evening will be
superfluous. My grandmother doesn't even like me to do the
dishes—ostensibly on the grounds that I do it badly, but in fact
because she wants to unburden me of all daily tasks. You have
to do everything by yourself over *there*; we might be getting a
little slow, and we're not much good for anything ("a mended
lid for a broken pot"), but at least we're two women *here*. Before
her determined generosity I am helpless. I am paralyzed by
thoughts of finality. There never will be time to return such
unmeasured generosity, let alone time to share again so extravagantly in the garden-sheltered house.

Experts declare that the surge of speculation in land and stocks
will turn Japan into a more American-style, visibly antagonistic
society. My grandmother blames Nakasone, the prime minister
who flattered Reagan and other Americans with resemblance.
Though she will not admit it, she broods over how much longer
she will be able to stay on the land where she has spent most of
her life. Like many Tokyoites, my grandparents own their house,
but not the land on which it stands. Current regulations provide
renters an uncertain blessing whereby they are entitled to 70
percent of the proceeds from the sales of rental rights. Not un-
reasonably, with her husband entering his tenth decade, my
grandmother worries that when the time comes for title change,
the temple owning her corner lot will raise the rent to the dizzying
heights of market value and then, driven to selling her rights,
she will be hard-pressed to pay the taxes on the proceeds.

Already across the street, next to my granduncle's house (now
quiet, with the three brothers who dutifully attended my birthday
parties grown up and gone), a bulldozer has come in to clear out
an old neighbor's house. The lot is modest, about the size of my
uncle's. His house has three rooms, not counting kitchen and

bath. The developer who bought the adjacent lot is putting up an eight-unit condo, known technically as a "mansion" in Japan. Such multiple-unit dwellings are being squeezed between the sober one- and two-story houses that used to line the streets of this old neighborhood. Taxes make it impossible for most sons to stay on the land inherited from their fathers. They sell to developers and try to buy in places within a two-hour commute of Tokyo, taking with them not only their families but the rising prices of their old neighborhoods. All over Japan, land prices spiral, advancing suburban sprawl. Where can people go on this mountain-crowded, typhoon- and earthquake-prone archipelago? What hubris to send those towers soaring into the sky in Shinjuku, in the heart of the capital, or on the land reclaimed, as it is said, by dumping garbage into an already suffocating Tokyo Bay.

The bulldozer across the street transmits its vibrations to the desk I share with my daughter. My grandmother knows every shrub and wildflower in her garden: that camellia planted when your aunt in Nagasaki graduated from high school, this strawberry geranium from the time we all went climbing in Hakone, do you remember? Her trees give off oxygen for the neighborhood. Her flowers are anticipated by passersby. When her garden is gone, where will the glance alight to find respite from asphalt?

The clichéd expense of subsistence in Tokyo still delivers an initial jolt. For many years the stability of life was ensured by the simple, if computationally awkward, equation of $1 = ¥ 360$. It has already been two decades since that equation, symbol of a seemingly eternal American world order, was dismantled. No numerical fixity has replaced it. This time it takes me a month or more to lose the instinct for instant conversion. Dejected by movie tickets at twelve dollars a person or five apples on sale for four, I would seize upon cotton T-shirts for three dollars each— made, of course, in an Asia that Japan has cast off—and, in a burst of rebellion against austerity, end up with an unusable dozen. I try to settle into the fringes of what is surely a historically fabulous middle-class existence.

It is a spectacle quite distinct from that earlier American paradise of pastel houses fringed with Astroturf-anticipating lawn and enticing gape of pool set discreetly in the rear. Fin-de-siècle Tokyo has no more room for houses of any color. But there are marvelous compensations. The vegetables are unfailingly perfect. The Chinese radishes are pearly white and crisp, the corn full-kerneled and candy sweet, the tomatoes soft vermilion, flavorful but firm. As for the fruit! Now, at the onset of a Chicago autumn, I picture sadly the fruit and vegetable stands of my birthplace with four varieties of delicately green, succulent pears nestling against figs lingering on as their purple deepens. They will be followed by ten varieties of apple; sweet persimmon, rich in vitamin C and thought to lower blood pressure; and finally the mandarin oranges, juicy, easy to peel, and seedless, obstacle to the California orange in bilateral trade negotiations. The mandarin orange reigns through the winter. Spring brings a spell of loneliness, inadequately assuaged by domestic citruses and Florida grapefruit, until the procession of summer fruits begins again with strawberries, loquats, grapes, and peaches.

But at what cost! I don't mean simply that one small melon costs anywhere from twenty dollars (in my grandparents' low-cost neighborhood) to fifty. It doesn't take a farmer to imagine the chemical investment required to maintain such unvarying perfection. I have heard that by some measures, pesticide use in Japan is ten times per capita what it is in the United States. But whatever the hidden threats to health, there are other risks to living in a society where consumers are told that it is they, with their discriminating taste coupled with selfless discipline, who demand, deserve, and receive the best that modern life has to offer.

In Japan, as elsewhere, the allure of late capitalism comes saturated with irony. In Japan, as elsewhere, the citizenry seem not to care. Perhaps it is easier to suspend doubts where general prosperity reinforces an apparent homogeneity, where there are neither obvious oppressors nor unsightly victims. Nature, that trusty aide, is pressed into ever more ingenious service. On television, scenes from the Swiss Alps, the Sahara, or unnameable native ponds sheltering plump birds serve as background, or in more subtle cases a foreground, for the promotion of life insurance, sports cars, and soft drinks. Where can those ponds be, I ask myself, recalling a conversation between a movie director and a publisher of fishing books who agreed it was no longer possible to film such scenes in Japan. Pristine images proliferate as coastlines are paved over and national and local preserves converted into golf courses and ski resorts with governmental blessing. And, as if to capture and transcend this process, commercials flaunt the biotechnological successors to the vegetables now bulging my mother's shopping bag: exquisite baby carrots grow from lush broccoli forests.

Several years ago, soaring land prices effectively terminated the dream of a minuscule home of one's own for most workers in the capital region. Relief from the regimen of work and commute comes at the same time for everyone in a country with more than half the population of the United States, a good part of which is squeezed into the nonmountainous, habitable 2 percent of the land, whose total mass approximates that of the state of California. On holidays (increasing in number as international opinion deems Japanese work habits unfair and duplicitous) and vacations (coming at New Year's and O-bon), there is a national migration in pursuit of a change of scene from the cramped apartment or even the modest house that enthralls its owners in "loan hell." No wonder that work comes to seem preferable to enforced recreation, not to mention familial intimacy. Everyday life in Japan compresses itself toward implosion.

It is unseemly for junior employees to leave before their seniors. In any case, the journey from workplace as office to work-place as bar is much shorter than the train ride sour with the exhalations of besotted men and OL (for "office lady," meaning the young women increasingly college- and junior college-educated who amass savings and spread their wings before leaving the work force for marriage in their mid-twenties).

The compulsory socializing dictated by work, in the form of drinking on weekdays for most men and golf on weekends for the supervisory class, absorbs all "free" time. No wonder, then, that there are children who literally do not recognize the men who are their fathers; and men, who, because of habitual or prolonged absence, find that there is no more room for them at home. A noontime television show posits a father's "home re-fusal" syndrome, so named after the long-established "school refusal" syndrome of children who take to their rooms, if not to their beds, and absent themselves from school for months and even years. The men described as suffering from "home refusal" syndrome have had their places usurped by their children, es-pecially those preparing for entrance examinations, who therefore command the unremitting devotion of their mothers. In acute cases the husbands begin to hallucinate, to commute to work from hospitals, and eventually, to renounce the gesture of home-coming altogether.

At present this phenomenon exists chiefly in the Harlequin sociology realm of the women's television show ("Checklist: Are You Driving Your Husband to Home Refusal Syndrome?"), but Japanese housewives indisputably manage their homes with an efficiency even less disrupted by the presence of infantilized hus-bands than was that of their American counterparts of the fifties, who mostly stayed home except for church, PTA, or scouting. Today a reasonably ambitious Japanese woman will have her children in cram school by fourth grade in order to position them for entrance into a desirable junior high school; if she is only mildly driven, or if her children are already deemed unpromising, the process will be delayed until junior high to prepare for high school entrance.

The process is arduous for both mother and child. The most dedicated mothers, those with children lucky enough to have won entrance to a prestigious cram school, attend their own study sessions on the Saturday afternoons or Sundays when their children are being tested on material engorged during the week. These mothers are told, and they learn to accept, that it is not unusual for children to stop eating altogether until they become habituated to the routine, a process that takes at least one month. Less privileged mothers contribute as they can, meeting their children with hot snacks before driving them to lessons if they are in the suburbs, staying up with them, preparing midnight snacks, and generally servicing them. (Incredulous, I try out on friends the suggestion that mother-son incest, widely acknowledged to be the more prevalent form in Japan, is associated with entrance-examination study. They say it isn't impossible.)

The sole expectation of children is that they study. This fact, and the nature of the study that is so inexorably imposed, have produced a host of side effects ranging from the disturbing (school refusal syndrome) to the terrifying (extreme bullying, tacitly condoned by insensitive or weary teachers, at times culminating in death). In compensation, children are showered with fantastically elaborate toys from birth, and when they get into university, if they work at all it is in order to travel to Canada, the United States, or Switzerland, that perdurable home of nature. Like Japanese adults, Japanese children accumulate savings: by sixth grade, many have all the material goods they can conceive of wanting. They therefore embark on the regimen of the passbook.

In the society they are growing into, the most significant and the only reliable freedom is the freedom to buy ever more refined commodities: exotic vegetables from Belgium or China to supplement the perfected domestic supplies; individual servings of sugar for coffee, sugar for tea in increasingly fanciful packaging; brand-name clothes, watches, and pens from Europe; and lately, a luxury car for the very rich who can't afford to buy homes. Presumably, satiation lies in an unforeseeable future, inasmuch as the yearning for a space to call one's own will go unfulfilled, and the subjection to discipline and the exercise of freedom will continue to meet in a useful confusion in the domain of consumption. For, on the one hand, the extraordinary, ever-intensifying daily sacrifices are justified by the abundance they evidently make possible, which also means there must be a per-petual escalation in the level and quality of abundance. On the other hand, the austere regimen imposed on men, women, and children is necessary precisely to maintain discipline in the face of voluptuous plenty, to ensure the continued production of the unnecessary. Recently, consumption as discipline has found its ideal expression in the exaltation of bodily hygiene to heights as yet unmatched even in the United States. Consequently, an ever-growing choice of sinks especially designed for the daily shampoo and electronic bidets (in a culture historically addicted to bathing) must be fitted into already bursting domestic spaces.

I retrace old patterns in the hopes of making myself at home. Most often, that means a trip to a shopping arcade in the neigh-borhood my grandparents occupied before evacuating to the countryside under intensified American bombing in 1945. The arcade, now covered with fancy plastic roofing with sliding par-titions for air and sunshine, is lined with mom-and-pop stores, the inevitable McDonald's, always bustling, and the occasional franchise of a chain claiming lower prices for televisions, rice cookers, camcorders, and batteries than Akihabara, fabled elec-tronics capital of the world. To the strains of "Three Coins in a Fountain," I wander past the gift shop with nested Lucite boxes, glass rocks, and other tempting baubles; glance at the kimono stores for items suggestive of tradition to serve as Christmas gifts to America; make my way through the miraculously low-priced children's shorts, pajamas, and socks to select a pair of pants bearing the words, "If your heart belongs to Daddy . . . Delicious, my dear! You've discovered my pet spread for cold cuts! *Celebrity* BRILLO. It works! And a 100%." My addiction to this form of shopping, with the clapping and calling of brash male clerks, samples of dumpling, aroma of roasting tea—so much celebration of buying and selling, living proof of the arcane distribution system contributing to the U.S. trade deficit—revives slowly but steadily.

I nurture this nascent sense of belonging by bringing back tokens of the arcade world to my grandmother and mother. My mother needs refreshment from her chief preoccupation, the administration of her father's existence. My grandfather is a man who broke a tray on his wife's head when he came home at two in the morning to find that she had let his rice burn (she was pregnant with my aunt next door, her third child, yet had no relief from her routine of cooking and cleaning, without running water or gas, for five live-in employees in addition to managing the business); who ran from the house with a five-thousand-yen bill clenched in his teeth, which he had squirreled away when family fortunes were at an ebb; who, in more prosperous days, outfitted a mistress with a set of false teeth and was foolish enough to record the same in a diary subsequently discovered by his wife. I should note, however, that he is also a man who was decorated in his early eighties for having "dedicated sixty years to the promotion of Western cinema in Japan."

Acute symptoms of high blood pressure in his fifties gave my mother and grandmother the first opportunity to encroach upon my grandfather's autonomy. The family doctor pronounced him a "drunk teetering on a rooftop whose fall should surprise no one." My grandmother promptly formulated an unvarying breakfast of peanut butter toast, powdered skim milk, and fresh fruit, reinforced by a draconian reduction in the use of soy sauce, principal source of flavor in Japanese cuisine, and in the absolute quantity of food intake. There were other challenges, however; for if it was one thing to ban domestic smoking, it was quite another to enforce it on my grandfather's daily rounds to the offices of MGM and Warner Brothers, the editors of movie magazines, the middlemen and retailers in the crammed and exquisitely tawdry entertainment district downtown. It was decided that he should be followed. These missions were usually undertaken by my mother and occasionally by my as yet unmarried aunt in Nagasaki. Lacking resources, they simply disguised themselves with glasses and struggled to keep up with my grandfather's prodigious pace, except, of course, as he paused at train stations or corner tobacco shops for a cigarette. Drinking was a similarly intractable problem.

Perhaps it was inevitable that efforts should eventually be redirected to monitoring his paper fetish, even though it involved no expense and the health risks were presumably negligible. My grandfather hoarded napkins from department store restaurants, posters from movie companies, envelopes and bags of all sizes from publishers. These were brought home to be piled in aggressively precarious stacks. Today, four decades later, along with his toothpaste and soap, my grandfather has his toilet and tissue paper rationed. Keeping her father from paper theft occupies a considerable portion of my mother's waking and even sleeping energies. (One night she clocked him asking to blow his nose at 1:32 and 2:05 a.m.) My mother, beginning to suffer from osteoporosis, is convinced that forty years' worth of calcium from the powdered skim milk has left the old man indecently strong. I try to distract her with sweets and sweaters from the arcade.

It is several years since I have spoken to my grandfather. What seemed several decades ago to be a willfully selective loss of hearing has grown into a massive imperviousness to the world. Other than through fierce gesticulation, communication entails writing. When confronted with the furious traces of his wife's black magic marker, he maintains a stony silence, except when impelled by rage to denunciation. The circumference of his activities has been vastly reduced since the days of his imperious forays into the vigorous chaos of Tokyo. Every Sunday, my mother draws up his exercise chart for the week. It is the same chart each week, with the days of the week written horizontally above a vertical column of prescribed hours. He himself draws loops in the empty blocks to indicate completion, four times a day, of the course leading from his room through the corridor filled with our spillover books and coats, past the kitchen, through the television room, then back to his room. He takes a good ten minutes for each circuit, a distance the rest of us traverse in twenty seconds.

Even this world is further reduced on those occasions of physical deterioration when he takes to his bed, moaning and even shrieking over back pain, provoking my grandmother's constant ministrations. These bouts are new, and come as a surprise after so many years of unwavering, reassuringly nasty activity. I should have guessed at changes in the dusty body when, during one of its exercise rounds, it struck out, without glance or pause, at its daughter, my mother. The combination of randomness and malicious accuracy was startling. During the bad spells, the randomness gains ground, and the intentionality of malice recedes behind whimpers. The progression is clear: he will eventually lose the desire, then the will, and finally the capacity to convert sounds into words. In the meanwhile, between bouts he is still able to harass his great-grandson, my son. By the end of our stay, my grandmother resorts to taping a purple ribbon down the center of the table between them. There will still be territorial skirmishes, with such instruments as drawing pads, markers, and speeding toy cars on the one side, stacks of old astrological calendars and hearing aid with long-dead batteries on the other. During cease-fires my grandfather watches his favorite TV show, a period piece in which a hero arrested in handsome old age wisely solves mysteries and lays swords to rest all over Japan. This series, tirelessly rerun, was the favorite of the late Emperor Showa as well.

When that figure collapsed on September 19, 1988, my grandmother was sympathetic. In age Hirohito was midway between her and my grandfather. (I should note that to write *Hirohito* is an awkward gesture. The monarch is never so intimately referred to in Japanese, yet this use of the first name is standard and therefore seemingly neutral in English. "His Majesty the Emperor," the Japanese newspaper mode of reference, suggests a bureaucratic reverence; "Hirohito" carries simultaneous reverberations of wartime vituperation and friendly postwar condescension.) After the unprecedented surgery of the previous year, performed only after much debate over the propriety of piercing the jeweled body with a knife, my grandmother thought the old man was finally being left to indulge his botanical and marine-biological fancies at the imperial villa. Like many others in a country where patients are not normally informed of terminal conditions, she believed the benign diagnoses assiduously disseminated by the media. She made no attempt to reconcile her sympathy with the tenets of an antimilitarist socialism she had innocently and passionately espoused since winning the vote after the war.

In the days, weeks, and then months after September 19, the citizens of Japan were treated to daily reports on the input and output of blood from the emperor's body. Two relatively unfamiliar words entered the national vocabulary: *toketsu* and *geketsu*. As terms, these occupy an ambiguous zone, more forbidding than "vomiting blood" and "rectal bleeding," less clinical than "hematemesis" or "melena." Throughout the fall, after the initial drama of *toketsu*, every newspaper carried a box indicating the detection of a slight amount of *geketsu*, the quantity of compensatory transfusion, and the reassuringly homely readings of temperature and pulse. By the time of his death three and a half months later, the emperor had received 31,000 cc, or approximately thirty liters, of blood in transfusion. I heard, but couldn't confirm, that it cost about $170 per cc. Vampire jokes began to circulate. Later, journalists assessing media coverage of the emperor's illness and death observed that use of the word *geketsu* was tantamount to a second human declaration. (The first took place in January of 1946 under American supervision.)

For the modern emperor of Japan, the name of his reign is the name by which he will be known posthumously. The birth and death dates of every Japanese citizen, as well as of all events, national and international, are expressed as a combination of reign name and year. The emperor himself lives namelessly ("His Majesty the Emperor") but intimately with the name of his death. Thus, he who was known in the West as Hirohito became Emperor Showa on January 7, 1989, and babies born on January 8 were celebrated for arriving with the dawn of Heisei, which is the name by which the present emperor will be known after he dies.

The death of the human being now safely remembered as Emperor Showa—"Shining Peace"—was surely one of the best prepared in history. The only unforeseen complication was the length of time the dying was to take. Hirohito was the first Japanese emperor to die under the postwar Constitution stipulating that sovereignty rests with the people. From the instant of his death to the staging of his burial some forty days later, the state choreographed an elaborate dance representing constitutionality and mystery, Western modernity and Eastern tradition. This dance had to suggest a history at once progressive and alluring, glossing adroitly over the interlude of war to elaborate the forty years of postwar prosperity. Above all, it had to imperceptibly accommodate the realities facing the world's leading economy.

For even the temporality of the emperor is comprehended within the temporality of contemporary capitalism. How many days could the stock exchange be closed? banks? government offices? Still, even if the banks had to close, their computers would keep running, maintaining the blood supply of the world.

Hirohito's collapsing without dying meant that these ingenuities had to be sustained over a far longer period than intended. Daily reverential reporting on the body of the emperor throughout the island nation both provoked and reinforced a massively orchestrated exercise in "self-restraint," or *jishuku*, a newly popularized word. Some of the losses—the expunging of felicitous wording such as "nice day" from commercials, and of alcohol from political fund-raisers—were not regrettable in themselves. But autumn is a time of renewed vigor, commercial and otherwise, of recovery from brutal July and August. So it was with a certain regret that neighborhood festivals were canceled one after another, along with weddings in November, the preferred month for matrimony. On field days at school, races began limply without the pistol shot. Not surprisingly, the costs of abstemious behavior were borne unevenly, by the makers and vendors of plastic masks, costume jewelry, and goldfish for scooping at carnival stalls; by caterers for weddings and other festivities; by taxi drivers who transported merrymakers and entertainers who kept them happy once they got there. Like the vampire jokes, the frustration of such people occupying the extensive periphery of prosperity circulated beneath the surface of official reporting.

In addition to the national promotion of "self-restraint," numerous preparations were made for the day of the unthinkable itself: movie theaters consulted department stores about whether to close, and for how many days, or how to stay open and still convey mourning. Athletic facilities consulted movie theaters. Decisions were made about supervising audience conduct at the instant of the announcement, about the status of the game, depending on the inning. Television stations, led by the government-owned NHK, wrangled only slightly over the number of days to be set aside for special programming: other than documentaries chronicling his late majesty's achievements, to be followed by documentaries chronicling the prolonged but altogether promising crown princeship of his son the new emperor, nature programs were to be the principal fare. FM stations stocked up on subdued recordings of Bach and Beethoven. Most of these arrangements had been in place for several years. In the course of "self-restraint" they were refined and often augmented.

Most of the measures other than media programming proved superfluous. Emperor Showa lingered well beyond baseball season into the new year. His death was announced early on January 7, a Saturday morning. Schools were in winter recess until the following Monday. The holiday rush was safely over for the stores. It was the last day of New Year's week, the crucial revenue-gathering period for Shinto shrines. The shrines, to be sure, had not altogether abandoned themselves to fate, for the national Shinto headquarters had discreetly announced in late 1988 that in the event of the unthinkable, worshipers would still be received for the customary New Year's observations. Like many religions, Shinto abhors pollution by blood and death. The emperor of Japan is the chief Shinto priest in his private capacity as the direct descendant of the sun goddess Amaterasu. Still, the shrines could not forgo the income to be generated by the sale of felicitous arrows and amulets appropriate for the forthcoming Year of the Snake.

So, on the crucial day, "self-restraint" amounted to minimizing the incessant announcements on public transport and operating stores with neon signs turned off and clerks wearing black arm bands moving to the notes of a Bach fugue. In his passing, the emperor of shining peace granted his nation respite from the incessant aural and visual stimuli of its fabulous economy. Rectal bleeding as sign of humanity.

Journalists, in reporting on the emperor's demise, were still under the spell of the "chrysanthemum taboo," so-called after the imperial crest, that crystallized in the 1960s through several episodes of right-wing attack on writers and publishers deemed guilty of transgressing imperial honor. Journalistic language used throughout Hirohito's illness and death revealed the continuing force of the taboo. Hirohito's death was reported as a *hōgyo* by every newspaper in the country except for the two dailies of Okinawa Prefecture and the *Red Flag*, the organ of the Japan Communist Party. According to standard dictionaries, only four Japanese can have this special word for death applied to their passing: the emperor, the empress, the dowager empress, and the grand dowager empress. All other Japanese, all other human beings for that matter, die ordinary deaths, linguistically speaking. There was considerable debate in journalistic circles as to whether Hirohito's death should be thus absolutely distinguished.

The issue was whether journalistic prose should be uniquely disrupted by honorific markers for actions and objects associated with the emperor and his immediate family. Japanese, like many languages, is extensively developed for the expression of social hierarchy. Prefixes, personal pronouns, and verbal endings vary according to whether speaker and addressee are mother and daughter, mother and daughter-in-law, father and son, employees separated by one year in seniority, teacher and parents, or seller and buyer (whether butcher and housewife, restaurant manager and diner, or banker and company president). That there are, of course, provisions for speakers and addressees of the same sex, age, and status, reinforces, rather than denies, the hierarchical marking of every utterance. I was once reluctant to address adults, typically teachers, in English because "you" sounded too baldly intrusive, being so flattening, so equalizing. Now, on visits to Japan, I fall prey to something like a sickness, as if table legs had lost their metaphoricity, before the oppressive, formulaic humility or arrogance I must assume in my daily dealings, all the while recognizing that the very possibility of intimacy is embedded in the tyranny of the language. The luxury of addressing my grandmother without honorifics is inseparable from the obligation to use them with her brother's wife, my grandaunt.

One of the achievements of modern Japanese writing was the development of a seemingly neutral mode that minimized such status and gender distinctions, effacing both distance and intimacy. In the instance of the emperor's death, the stylistic objectivity of journalistic Japanese had been irredeemably compromised by the repeated use of honorifics in reporting his illness. No wonder that, for all their soul-searching, journalists uniformly produced the event as a *hōgyo*.

Not that they were alone in their abjection. There were the masses of nonbelieving practitioners of "self-restraint," for instance; there were nonbelievers who even thronged to the palace to sign their names during the bleeding and after the dying because everyone was doing it, because they might get on television, because they—the young ones—thought of the emperor as a sweet, vulnerable old man who reminded them of a teenage idol who had recently committed suicide. There were also the cynics who emptied the shelves at rental video stores because they knew the emperor had nothing to do with them and they found the reverential programming insufferably dull.

I fear the nonbelieving observers of social custom and the confident cynics more than the believers who embarrassed their cosmopolitan compatriots by kneeling and touching their heads in grief on the ground outside the palace, and more than the right-wing extremists with their blaring trucks. I am fearful of the latter, too, because rarely, but memorably, they have killed and maimed, and their terrorizing behavior all but obliterates the fragile impulse to dissent. The sophisticated cynics do not see that they cannot disengage by choice: in their submission to an education that robbed them of their childhood, that holds their own children hostage through secret records passed from school to school, reinforcing an ever more tyrannical regimen of competition, in their surrender to a crushing routine of work and commute, they are participants in a compulsory game in which the emperor card will turn up as the joker.

This is not to say that the emperor, or even the emperor system, as intellectuals would more chastely put it, is to be held solely responsible for the state of affairs in Japan today. Contrary to propaganda, the foundations of the contemporary system are hardly ancient. The nineteenth-century statesman Itō Hirobumi lamented the absence of an indigenous belief system adequate to providing the psychic fuel and discipline necessary to hurtle society into a Western-style modernity overnight. The solution, at that point, was to snatch the young Emperor Meiji from the shadowy court life of Kyoto and transform him into a monarch in Western military costume for deployment in the new capital city of Tokyo and throughout the nation. The image of this emperor, who died in 1912, is still familiar in Japan. Heavy eyebrows and braided uniform suggest a warrior in commanding stillness. This was in fact a photograph of a painting, for even the image of a god-king could not be exposed to ordinary eyes. There we have it: modern technology in the service of mystery in the service of a ruthless rationalization and industrial capability. The mystery makes the rationalization palatable, hence feasible; the rationalization ensures a continual hunger for mystery—for transcendence of the economic through an uncalculated leap into a past that never was.

Hirohito's funeral in February of 1989 was a celebration of the successes of Japanese capitalism. How else explain the unseemly media preoccupation with the number of heads of state in attendance, reminiscent of an Olympic medals count? In spite of strenuous precautions, the long-repressed question of war guilt had resurfaced during Hirohito's dying. The gathering of world leaders made that question moot by bearing witness to the stunning achievements of Japanese modernity. Not only was the dead man not guilty, but the Japanese economic miracle was subtly but ineluctably linked to a culture that reveres emperors and provides them with ancient, august burial.

The equation of economic success with kingly presence is of course a venerable one, detectable even in myths of archaic rulers as the embodiment of cosmic order, most crucially demonstrated by agricultural abundance. In the Japanese nineteenth century an imperial system refurbished to serve as potent symbol for unchanging tradition was harnessed to an economic transformation envisioned initially without but subsequently within a cosmos defined by the terms of Western modernity. After World War II the American Occupation sent Hirohito on a tour of the war-ravaged land, above all to be seen by his people (American republicanism being willing to subscribe to royal magic where expedient), and occasionally to inspirit them with the bisyllabic utterance that became his trademark: *ah sō*, "is that right," delivered when, for example, the man in the crowd whom he had favored with conversation indicated that he had lost his house and all his family in the firebombing of Tokyo. Visibility was incomparably expanded in 1959 when his son Akihito, now emperor, married Michiko, miller's daughter or princess of the flour industry according to one's perspective, before the eyes of all Japan, for virtually every household had purchased a television set for the occasion.

The domestic style of the new couple, Akihito and Michiko, was widely disseminated through television and women's magazines. It was an appealing household, blossoming under the gaze of the benevolently aging emperor and empress. The image called out to the youth of Japan: work hard and you, too, may one day have a living room where children play musical instruments and read books at your knee. Erstwhile student activists who had joined the staffs of such magazines thought they could still undermine imperial ideology by displaying the once-sacred images on pages to be tossed into train station rubbish bins or traded in for toilet paper. Twenty years later, the same magazines would carry portraits of the now middle-aged couple in elegant mourning to complement chronicles of the human side, so-called, of Hirohito's life.

One month after the funeral, it was a thing of the remote past. The passage of a thousand years is as nothing compared to the power of the media to make births, deaths, earthquakes, famine, and genocide fade into a dusty past. As it happened, the media did not have to strain to distract the public during the spring and summer of 1989. Pursuit of a major bribery scandal, which had been disrupted by the imperial dying, was restored to the lime-light, to be fortified by disclosures of sexual indiscretion and the imposition of a hated sales tax. As the majority of the print and visual media relentlessly converted controversy into entertain-ment, some citizens insisted on contesting the general presump-tion that they neither could nor would choose to see, to think, or to care about the world in which they lived. Thus, the great Socialist victory in the upper house elections of July 1989 created a painfully hopeful moment when it almost seemed as if one-party rule, which had already blanketed four decades, did not have to stretch into infinity.

I left, once again, in spirit-haunted August. I wish I could have stayed, not to witness the wasteful anachronism of the mak-ing of a monarch but to savor a while longer the rupture of smugness by Socialist chairwoman Doi Takako and her cohort of women. I wish I could have stayed to hear the new stories being told about the war, stories newly introspective about Jap-anese aggression in Asia, which render more compelling the old stories about Japanese victimization by America in 1945. I wish I could have stayed to follow my grandmother's garden into au-tumn: the merely reliable phlox growing brilliant, the chrysanthemums in wild abundance, the oleaster sweetening the sharp dusk air.

I would have stayed, but I couldn't, so I content myself with my mother's letters, filled with suggestions for taking the bitterness out of eggplant and recipes for replenishing my repertoire, luxuriously depleted after a year of my grandmother's indulgence; tinged with angry sorrow over the distraction produced by media flutter over the prospect of princely marriage and anxious watchfulness over the inevitable bickering, slander, and even serious discussion as the Socialists imagine taking power after forty years of abstract opposition.

From across the Pacific and half a continent, I sense an autumnal cooling of those impulses to question the conditions of membership in the world's most orderly and prosperous society. My mother's letters grow dispirited. I force myself to read on, knowing she doesn't have the luxury of denunciation, dismissal, and departure. Nor do my new friends and acquaintances, met through the very despair born of the year of the emperor's dying and death. Where there are neither visible oppressors nor victims, and where the memory of historical suffering has grown remote, freedom becomes subtle, banal, and finally, elusive. To call attention to its flight amidst pervasive prosperity is a thankless undertaking. Most who embark on such a venture have not chosen it. They have been driven to it, by vivid confrontation with the residues of historic oppression, by encounters with victims and oppressors, who are, after all, produced even in times of prosperity and peace as well as war, and finally, by recognition of the repressiveness of everyday life, a recognition they cannot dispel in spite of the potency of common sense, most especially the belief in the existence and importance of social harmony. I had the good fortune to meet such people, ordinary people— that is to say, extraordinary resisters in a fin-de-siècle Japan that issues no calls for resistance. They are bound to this society. And refusing, against overwhelming odds, to surrender to its rewards.

I need to remember what I came to know of their lives, both familiar and strange, to learn it and imagine it against the continued celebration of coercive consensus on one side of the Pacific and mounting fury over waning supremacy on the other. Here, then, are my sentences of learning and imagining: for bearing witness against the indifference of time and the hostility of space.

October 1989

I

OKINAWA

A SUPERMARKET OWNER

EVERY NIGHT, on the weather report in Tokyo, a section of the television screen is carved out to make room for Okinawa. First comes a satellite view of east Asia with the Japanese archipelago arching from the continent. This image translates what could once have been a map of the Greater East Asia Co-Prosperity Sphere into splotches of differing density. It is a display of science, with an excess of precision that to the untrained eye fails to supply the gratification of unambiguous boundaries. These emerge in the next screen, in which Japan is isolated with Okinawa pasted on to the corner. It might be better to refer instead to "the Ryukyuan archipelago," since "Okinawa," strictly speaking, is the name of the main island, which is, to be sure, the only blip visible in that segregated part of the screen. (Okinawans say that the relation of Okinawa to the rest of Japan is reproduced in the combined abjection and pride of the outlying islands toward Okinawa Island.) Geographic appellation always carries the burden of history, and it is therefore not easy to decide which name is less tainted by the record of oppression.

For, from the vantage point of a Japan centered in Tokyo, even when Tokyo was known as Edo, both names have signaled the alien and the lesser. These fifty-odd islands, jewels of the sea, did not belong to Japan until recently. Unified under a monarchy in the early fifteenth century, Ryukyuans ranged the seas, prospering through trade with various regions in Japan, China, Korea, and southeast Asia, and enriching their own practices in weaving, dyeing, dance, and music. In the beginning of the seventeenth century, the kingdom fell under the control of the Shimazu clan from southwestern Japan, and Ryukyuans became vassals of a powerful vassal of the shogun in Edo. In 1868 Edo became Tokyo, and the following year, Edo Castle became the Imperial Palace for the young man to be known posthumously as Emperor Meiji. Nine years later the Meiji government incorporated Okinawa Prefecture into a centralized, bureaucratic state apparatus, and the zealous modernizers in Tokyo, perhaps displacing their own anxieties vis-à-vis the West, proceeded to treat it as a retarded child in need of special disciplinary measures. During the last months of the Pacific War, Okinawa Prefecture was uniquely subjected to land battle in a strategy for deferring defeat for mainland Japanese and their emperor. After surrender, the scorched, corpse-filled island prefecture was ceded to U.S. forces for indefinite occupation, and once again it became known as the Ryukyus. This arrangement lasted until 1972, when the islands were reincorporated into Japan as Okinawa Prefecture. The process was represented with affected innocence as either a "reversion" or a "restoration."

It is commonly said that the Japanese islands can be fitted into the state of California. (And also that the value of that land, which is one-twenty-fifth the land mass of the United States, is twice the value of the latter.) Of that one-twenty-fifth, Okinawa occupies less than one-one hundredth, but that fails to take into

account the startling, cobalt-green sea, where so much of Ryukyuan history has unfolded. How is sovereign territory calculated?
Do those secure entries in almanac, encyclopedia, and dictionary
pursue the alterations of coastline, whether by silting of the red-
clay Okinawan soil into the sea, or by the concrete solidification of
mainland coastal waters? If its seas were included, Okinawa would
claim a territory amounting to 50 percent of the mainland. There
is, of course, a certain absurdity in solidifying the other islands
into a "mainland," especially with the Asian continent looming
just behind, but that succinctly reflects the double isolation of
Okinawa, sole island prefecture in a nation of islands, inclined to
represent itself, with a hint of proud grievance, as an island nation.

A memory from my own adolescence: the participation of a
team from Okinawa, still under American rule, for the first time
in the summer Japanese high school baseball championships in
Kōshien Stadium, Osaka. Unfolding under the August sun, this
sports event was accentuated in those days with traces of the
Pacific War. Widows of once-promising pitchers attended in re-
membrance. (They wouldn't have been called "pitchers" then,
but *tōshu*, "throwers"; for after Pearl Harbor, those aspects of
enemy culture still to be tolerated had to be cleansed through
awkward transposition into sinicized Japanese neologisms.) Unused to national competition, the Okinawan team predictably lost
in the first round. High school baseball is normally charged with
ritual: crew-cut players line up at home plate to bow to each
other and the umpire before the game; at the end, the winning
team returns for the school song, and lyrics extolling youthful
purity, lofty ambition, and harmony with nature fill the television
screen against the background of the school flag sliding up the
pole; the defeated, meanwhile, bow in tearful chagrin before the
first- or third-base stands. Managers have been known to im-
molate themselves for Kōshien-related failures. Given this training of national sensibility, powerful chords were struck when the
Okinawan team began scraping up soil from the stadium—soil

of the homeland—and putting it into plastic bags to take back along with their passports. Upon their return, however, American authorities confiscated the precious keepsake. Poor Okinawa, I thought. Poor Okinawa, wicked America, and possibly, even probably, poor Japan.

That was all the imagination and knowledge I had then, growing up in the shadow of American military bases during the Occupation and ensuing Pax Americana. The 1964 Olympics in Tokyo celebrated the hard-won independence of African and some Asian nations and most especially the miraculous rebirth of Japan from the ashes of defeat. Not only had the Japanese cleaned up wartime rubble, but they were steadily stripping themselves of Asian backwardness to concoct an original imitation of American life. The promotion of an American-style democracy under American tutelage, spurred by the need for a pillar of freedom in the Pacific, was rewarded with U.N. membership in 1956. I didn't foresee that Japanese would soon happily accept designation as honorary whites by the South African government. Or that the Olympics were a display of High Growth Economics, a dress rehearsal for the funeral of Emperor Showa in February 1989, by which time Japan would have overtaken America even in Overseas Development Assistance (ODA)—building bridges to nowhere in Nigeria and sending wrong-gauge railroad cars to the Philippines—such being the more beguiling examples of how "we Japanese don't have much experience in world leadership."

Wicked America. By which I meant the America of officers' clubs, dependent schools, chapels, PXs, and native maids and drivers. The Olympic Village for the 1964 Tokyo Games sprung up on the former site of one such never-never land, Washington Heights by name, where I went to school for six years. Although I had been taken to the Ernie Pyle Theater to see *Peter Pan* and to the dispensary with its strange smells and huge pink-and-white nurses in order to be kept on an American immunization schedule, my first serious introduction to America came with school registration in Washington Heights. That marked the beginning of my struggles to produce color with waxy Crayolas; to sing songs with incomprehensible, evidently silly lyrics such as "she'll be coming 'round the mountain when she [who?] comes" or "Yankee Doodle went to town a-"; to Plédge Ăllégiănce tó thĕ Flág, a mysterious enough affair even without the insertion of "under God" in my second-grade year, the year my father abandoned, or was expelled from, the family; to negotiate my way around the labyrinth of classrooms, first in the main building, then in Quonset huts surrounding Play Area A or later Area D, after the inspired nomenclature of military administration.

Every day a fleet of chocolate-colored buses brought the children who lived off-base to the grandeur of the Heights, and every afternoon at 3 p.m., we ran across gravel and slope from the Quonset huts to the parking lot. We rushed because there was always a certain anxiety about missing our buses, an anxiety abetted by the timing of the color guard in lowering the flag. We had to halt in our tracks when that happened, and we watched with a pleasurable tension because it was said that if even one corner of the Stars and Stripes touched the ground, it would have to be burned. I should have known that there was no need to worry, for the bus drivers were as transfixed as we.

On the bus there was much talk about colonels, lieutenants, and majors, which I didn't understand since my father was by then a civilian employee of the U.S. Armed Forces. What I did understand was that the zone between base and maid-cleaned home swarmed with germs. No matter how sultry the wait when the bus had a flat tire during summer school, we sat stoically rather than sip "native" water. When the bus dropped me off, I was always met by my grandmother, even though I had only to cross an eight-foot-wide street to reach the gate. It was an unmistakably native woman waiting to lead me to an unmistakably native house. How did I explain her to my bus mates? Did I tell them she was the—my—maid? Did I wait until the bus turned in the dust to cross the street and pass through the gate?

On the other hand, once I was in the house, my father's oversized frame was equally embarrassing. He never learned to stoop in passing from room to room. His hulking frame kept my playmates away on weekends. He listened intently to the Far East Network. At night, as I lay beside my grandmother, I could hear the refrain to "The Yellow Rose of Texas" drifting from my parents' bedroom. He read the *Pacific Stars and Stripes*. He argued with my mother over Eisenhower versus Stevenson and U.S. atmospheric testing of hydrogen bombs over Bikini, another island in the Pacific. This was the man who, two years into the marriage and extended-family living, walked into my grandparents' house without pausing to remove his combat boots and demanded to take me home, as he put it, to Los Angeles. My mother was out; my grandmother, thinking her daughter would be sad to find me gone, rushed out of the house barefoot with me on her back, swallowed her pride, and sought refuge in a neighbor's house from her son-in-law. I didn't know of this episode in the years I was growing up with my father, but the presence of gum-chewing, camera-toting GIs in the Tokyo of my childhood caused me deep chagrin, mostly on my own account but probably on theirs as well, though I couldn't have said so at the time.

It was my grandfather who had brought my father, along with other GIs, home to meet his daughters who spoke English. I read, in a collection of Okinawan poet Takara Ben, about island girls, their arms bare to the pits, staring into the sea, waiting for black-skinned, white-skinned GIs.[1] My mother was not an island girl. She was privileged, though not lucky, and she was married to my Scottish-American father at the American consulate in Yokohama. That was in 1946, when food and supplies were still scarce and the black market vigorous. That was how I came to

---

[1]Takara Ben, "Yume no Mokushi" [Dream Revelations], from *Misaki* [Promontory] (Osaka: Kaifūsha, 1984), pp. 18–19.

grow up in Tokyo with parents, maternal grandparents, unmarried aunts, an assortment of cats, and organdy dresses: custom and ceremony indeed for a half-breed daughter in a defeated land.

The subtle shame that clung like an odor to those years of American male presence in the form of military occupation marked Okinawa as a place I would unintentionally avoid. There, the ubiquity and the seeming sempiternity of American bases made the shame more palpable than on the mainland. Seventeen years after Okinawa's reversion to Japan, I find myself recounting my first, recent visit there to a friend from a classical literature research group. We are drinking. He is surprised: I hadn't been there as a child? I am not sure what I am being asked. Whether, after all, I was illegitimate? Or more simply, being a half-breed of my generation, I must surely have been there where my kind are concentrated? Many years into my growing up, I thought I had understood the awkward piquancy of biracial children with the formulation, they are nothing if not the embodiment of sex itself; now, I modify it to, the biracial offspring of war are at once more offensive and intriguing because they bear the imprint of sex as domination.

The reversion of Okinawa to Japan in 1972 effected only telling variations on the motif of inferiority. As the Vietnam War wound down, prostitutes had to shift their attention from American GIs to the construction workers descending from the mainland for a succession of projects that were to bring the trappings of Japanese prosperity to the islands. These efforts dotted the landscape with gleaming white high-rise hotels, palm trees, and in the areas condemned to be deluxe, white sand replacing the original coral-strewn beaches. "Blue skies, blue seas" became the Homeric epithet for Okinawa in travel posters. Pineapple, sugarcane, and easy—that is, dark—women; tropicality, relative undress, pleasure, and second-class citizenship. Before reversion, words such as *kāpentā*, *randorī*, *gāden bōi*, and *hausumeido* created a new Japanese to go along with the coveted jobs of carpenter, dry-cleaner, garden boy, and housemaid to American military personnel and their families. I've also come across *hanī* and *onrī* in Okinawan fiction as well as in discussions of prostitution economy: furniture stores were the ones to profit when a girl became a "honey" or an "only" to a GI because protocol demanded new beds on such occasions.

In recent years the dark women have mostly been cancerously tanned girls frolicking from the mainland, while the maids and bellhops at their hotels are still natives. Profits from these resorts find their way back to the mainland department stores and airline companies that built them. They are playgrounds for the youth of Tokyo, Osaka, and the dozen other cities connected by air to Naha, the prefectural capital. Pictorially and linguistically, at least, capitalism as exotic self-indulgence has replaced American masculinity as the expression of military occupation.

It was by luck that I was made to overcome forty years of studied indifference and turn my eyes to Okinawa. Luck in this case came in the form of a small news item I read in September, soon after my arrival in Japan. An Okinawan almost my age, on trial for having removed and burned a Japanese flag during the National Athletic Meet of 1987, had just published a book. Flag burning was a quaint enough gesture in 1980s Japan; perpetrated by a supermarket owner, it was incomprehensible. I noted the name, Chibana Shōichi, recorded the title of his book, and stored it away as information for which I then had no category of use.

Yet, like an unidentified seed fortuitously exposed to optimal conditions for germination and growth, that bit of information exploded into urgency during the ensuing months of life under conditions of "self-restraint." I made my first trip to Okinawa about one month after Hirohito's funeral, in late March of 1989.

The prefectural capital Naha is approximately two and a half hours by jet from Tokyo. Before 1972, the trip would have required a passport for a Japanese or an Okinawan traveler, though not for one in my position, a U.S.-passported, Japan-registered, fingerprinted alien since birth. The American presence remains palpable. Airspace over Naha is not only perilously crowded, what with traffic from the U.S. bases at Kadena and Futenma, but civilian aircraft are forced to maintain questionably low altitudes during takeoff and landing so as not to interfere with American military craft.

Naha, a city of 300,000 or 700,000 according to whether the adjoining, subordinate townships are included, sprawls in the southern part of Okinawa Island. "Sprawls" refers to its disorderly appearance, not to a plenitude of land available for expansion. There is no such space on this largest island of the prefecture, which is so narrow in places that the sea spreads out in vivid intensity on either side. The construction that one becomes accustomed to everywhere in Japan approaches frenzy here, which is surprising given the sleepy, subtropical image scornfully purveyed by impatient mainlanders and ambitious locals and affectionately affirmed by once-harried, transplanted mainlanders and proud Ryukyuans. High-rises emerge from disgorged hillsides, trucks and bulldozers choke the perennially clogged traffic. Unlike the rest of Japan, Okinawa has no rail system. It would be impossible to create one now through the obstacle course of American bases. Buses and taxis are hardly sufficient. The result is the proliferation of two- and even three-car families driving on a handful of trunk roads.

Off those routes, the roads, even near the center of Naha, narrow to barely admit one car. The houses, some still picturesque with soft orange-tiled roofs, become low-slung, evoking centuries of typhoon fear. The new construction is fearless, and as if to cast its lot with the spirit of progress, or to delude it to the heights of hubris, nature has withheld its fury for some years now.

Okinawans were initially barred from the city of Naha by American Occupation authorities; when it was partially reopened they returned, but of course all their records had been burned. The city reassigned land arbitrarily, even to those whose property was still under American control. The effects of wartime devastation and peacetime prosperity commingle in the dust of the landscape.

Yomitanson, the village of flag burner Chibana Shōichi, is approximately one hour's drive from Naha on a spacious expressway lined with palm trees, rhododendron, and barbed wire. Central Okinawa Island is dominated by Kadena Air Base. Prior to reversion, American bases took up 71 percent of Yomitanson; even now, they occupy 48 percent of village land. Fighter planes cross the expressways with unapologetic frequency, especially on certain weekdays. These are favorite spots for military buffs, for the spectacle here is as varied as any in the world.

I'd hesitated at first to bring my family, but now I am glad to have their company. I'm grateful, too, for my new circle of friends and friends of theirs, one of whom gave up a precious Sunday with his five children to serve as our driver. Our guide Toshiko has been here several times with old schoolmates, fine matrons now, who, for instance, will join thousands in forming a human chain around Kadena Air Base in driving rain, and who therefore were quick to visit Chibana when he was under siege for the flag burning. Toshiko is my mother's age. I don't know how to approach strangers and ask them why they do things that irreversibly change their lives. Toshiko can ask people their income, chide them for cowardice, and generally overwhelm qualification and hesitation without giving offense. She is from a prominent Okinawan family that had safely evacuated to the mainland during the war. Not having witnessed the devastation, she is insatiably curious and indefatigably impassioned about it.

We are early, so when we get off National Route 58, we visit the village pottery center. It was built on the site of American facilities for the "disposal" of staggering quantities of undetonated American and Japanese explosives from the war. "Disposing" of bombs means detonating them, which is not pleasant for surrounding communities. As I later learned, it is entirely characteristic of Yomitanson both that its village administration should have fought alongside citizens to compel U.S. authorities to desist from such operations, and that when the land was finally returned, it should have become a home for potters. Yomitanson's leadership is committed to viewing as linked activities the struggle for peace and the pursuit of an autonomous economy through the promotion of indigenous culture.

After lunch we lose our way in the labyrinth of sunny, winding streets. Toshiko, a woman who is accustomed to being driven about without maps to clutter her mind, fulfills her duties as guide by leaping from the van to hail the driver caught behind our crawl as "young man of the village" and persuading him to guide us to Hanza Supermarket, Chibana Shōichi's store. Hanza is the old, local reading of Namihira, the name by which the hamlet is known today. The store façade is nondescript. It is only from having seen photographs that I can detect what might be traces of the fire set by right-wingers shortly after the flag burning. Shōichi's supporters, including some of his wholesalers, had pitched in to restore the shop. "7-UP" banners flutter gaily over stacks of disposable diapers. Toshiko goes in to find Shōichi but comes out clucking her tongue: "He's gone off to the cave again, to guide some people who just showed up. And we had an appointment." We decide to wait at his house.

The Chibana house was one of the first to be built in the neighborhood after the war. It occupies an impressively sized corner lot with a view of the Pacific, but since it doesn't border the beach, by Okinawan reckoning it is not close to the sea. In late March the garden walls drip with scarlet bougainvillea. Inside, carp and goldfish dart and dream in an arbor-cooled pond. The garden is Mr. Chibana senior's handiwork. The house sprawls in ungainly fashion. We are led to a room off to the side, which Toshiko has dubbed the Combat Hut. It comes equipped with copy machine and word processor.

We exchange greetings with Mr. Chibana, a robust man of seventy busy with the care of his young grandchildren, the younger of whom was born while Shōichi was in detention; and Shōichi's wife Yōko. I know from his book that Shōichi had always shared his views with her so that she was not shocked when she heard that he had burned the flag at the youth softball event of the National Athletic Meet. It was his mother, also a confidante and usually a stalwart supporter, who was furious when he called just as Yōko was going into labor. She had hung up abruptly: didn't he understand how hard it was for a woman to give birth? Couldn't he remember the difficulties with the first delivery? Today, Mrs. Chibana senior is spending the afternoon with her traditional music group, and Yōko confines herself to bringing us a succession of treats, including fried savory sea grass that her mother-in-law had gathered off the rocks early that morning. I wonder if Mrs. Chibana is annoyed with yet another intrusion into family life.

Shōichi is instantly likable. Tall, striking, and unaffected, he is a warm host. He doesn't show a trace of irritation with questions he has doubtless answered a hundred times over in the eighteen months since the event. He speaks with a freshness undiminished by repetition and a conviction free of ostentation. Indeed, the conviviality he generates threatens to obscure the seriousness of his act—burning the Rising Sun flag at a national athletic event as a deliberate gesture of civil disobedience—and the chain of reactions it unleashed: arrest, detention, and trial on the one hand, death threats and village besiegement by right-wing groups on the other. The last resulted, most painfully of all, in his estrangement from the elderly members of the community, whose suffering in the war under the sign of the Rising Sun had driven Shōichi to burn the flag in the first place.

We begin with generalities. What have the police done to protect him? Almost nothing. For a while, a police car was parked near the house. But they haven't done anything at the supermarket, even though it was burned and attacked several times. Yes, the ones who burned it were caught and sentenced to one- and two-year terms. Does he still hear from the right-wingers? They wrote him in December of 1988 (more than one year after the event) that they would get him before the year was out, so he should settle his affairs. Year's end is the traditional time for cleaning in Japan: office, house, accounts, and finally, around midnight, the exhausted body itself.

In postwar Japan with its constitutional guarantees of free speech, the "chrysanthemum taboo" has effectively eliminated nonsanctioned, that is to say noncelebratory, discussion of the imperial family. Not that this constraint should be attributed solely to domestic circumstances, most particularly that conveniently elusive entity known as "Japanese culture." The American Occupation under MacArthur deemed Hirohito's continued presence indispensable to its operation locally and to American priorities globally as the Cold War congealed into the new national preoccupation. Thus, American interests dovetailed with the emerging interests of the rehabilitated Japanese leadership to reinforce the dispensation from reflection afforded by devastating defeat. It became virtually impossible, for instance, to recall that Japan had been waging a war of aggression prior to Hiroshima and Nagasaki. In fact, right-wing bullets and knives not only enforced the chrysanthemum taboo in a narrow sense but, by discouraging dissent of any form, contributed to the implementation of both the American agenda for Japan and that of the conservative Japanese leadership eager to suppress union activity and educational reform in the interests of economic recovery. The difficulty of discussing war guilt in general and of imperial responsibility in particular produced a national amnesia that first mobilized a labor force for stupendously hard work and then facilitated the transition to unreflective prosperity.

Shōichi knows about the cases of right-wing violence in the 1960s that made the chrysanthemum taboo virtually unbreachable. Especially persuasive was the fate of a novel depicting the violent deaths of members of the imperial family. Attackers charged the home of the prestigious publisher, found him absent, wounded his wife and killed their maid. The author himself had to go into permanent hiding.

Shōichi's life has been threatened even in court. He has asked the judge to have such threats—shouted out by spectators—entered into the record, but the judge has refused. "Why should people who say they are going to kill you be allowed into the same courtroom?" he asks. Not only are they allowed in, they are guaranteed space in the gallery, which seats only twenty-seven people. The authorities instituted order in the early days of the trial at Naha District Court by having the Chibana supporters and the right-wingers draw lots for seats, but allocated the right wing the extra seat, for a total of fourteen. The proceedings unfold before the massive presence of riot police in battle gear. They usually face the Chibana crowd with their shields and spears, effectively protecting the right-wingers who are behind them, while Shōichi is told not to leave the courthouse by the front entrance because the police cannot guarantee his safety.

Not only are those who threaten the defendant's life permitted into the courtroom, but their shouts and harassments (hitting fellow spectators, jerking them back by the collar) go largely ignored. A hallway sign warns against "dozing, smoking, reading newspapers and books" and other forms of inappropriate behavior.

One day, there appeared a supplementary notice refusing entry to "those who have infants" with them. Shōichi's wife and other women supporters had been coming with their babies from time to time, there being virtually no institution of baby-sitting in Japan. When their babies fussed, the mothers had of course scurried out before anyone needed to tell them to leave. But that had been deemed insufficient. As Shōichi speculates in his book,

> . . . the trial today is an occasion for the state to pass judgment, as an exercise of its "sacred right," or more precisely, through its "authority," upon a defendant who is presumed to have committed a crime. So, it is probably thought that for a child to cry in this "sacred space," or to create a stir by coughing, for instance, is to rupture the "authority of silence." Shouldn't we be questioning an "authority" or a "sacredness" that can be undermined so easily?[2]

Mothers with young children are not all that's missing from the Chibana trial. There is no court stenographer. Instead, a secretary with a tape recorder produces summaries of the proceedings. In other words, there is no verbatim transcript available to the defendant and his counsel. In all of Japan only the Naha District Court has no stenographer. Even Kushiro, equally as remote in Hokkaido, has recently added a stenographer to its staff. Tenacious Shōichi continues to demand a stenographer. The chief judge, an Okinawan, temporizes and threatens to throw Shōichi out of court. This isn't the way the legal system was presented in his textbooks, observes Shōichi. "Don't you think something's wrong here? The same law's supposed to apply across the land. But the courts are different."

At the first hearing Shōichi attempted to make his own statement after his lawyers spoke, but he was stopped by the judge.

---

[2]Chibana Shōichi, *Yakisuterareta Hi no Maru: Kichi no Shima Okinawa Yomitanson Kara* [The Burned and Discarded Rising Sun: From Yomitanson, Okinawa, Island of Bases] (Tokyo: Shinsensha, 1988), p. 178.

He writes, "I had no intention of being 'judged' by the court. Rather, I thought of it as an occasion to 'pass judgment on the Rising Sun [flag].' I thought of the trial as *my trial*." (p. 175) In the same spirit, Shōichi is annoyed by the prosecution's practice of providing only two copies of every document so that he can never get a look at them while in court. Likewise with the practice of referring to statutes and codes by number. The absence of a jury system in Japan means, among many things, that there is no need for legal experts to accommodate, let alone appeal, to the comprehension of amateur citizens. It also means that witnesses face the judge, and some judges complain if witnesses turn too far toward their interlocuters, the examining prosecutor or attorney. It bothers Shōichi that he, the defendant, cannot follow the proceedings. The chief judge commonsensically reminds him that that is the reason for counsel. Shōichi disagrees.

> My attorneys are only my legal advisers, my technical advisers. The very notion of a trial in which the principals are made to sit in silence is disgusting.
> The same with spectators. Surely the principle of the open trial doesn't mean, here, you have the right to be a spectator. If all you have is a trial in which legal experts manipulate legal terms, then that "openness" is mere hypocrisy. (p. 177)

I am struck by the contrast between the uncompromising tone of such analyses and the softness of Shōichi's demeanor in person. What underlies both, though, is the force of his radical innocence.

I wonder why most of us hadn't known about the absence of a court stenographer. Had it been taken up by the Okinawan newspapers, those that refused to present the emperor's death as a *hōgyo*? My friends seem to think not. Why not? "Maybe they're afraid of the right wing, too."

Recently, those supporters who gain access to seats go into the courtroom armed with pencil and pad. This is because of a

favorable ruling by the Supreme Court of Japan early in 1989
on a remarkable suit brought by an American lawyer, which
established the right of spectators to take notes at judicial proceedings. Previously, spectators could not introduce writing instruments into the courtroom. Though tape recorders are still
eliminated by metal detector, there are now several supporters
taking verbatim accounts. Do the right-wingers keep records, too?
No, Shōichi chuckles. They don't do much writing.

Who are these right-wingers? Mostly thugs. There are two
main groups, and the bosses come from the mainland. You can
tell right away because Okinawan gangsters could never afford
those fancy cars. Mostly, however, as elsewhere in Japan, they
make themselves conspicuous aurally as well as visually in their
black trucks with inflammatory signs and blaring loudspeakers.
Theirs is a tyranny of sound, shattering concentration and razing
daydreams with a relentless barrage of military songs and vitu-
perative slogans. "Execute the traitor Chibana Shōichi," they
screamed in the weeks and months following the flag burning.
(The detectives from the Public Security Investigation Agency
used the same forms of address during their interrogation of Shōichi while he was in detention. There is considerable speculation
and even consensus in Japan about the proximity of the right
wing to the police forces; Shōichi, for his part, rejoices at the
thought of spreading his "traitor's blood" by participating in the
Yomitanson Chamber of Commerce youth blood drive.)

These right-wingers do not content themselves with aural violence. After the flag burning they set fire to Shōichi's store and
threatened his customers. When Shōichi was released after
twenty-five days of detention, the old women of the village wept
and embraced him and said no one was going to keep them from
shopping at his store. Shōichi's reference to the elderly in his
community, whether in speech or in writing, is always affectionate, indeed, intimate: *ojī* for old men, *obā* for old women,
unindividualized terms evoking the archetypal Grandpa and

Grandma of folklore. Such forms of address and reference have begun to sound age-discriminatory to some, especially in urban settings. In Yomitanson there is still a world where, for the moment, these forms denote relationships at once general and particular, familiar and respectful.

For all the courageous loyalty of the *ŏbā*, business at the supermarket fell drastically for a time, from an average of 470-odd customers a day to the 270 range. Supporters organized shopping excursions not only from Naha but from Yambaru in the far north of the island, which meant at least a three-hour drive each way. Thanks to such efforts, and the cooperation of store suppliers, numbers have gone up to about 420 customers a day.

During that first traumatic period, especially when Shōichi was in detention, members of the village chamber of commerce, of which Shōichi was vice president, as well as those of the Yomitanson Executive Committee for Peace organized shifts to protect the store. The executive committee, as it became known, is an informal but effective group of villagers whom Shōichi helped organize because, being self-employed—farmers, artists, and businessmen like himself—they had no natural forum of communal activism such as a union. "We were never afraid," Mrs. Chibana told me later, "because there were always supporters around." She herself has engaged in conversation the right-wingers who came looking for Shōichi. Wasn't she afraid? "Well, I've always thought they have to be human, too. I told them Shōichi wasn't home. They said, 'Do you think it was a good thing, what your son did, bringing down the Rising Sun?' I said, 'No, I don't think it was a good thing.' I lied. 'You shouldn't let him do things like that.' I agreed. But then I said, 'For your part, please don't corrupt our young people.' "

Shōichi is a serious entrepreneur: co-owner of a second supermarket, owner of the Marco Polo coffee shop, and the impressively indebted would-be developer of a village shopping mall.

He has traveled extensively in southeast Asia on business for the chamber of commerce. Yet he is no longer its vice president. Even in this U.S. base–surrounded community, known for its peace activism, a majority of the board could not reconcile themselves to a flag-burning vice president. The decision was the so-called moderate one of allowing Shōichi to submit his resignation. Over and over again it is said that it was all right for Shōichi to bring down the flag; he just shouldn't have burned it. As Shōichi puts it, most of the local people accept what he did "on an emotional level." Outside Okinawa, though, he has generated support precisely because he went so far as to burn the flag.

It is, to be sure, always easier to cheer a subversive act from a distance, where there is no threat of rupturing the weave of one's own everyday life. But the specific vicissitudes of Okinawan/Ryukyuan history are also reflected in these differing valuations of Shōichi's act. The now-elderly, in striving to prove themselves as authentically Japanese as mainlanders, had sacrificed their flesh and their land to the cause of the Rising Sun. They were, though they do not like to acknowledge it, betrayed by it—in the form of mainland soldiers who drove them from their shelters to certain death or killed them with their own hands during the last months of the war, as well as in the form of Emperor Hirohito, who chose to prolong the war through those months against the urgings of his closest adviser. After a quarter of a century of life under the Stars and Stripes, their children, including Shōichi, conducted the reversion struggle under the sign of the Rising Sun. At the time of Okinawa's return to Japan in 1972, much of the land was occupied by U.S. military forces (and in areas such as Yomitanson, still is). The American base and the Japanese resort are the present incarnations of the forces mobilized by the two flags. They bring with them overlapping blessings and curses. The common irritations and occasionally tragic mishaps of life in the shadow of a military base are countered by revenues in the form of employment opportunities and irresistibly handsome compensation to landowners leasing their property to U.S. forces. Although the lion's share of profits generated at the Japanese resorts finds its way back to the mainland and, moreover, their presence degrades the natural and human environment, the high-rise hotels stimulate the local economy and simulate the sensation of participation in Japanese prosperity for Okinawans.

Such circumstances breed ambivalence. Most people prefer to leave it unexplored, with the consequence that any sort of confrontation feels abusive. This is precisely what happened to Shō-ichi's community just a few days before his flag burning. The entire village had been mobilized to host the youth softball event of the National Athletic Meet at the Forest of Peace Stadium. Perhaps because he had gotten wind of the peace-activist village administration, the head of the Japan Softball Association, a mainlander, suddenly announced that he would take the games elsewhere unless he had assurances that the Rising Sun would fly from the main flagpole of the stadium. Mayor Yamauchi Tokushin, for many years a teacher of world history at Yomitan-son High School, is known as an ardent explicator of the values of liberal democracy. He is on record as having denounced the recent escalation of efforts by the national government and its regional representatives to impose school observance of the Rising Sun flag and "The Reign of Our Lord" anthem as lacking in historical reflection. Chibana Shōichi was one of his students, since grown into a trusted and innovative adviser to his administration. The evening before the games, after tense negotiations, Mayor Yamauchi Tokushin announced that he had agreed to ("caved in," in Toshiko's phrasing) raise the flag.

It is entirely characteristic of Shōichi not to criticize the mayor for having yielded on the flag or for bringing charges against him for burning it. On the former, he believes that he took up the fight where the mayor had to leave off. On the latter, he even sent word through his lawyer asking the mayor not to hesitate to bring charges, again because he thought an elected official could not do otherwise. It was precisely an understanding of his own position that made him take the initiative on the morning of October 26, 1987, climbing the flagpole platform and turning his cigarette lighter on the Rising Sun, since, shopkeeper that he was, no one could fire him.

I ask Shōichi why he thinks the community has drawn the line at burning the flag. "Well, bringing the flag down is okay as a protest against having it forced on us. But burning it seems like a rebellion against the state." Why did he burn it? "I thought they would put it up again if I didn't."

One of the goals of Shōichi and his defense team is to remind the nation that the Rising Sun is nowhere documented as the official flag of Japan. The charges brought by Mayor Yamauchi refer only to an incidence of trespassing (the flagpole platform of a village athletic facility) and of vandalism (burning a "Rising Sun" flag belonging to the Yomitanson Executive Committee of the National Athletic Meet). Yet the indictment drawn up by the state consistently refers to a "national flag."

This is a critical slip at a time when the Education Ministry has mandated the raising of the flag and the singing of the anthem praising the imperial reign at the beginning and end of semesters and graduation ceremonies at all schools, private as well as public, throughout Japan. The practice has long been encouraged, but the directives issued in March of 1989 make it compulsory, with penalties for violation. Most citizens do not know that the Rising Sun has never been designated the national flag, just as few remark upon Japan's distinction among the Axis powers in not taking steps to alter its national symbols after the war. Members of Shōichi's nationwide network of supporters suspect that the state's real interest lies in using his trial to establish the official character of the Rising Sun.

The legal distinctions are important, but it is the memory of Okinawa's disproportionate sufferings in the war, sufferings easily

forgotten insofar as they were never known by the rest of Japan
in contrast to the tragedies of Hiroshima and Nagasaki, that com-
plicates the status of the flag in Okinawa. According to a 1985
Education Ministry survey of school observance of flag raising
and anthem singing, Okinawa ranked decisively at the bottom of
the nation in both the former (6 percent on average) and the
latter (0 percent). By spring of 1987, with the National Athletic
Meet just six months away, 97.6 percent of prefectural schools
were raising the flag and 18.75 percent of elementary schools,
7.85 percent of junior high schools, and 8.8 percent of high
schools were singing the anthem.[3] This altogether remarkable
increase in compliance was politically effected through bills
passed without discussion in Liberal Democratic Party–dominated local assemblies and in the Okinawa Prefectural Assembly
in the fall of 1985. In November of that year, the prefectural
superintendent of education sent out a notice outlining how it
was only "natural" or "proper" (the word *tōzen* strategically contains both notions) that Okinawans, as "citizens of Japan," should
"respect and venerate" the national flag and anthem. High school
principals and local superintendents were charged with the task
of advancing student understanding of the "educational significance of the national flag and anthem."[4] This was achieved
through the use of subtle and not-so-subtle threats of reassignment
to inconvenient locations for teachers and diminished employment prospects for graduating students, measures reinforced by
the posting of plainclothes policemen at schools where resistance
seemed likely.

Okinawa's instant patriotic respectability was not won without
incident. In the municipal assembly of Naha, the prefectural
capital, the Communist assemblyman leading the opposition was
disposed of with a karate blow by a Liberal Democratic repre-

---

[3]Taira Sōjun, "Ima Naze Tennō Ka" [Why the Emperor Now], *Okinawa to Tennō*
[Okinawa and the Emperor] (Naha: Akebono Shuppan, 1987), pp. 148–49.
[4]Quoted in ibid., pp. 152–53.

sentative. In Chibana Shōichi's village, the chairman of the Citizens' Conference to Consider the Future of Yomitanson, who
happened to be the former vice speaker of the village assembly,
appeared on graduation day at Yomitan High School in suit and
tie, lay down on the ground before the entrance to the gymnasium, and said to the principal, " 'If you really want to raise the
Rising Sun, you're going to have to walk over me first.' "⁵

In March of 1987, in spite of the passage of a village assembly
resolution against the imposition of the flag and anthem, in spite
of a petition to the school with eight thousand signatures (out of
a total village population of thirty thousand) protesting such imposition, Yomitan High School opened its graduation with the
Rising Sun flag onstage. Since there had been talk that something
was likely to happen at one of the area high schools, television
cameras were ready when a girl from the junior class walked up
onto the stage, snatched the flag from its stand, and walked off
with it, quickly followed by two female friends.

The gestures of the friends, as viewed on film, are ambiguous.
Mostly it looks as if they are trying just to stay near their friend,
perhaps to shield her in the ensuing scuffle. The dean of the
night division tells the girl excitedly, "If you were twenty, this
would be a crime." The girl, hanging her head and weeping,
responds firmly, "That's all right," and asks, "Who said you could
do this? Did you get the students' permission?" I have written
"scuffle," but the exchange between the dark, bent form of the
girl and the agitated figure of the dean is slow and heavy. The
gravity comes from the girl. The dean presses her with her hy-
pothetical criminality. Finally, she breaks loose like a hunted
animal and in sad triumph thrusts the flag into a gutter filled
with muddy rainwater outside the gymnasium.

Why was the girl so upset by the sight of the flag at her school
as to take matters into her own hands? But even more, why have

⁵Ibid., p. 26.

Okinawans so successfully enforced and accepted compliance with national educational policy on the use of the flag and the anthem? Is the bullying by elected officials and school authorities explanation enough? And why should it matter in the first place? Is there more to it than sentiment, whether and how Okinawans will remember those who died in the name of the emperor of the Land of the Rising Sun? Why did Chibana Shōichi, a man by general agreement fated for the heights of commercial and civic success, find it necessary to burn the flag at a national sports event hosted by his village, on the eve of the birth of his second child?

At some remove from the village center, next to a narrow path through sugarcane fields, a set of small concrete steps leads down to Chibichirigama. It is a natural cave formation of the sort found throughout Okinawa. This one is covered with thick brush, and the entrance is so low that one must double over to get in. From his boyhood Shōichi remembers it as a place where he wasn't supposed to play. It wasn't until his mid-thirties that he learned why.

April 1, 1945 was at once Easter Sunday, April Fool's Day, and L, that is, Love Day, the code for the beginning of the American invasion of Japan. One hundred eighty thousand troops landed on the beaches of Yomitanson and Kadena in Okinawa. This is conventionally described as a "bloodless" landing in English-language sources because, to American perceptions, Japanese troops had lost the wherewithal to resist. After the October 10, 1944 bombing of Naha, the prefectural capital, a number of Yomitan families had taken refuge in Chibichirigama. Intermittent but increasingly intense American bombing after the first of the year drove those who had been burned out of their homes or those who were not able-bodied to take up permanent residence in the cave. Others continued to farm and cook in their homes when they could, taking refuge in family shelters when that seemed sufficient and retreating to the cave when danger seemed more imminent. American bombers were not the only threat facing these Okinawans, however. Those who happened to be in the cave on March 29 were driven out by Japanese soldiers armed with hand grenades. What awaited them outside was the concentrated bombing that has produced the expression, "the iron storm," that Okinawans use in describing the Battle of Okinawa.

It is now known that similar episodes took place throughout Okinawa. Desperate for food and shelter, Japanese troops drove local civilians from the great family tombs or natural caves where they had taken refuge. Oral-history accounts show that even when civilians and Japanese troops shared hiding places, babies' cries were stilled by soldiers fearful of detection by the Americans, or worse yet, by their own mothers fearful of the Japanese soldiers. Still, older people I have talked to unselfconsciously continue to refer to the Japanese forces as *yūgun*, the friendly forces.

In Yomitanson the Japanese soldiers who had driven out the villagers on March 29 moved on, leaving the cave free for local occupation once more. By Love Day some 140 people had taken refuge in Chibichirigama. Then one of the women, approaching the opening in order to start cooking, saw soldiers whom she knew could be none other than the dreaded *Hījāmī*: Goat Eyes, the name Okinawans had given Americans because they invariably stopped bombing at night, and it was believed that goats couldn't see in the dark. In the charged atmosphere produced by the discovery, one young woman challenged the men to march out with bamboo spears and prove their worth. Two did so, and were promptly greeted with a barrage of hand grenades and machine-gun fire. Severely wounded, they retreated into the cave. Soon American soldiers came in with an interpreter, who assured the villagers that they would not be killed if they would vacate the cave and surrender. That no one believed this message was the immediate cause of the tragedy about to take place.

Two of the men decided that the time had come to prepare for an honorable end. They had been in Saipan and had witnessed what is known as the "Saipan *gyokusai*." The term *gyokusai* means honorable death in lieu of surrender; it is ubiquitous in Japanese accounts of war, and the constituent Chinese characters are assiduously carved on monument after monument. My eyes catch on them each time, for they literally mean "jewels shattering." The Japanese body in an honorable dying, having shouted *banzai* to the emperor, is as beautiful as a shattering jewel, perhaps itself a metaphor for the scattering petals of the cherry blossom. *Gyoku* is also a prefix for words pertaining to the emperor's body, as in *gyokutai*, "jeweled body," the item which so freighted discussions of the appropriateness of surgery for Hirohito. To prepare for the enactment of an Okinawan *gyokusai*, the two veterans of Saipan gathered bedding and clothes, and all other combustible implements of daily life the villagers had brought to the cave in that stubborn determination to maintain routine, and without further ado, set the pile on fire. There was, however, no consensus that the time had come to die. In the end four women, all mothers with babies, managed to put out the fire.

Another visitation by American soldiers, this time bearing cigarettes, water, and chocolate, failed to convince even those who had opposed the fire. One of the older men again started blocking the entrance with combustibles. Perhaps it was because he had been in the army and had seen what the Japanese did in China that this man thought it would be better to dispatch themselves before the enemy could get to them. There was still violent disagreement within the cave, however. Then a woman gave in to her eighteen-year-old daughter's pleas that she kill her with her own hands while "she was still pure." The mother thrust a kitchen knife into the girl's neck. Next, a twenty-five-year-old army nurse who had observed the behavior of the Japanese army in the course of its advance on the continent called her family together, confirmed their identities (for the cave was dark), and injected them with the poison she kept in her kit. Many others begged her to inject them, but she refused, saying she had just enough for her own family and relatives. By this time chaos had overtaken the cave, and the pile at the entrance was ignited. Not everyone was ready to die, but the smoke threatened to suffocate them all. Some managed to walk out, not in hopes of escaping, but simply because the smoke was unbearable and they thought it would be easier to be shot dead by the Americans. In the end eighty-two people were dead, forty-seven of them children under the age of twelve. This is one aspect of the bloodless American landing.

The survivors of Chibichirigama left this story buried with their dead for thirty-eight years. Those who tried to unearth the secret met with a silence surpassing the conventional reticence of country folk. It was only in 1983 that it was broken by the devoted, even driven efforts of three men. The most senior of them was Higa Heishin, a villager who lost fifteen relatives in the cave while he was with the Japanese army on the continent. When he returned, no one was willing to tell him how his relatives had met their end. He had no way of knowing, for instance, that a cousin of his, the young nurse, had poisoned her family by injection. But Heishin was as quietly obstinate as his fellow villagers, and decades later he found a collaborator in an outsider, Shimojima Tetsurō, an artist and writer of children's books from Tokyo. Shimojima was pursuing a successful career as a commercial artist when the 1973 suicide of an acclaimed commercial filmmaker caused him, like many others in his cohort, to veer sharply from his chosen path. The filmmaker, Sugiyama Toshi, who was known for his understated, romantic TV commercials for Shiseido cosmetics, left behind this note:

Not being "rich,"
How can I understand a "rich" world.
Not being "happy,"
How can I depict a "happy" world.
Not having any "dreams,"
How can I possibly sell "dreams" . . .
If you lie, you usually get caught.[6]

Shimojima began collecting tales from old folks in rural areas, writing and illustrating his own books for children because, as he puts it, he was giving up on adult Japanese. The long journey begun from Sugiyama's suicide eventually led him to Okinawa and circuitously but fatefully to Yomitanson. There he became possessed, though with the diffidence and disciplined patience necessary for the outsider, by the desire to wrest the truth of the cave. His fervor and his banter ("You'll never get yourself a wife until you prove you're a man") eventually overcame the hesitations of the youngest member of the trio, Chibana Shōichi. Shōichi belonged to the immediate postwar generation. His parents were prominent figures in the men's and women's groups of the village, and he was liked and trusted by everyone.

These three men—the World War II veteran and night watchman at the village community center, the youthful owner of the village supermarket, and the outsider artist—slowly came to conjoin their obsessions. Even after they had decided to act together, they had to submit to an exquisite regimen of patience, for they could only inch toward that moment of violence when the survivors would open their lips. It was Heishin who laboriously ensured that those who said they would attend a meeting in fact showed up. At first the survivors consented to speak only on condition that the discussion be confined to names and numbers.

---

[6]*Asahi Shimbun*, December 26, 1973. "Rich" and "happy" are in English in the original.

They could bring themselves to acknowledge the need for an accurate record of those who died in Chibichirigama. But speaking and counting their names quickened the survivors' memories of the dead and of the nightmare of their dying. The survivors began to meet in groups of two and three. Their stories trickled, then poured, into a tape recorder, freely in dialect, incomprehensible to the artist, who struggled to restore every member of the lost community through imaginative portraiture.

What happened in Chibichirigama in Yomitanson is usually referred to as a *shūdan jiketsu*. *Shūdan* means "group" or "mass." The first dictionary entry for *jiketsu* is "self-determination," as in "ethnic self-determination." The second meaning is "suicide," with the added nuance of suicide resulting from a sense of responsibility. Accordingly, the neutral translation of *shūdan jiketsu* might be "collective suicide." In this instance, the neutral choice is inadequate. For if the end of life was "self-determined," indeed, auto-executed, the determination was made under duress, both in the form of the presence of the two armies and in the long discipline required for the production of Japanese imperial subjects. For this reason I think of *shūdan jiketsu* as "compulsory group suicide."

Similar forms of civilian communal death occurred in various parts of Okinawa during the spring of 1945, and indeed in Manchuria and elsewhere in the Japanese Empire. One of the commonest implements was the hand grenade supplied by the Japanese army. There were usually not enough to go around, so people huddled in groups for efficiency. On Zamami Island rat poison was the instrument of choice. The have-nots envied the haves while the latter gulped down as much of the substance as they could. It was a misplaced envy, however, for excess consumption led to vomiting and excruciating discomfort but not to death. For that, more active intervention was required, as illustrated by the case of a frenzied mother who held her baby by the feet and pounded it to pulp against a rock. Families often hanged themselves from single ropes. This worked well enough for those in the middle, but not nearly as effectively for those on the ends. Finally, there were the stones, farm tools, razor blades, and kitchen knives, the implements brought in along with dishes, pots and pans to sustain life in the natural caves or great family tombs throughout that dark spring.

The official view of this history, as represented by the Education Ministry, requires that collective suicide be strictly distinguished from the purportedly insignificant, difficult-to-substantiate instances of civilian murder by Japanese military personnel. The ministry approvingly describes textbook references to collective suicide as contributing to an "objective understanding" of civilian casualties during the Battle of Okinawa.[7] Above all, collective suicide, unlike civilian killings, enhances the narrative of courageous Japanese—even if they happen to be Okinawan—united in the spirit of honorable sacrifice.

Not only can the Education Ministry dictate the use of the flag and the anthem, but through the exercise of its prerogative of screening textbooks for all grade levels in all schools, public and private, throughout the nation, it is able to fashion history after its own preferences. This doesn't always proceed with bureaucratic ease. In the early 1980s, for example, the Republic of Korea and the People's Republic of China sharply protested instances of "screening" in which the Education Ministry demanded that agitation for Korean independence following the 1910 annexation by Japan be described as "rioting"; that the movement of the Japanese army into the Asian continent in the 1930s be described as an "advance" rather than an "invasion"; and that in accounts of the 1937 episode known in the West as the Rape of Nanking, when Japanese forces entered that city and 200,000 to 300,000 Chinese women, children, and POWs were left

---

[7]Quoted in Arasaki Moriteru, Ōshiro Masayasu, Takamine Tomokazu, et al., *Kankō Kōsu de nai Okinawa* [Okinawa off the Tourist Course], 2d ed. (Tokyo: Kōbunken, 1989), p. 152.

dead,[8] the event be described as an effect of the "confusion" of the times and the casualty figures be reduced.

The eminent historian Ienaga Saburō, who has served as plaintiff for a quarter of a century in a number of suits involving just such ministry activities, has insisted that textbooks be permitted to refer to Japanese army killings of Okinawan civilians. His lawyers and supporters deny the validity of the government's categorical distinction between collective suicide and civilian murder. Not only did Japanese soldiers drive Okinawans from their shelters into certain death, suffocate their crying babies, and kill those who had already surrendered and were then sent back by Americans to persuade their fellows to do the same; their presence both explicitly and tacitly prompted episodes of Okinawan collective suicide.[9] Through emphasis on the "nobility" of the Okinawan "choice" of suicide, as suggested by the novelist Sono Ayako as state's witness in an Ienaga textbook trial,[10] civilian suicide becomes comparable to military death, and therefore fit to memorialize as *gyokusai* in the rhetoric of shattering jewels and falling petals. Putting aside the question of whether most soldiers from the mainland "chose" their glorious deaths, the sort of homage proposed by Sono and government officials conveniently forgets the history of Okinawa's second-class citizenship, the sort of history produced by a racist colonialism in which lagging natives are disciplined in the name of civilization.

Civilization, in this context, meant the opportunity for Okinawans to sacrifice for the emperor just like other Japanese. During the war, however, the condition of being Okinawan was often

---

[8]"Nankin Jiken" [Nanjing Incident], *Kadokawa Nihonshi Jiten* [*Kadokawa Dictionary of Japanese History*], 2d ed. (Tokyo: Kadokawa Shoten, 1981), p. 719. As is inevitably the case with such episodes, reliable estimates are hard to come by. Continuing controversy exacerbates this instance.

[9]Maps in Arasaki, *Okinawa off the Tourist Course*, p. 139, and Okinawa Kenritsu Heiwa Kinen Shiryōkan [Okinawa Prefectural Peace Memorial Museum], ed., *Heiwa e no Shōgen* [Witnesses for Peace] (Naha: Okinawa-ken Seikatsu Fukushibu Engoka, 1983), p. 45, document these episodes.

[10]*Asahi Shimbun*, April 6, 1988.

sufficient to put a civilian at risk before Japanese troops. Survivor testimony is graphic on this point. Nakajō Mitsutoshi, male, then sixteen, tells what happened after Japanese soldiers entered the cave where his extended family had taken refuge:

> By then we only had a few half-rotten, sticky rice balls made from rice boiled a few days before. Only the children had them, and we adults didn't eat anything. We just sat there, looking at what the soldiers were doing. Perhaps they thought we knew nothing. They said they were going on a surprise attack mission and took away our food, threatening us with their pistols, but we knew they just wanted to stay alive and get back to the mainland.
>
> The next day, they told us they were going to "dispose" of all children under three years of age because they said children would attract enemy attention and Americans would throw explosives into our cave. There were five children under three, including my brother and my niece. . . .
>
> When they said they were going to kill the five children, we asked the commander to let us go out of the cave with the children. But he said no. He said we would become spies. He posted guards at the entrance of the cave and would not let us go out. Then four or five soldiers came to us and took away the children from us one by one, including my brother, and gave them the injection. . . .
>
> Then, the next morning, they said we were the only civilians alive in the area, so they were also going to "dispose" of us before the Americans captured us and crushed us under their tanks. We knew they were going to kill us all just to take our food.

Maeda Haru, a nineteen-year-old woman from Maehira village, recalls what happened when surviving Japanese troops, desperate as Americans closed in on them, raided her cave:

> There was no bombardment in the morning, and everybody went out of the cave to get water. Then I found my younger brother and sister crying and calling me from a pile of sugar

cane bagasse at Miisumo. They said they got hurt in front of Mearakagua [household name] and had come crawling on their hands and knees.

I brought them one by one to the cave and laid them down. I asked them if anything'd happened to Mother, and they said Mother was dead. Maybe Seiyu was also dead, they said. I asked them why Mother was killed. What they told me was that a Japanese soldier came and asked Mother how many people were in there, but as my mother couldn't speak Japanese well, she answered, "Hui, hui?" Of course, what she meant to say was "Yes? What is it?" but the soldier instantly cut her head off. The head landed in my sister-in-law Yuki's lap. Everybody panicked. My younger sister got away, carrying our younger brother on her back, but when she got as far as Mearakagua, the soldiers caught up with her, took her inside the gate of the house and stabbed her, so she let go of our little brother. She was stabbed three times in the abdomen and her intestines came out here and there. My brother'd been stabbed deep and cut wide in the stomach, and all his tangled intestines came out. He died soon.

Going out to fetch water for the injured brother and sister, Haru passes by several bodies, including those of her youngest brother and her sister-in-law Yuki's father, whose head was also lopped off so that he was left in a sitting position holding his own head in his hands. An uncle lies dead at the well. After the younger brother and sister die, she tries but fails to strangle herself. She goes out in search of her mother's body:

The soldiers had dragged her body several yards away from the spot where they'd killed her. When I saw her lying there, I couldn't control myself. I screamed at the soldiers and asked why they had to do all this to my mother. They only said they couldn't help it because they were fighting a war. . . .

Now that all my folks were dead, I told them to kill me, too. One of them told another to kill me, but he didn't have any weapons. Another soldier said I was too young to die and that I should go with him to northern Okinawa. I said no and told him I would die right where they'd killed my folks. This soldier had a bayonet, but he didn't do anything to me.

The next day, I saw Americans coming and going outside our cave.[11]

No doubt Japanese soldiers killed Okinawan civilians both out of desperation for food and shelter and from deeply ingrained beliefs about their incomplete Japaneseness. Okinawans, for their part, had been imbued with both the horror and the shame (as Japanese) of falling into American hands. No doubt this sense of horror and shame helped them grasp the meaning of hand grenade distribution. No doubt, at the same time, that the forty-two children twelve years or younger who died in Chibichirigama had no "philosophy" of collective suicide.

The civilian atrocities perpetrated by the Japanese army and the collective suicide committed by Okinawan civilians are inseparable. Ienaga Saburō and his supporters emphasize the former, against Sono Ayako and the Education Ministry, who dramatize the latter. Neither Okinawan nor Japanese deaths in the war should be reduced to the appealing simplicity of noble suicide. Nor, on the other hand, should Okinawans be made into pure victims of Japanese militarism, any more than Japanese should continue to recall the Pacific War only as a story of their own victimization by American aggression.

In the present day, in Okinawa and in the rest of Japan, to adopt the narrative of victimization, of Okinawans to Japanese and Japanese to Americans, is to forget the history of Japanese aggression in Asia, a history that in turn entailed profound suffering for Japanese, both mainlanders and Okinawans. Such disregard reinforces inattention to the far more subtle repression

---

[11]Welfare Department, Okinawa Prefecture, *An Oral History of the Battle of Okinawa* (Naha: Relief Section, Welfare Department, Okinawa Prefectural Government, 1985), pp. 27 and 29, emended slightly for idiomatic usage.

exercised by the imposition of models of success throughout Japan, the mainland as well as Okinawa, and increasingly, throughout the world in relentlessly familiar though deceptively various forms. Inattention inexorably spells the loss of critical capacity. The paradoxical phrase "compulsory suicide" is meant to suggest the dark inmixing of coercion and consent, of aggression and victimization at work in the story of the caves. It is his sensitivity to the ways in which inattention to the present overlaps with oblivion of the past that compels Chibana Shōichi, supermarket owner, to resist the imposition of the Rising Sun.

Like those fellow Okinawans who condemned his act, Shōichi had wanted his prefecture to host the National Athletic Meet, and he had worked hard to bring the youth softball games to his village. Given his role in the chamber of commerce, such enthusiasm is not surprising. Hindsight might charge him with naïveté, but as is often the case, it is only when one has taken the extraordinary step, gone beyond the pale, that the structure of the ordinary is revealed. Without having burned the flag and faced the consequences, Shōichi would not have understood the nature of the National Athletic Meet as he now does.

The National Athletic Meet was established in 1946 on the theory that sports would help to revive spirits from the devastation of war. At the first meet, held in Kyoto, there was no entrance march, no appearance by the emperor, no raising of the flag, no singing of the anthem. Athletes gathered from around the country with blankets for camping out and food for picnicking. That same year, the emperor began his journeys through the land at the behest of the American Occupation. He appeared at the second National Athletic Meet in Ishikawa Prefecture, and contrary to earlier GHQ policy strictly forbidding display of the Rising Sun, permission was granted to raise the same, whereupon "unex-

pectedly" the "assembled crowd sang out the *Kimi ga Yo* [The
Reign of Our Lord]."[12]

Once the emperor had visited every prefecture in the country
other than Okinawa, his appearance at the National Athletic Meet
could no longer be staged as a happy coincidence. The new,
more explicitly ritualized age of imperial attendance was marked
by the awarding of the Emperor Cup to the victorious prefecture
and the Empress Cup to the runner-up. Determining the criteria
for victory was a vexing task. During the first few years, regardless
of where the meet was held, Tokyo scored highest, which violated
a general sense of propriety dictating that the host prefecture
should be the winner. The solution adopted for some years was
to rotate the most talented trainers and students from prefecture
to prefecture, a practice that even the most cynical organizers of
imperial and athletic ritual eventually found difficult to defend.

Okinawa's turn to host the meet and to receive an imperial
visit did not come until 1987. Nishime Junji, the Liberal Democratic governor, hoped that the occasion would mean the end
of Okinawa's long and troubled postwar history. In preparation
for the visit, the prefecture budgeted 600 million yen, or over 4
million dollars, for security measures. Previous host prefectures
had engaged in such tactics as stationing sharpshooters on roof-
tops, investigating mental patients, and excluding outcaste Burakumin from welcoming events. In Okinawa, visits by the crown
prince (now Emperor Akihito) were met with shrub pruning and
open curtains on all second-floor windows along his route.[13]

Kokutai, the abbreviation by which the National Athletic Meet
is known, is an exact homonym for *kokutai*, commonly translated
as the "national polity," for which the familiar English phrase

---

[12]Quoted in Toguchi Akira, "Kokumin Taiiku Taikai (Kokutai) to Tennō" [The National
Athletic Meet and the Emperor], *Okinawa and the Emperor*, p. 183.
[13]Such measures are described in many sources; these examples come from Toguchi,
ibid., p. 198.

"body politic" more adequately captures the crucial organicism. The essence of the *kokutai* was declared by a notorious Education Ministry formulation of 1937 to be manifest in the unbroken imperial line and in the absolute loyalty to parents and sovereign through which the individual died to himself but was reborn to a more authentic existence. The early association of the emperor with the National Athletic Meet was symptomatic. The surveillance that has become associated with the sports event suggests a commonality of more than sound; indeed, it hints at a continuity between the disciplining of the prewar body politic and the postwar body athletic.

The Kokutai was late in coming to Okinawa because Okinawa was late in coming to Japan. But precisely because of its belatedness, Okinawa's schools received the most important icons of the age, the Rising Sun flag and the imperial portrait, beginning in 1873, in advance of the rest of the nation.[14] The protocol for transporting these images, which were in fact photographs of portraits; their housing in structures called *hōanden*, especially built on school grounds; and the ritual developed to signify veneration—above all, the daily bow before the *hōanden*—united children and their teachers throughout Japan in a common discipline and served to instill belief in the sacred being of the emperor and to promote the instinct for obedience to his wishes. No mishap was tolerated in the handling of the portraits. As civilians were maimed and slaughtered in the Battle of Okinawa, the imperial portraits were moved progressively northward for safekeeping. To get them wet in the rain, lost in the confusion, or worst of all, captured by Americans was to invite execution.[15]

Okinawan children also became Japanese by memorizing the Imperial Rescript on Education, promulgated in 1890. They

---

[14]Yamakawa Munehide, "Okinawa to Kōminka Kyōiku" [Okinawa and Education for the Production of Imperial Subjects], *Okinawa and the Emperor*, p. 81.
[15]Ibid., p. 83.

learned to listen to it every morning, heads bowed, bodies still, fearful even of clearing their throats. The following is the official translation of the Rescript:

Know Ye, Our Subjects:

Our Imperial Ancestors have founded Our Empire on a basis broad and everlasting and have deeply and firmly implanted virtue; Our subjects ever united in loyalty and filial piety have from generation to generation illustrated the beauty thereof. This is the glory of the fundamental character of Our Empire, and herein also lies the source of Our education. Ye, Our subjects, be filial to your parents, affectionate to your brothers and sisters; as husbands and wives be harmonious, as friends true; bear yourselves in modesty and moderation; extend your benevolence to all; pursue learning and cultivate arts, and thereby develop intellectual faculties and perfect moral powers; furthermore advance public good and promote common interests; always respect the Constitution and observe the laws; should emergency arise, offer yourselves courageously to the State; and thus guard and maintain the prosperity of Our Imperial Throne coeval with heaven and earth. So shall ye not only be Our good and faithful subjects, but render illustrious the best traditions of your forefathers.

The Way here set forth is indeed the teaching bequeathed by Our Imperial Ancestors, to be observed alike by Their Descendants and the subjects, infallible for all ages and true in all places. It is Our wish to lay it to heart in all reverence, in common with you, Our subjects, so that we may all thus attain to the same virtue.

The 30th day of the 10th month of the 23rd year of Meiji.

Now, well over half a century later, my mother and grandmother can stumble through a recitation of these words which they claim not to have understood as they stood with their heads bowed. Japanese children absorbed through ear and posture reverence for a remote and mysterious being. Learning to sustain that posture and to endure the recitation of incomprehensible syllables were forms of discipline indispensable to Japan's excruciatingly rapid industrial and military mobilization.

Okinawans had a special challenge as recently constituted imperial subjects. Their many dialects and their geographic remove posed a barrier to the newly standardized national Japanese language. They came with a range of embarrassing customs, prompting their leaders to embark on a concerted campaign to stamp out signs of backwardness—dialect, tattooing on women, long hair on men.

In short, Okinawans had to remake themselves in an effort to become proper imperial subjects. This proved to be insufficient. At the culmination of the Pacific War, they were called upon to sacrifice their land for the sake of the mainland. Specifically, in February of 1945, when Konoe Fumimaro, prime minister prior to Tōjō Hideki, urged Emperor Hirohito to enter into immediate negotiations to end the war, Hirohito refused, citing the need to achieve military gains once more. Had Hirohito heeded Konoe's words, there would have been no Battle of Okinawa, no Hiroshima, no Nagasaki. Since "military gains" were already a fanciful notion at the time of the discussion between Hirohito and Konoe, the Battle of Okinawa was simply a strategy for delaying mainland invasion. Civilians were mobilized to tear up just-completed airstrips because there were no more kamikaze planes available, making it likely that these would serve only too conveniently for enemy landing; healthy boys and girls were chosen to run into American tanks with bombs strapped on their backs; adolescent girls served as nurses on endless retreats during which wounded soldiers and civilians were subjected to "disposal."

Those Okinawans who survived these barbarisms found that their scarred land had been offered in apparent perpetuity to the military forces of the United States, and that they had to engage in battle once more over scraps for their own subsistence. No wonder, then, that "parity with the mainland" became the rallying cry of the reversion struggles: reduction of the American military presence and the guarantee, above all, of a nuclear-free return to Japan.

Nearly twenty years after reversion, three-quarters of the American military presence in Japan is still concentrated in Okinawa; there are strong suspicions, amounting to conviction in local circles, that nuclear weapons are stored at Kadena Air Base. Okinawa today presents the disheartening if familiar spectacle of those who have been treated as second-class citizens embracing the values of their oppressors and laboring to become identical to them through stupendous and stupefying effort. Thus, the marvelous rate of school observance of the Rising Sun flag; the establishment of cram schools sufficiently demanding as to produce first-graders who can handle calculus; and the reduction of several hundred dialects thriving before the war to a mere handful.

There is still pervasive anxiety about speaking "correct" Japanese. Language is the most elusive, because subtle, traitor. If all visible difference between peoples could be effaced, speech would still threaten to betray cultural difference, too easily thought to have a genetic, and therefore racial, origin. The waves of programs to eradicate this difference in the Okinawan prewar continued into the postwar. In the late fifties and early sixties, teachers hung "dialect tags" from the necks of offending students, which could only be gotten rid of by finding other students slipping into the tabooed sounds. The hapless student who was still tagged at the end of the day had to go home wearing the badge of humiliation. Sometimes, in desperation, an offender would hit an unsuspecting classmate in the hope of eliciting an exclamation, which, naturally, would come in dialect rather than in standard Japanese.[16]

Food is another source of elemental satisfaction and humili-

---

[16]Takara Ben, "Yami no Kotoba o Tokihanate" [Set Free the Words of Darkness], *Ryū-kyūko: Shi, Shisō, Jōkyō* [The Ryukyuan Archipelago: Poetry, Thought, and Situation] (Osaka: Kaifūsha, 1988), pp. 19–31.

ation. In preparation for the National Athletic Meet, Okinawan women were mobilized to greet, house, and feed the youths who could not be accommodated in hotels. Their unquestioning readiness, young and old, to perform according to demand prompts one of my friends, also an Okinawan woman, to shake her head and say, "They're no different from the Greater Japan National Defense Women's Association"—that prewar institution of women mobilized to wave flags to soldiers at train stations, to comfort the bereaved, and to generally make themselves useful during air raid drills. The National Athletic Meet organizers had the women taking bowing lessons so that they would lower themselves to a uniform depth, and cooking lessons with standardized menus—no embarrassingly grotesque Okinawan specialties. The same friend tells me how one grandmother in her neighborhood panicked on the eve of the event because the lessons had been given too far in advance and she could not remember how to prepare the requisite fare.

Hirohito never came to the Okinawa Kokutai. He fell ill with the cancer that was to leave him dead two years later without having set foot in Okinawa as emperor. Chibana Shōichi likes the explanation of the *ojī* and *obā* of Yomitan: "It's a curse, it's divine punishment from Okinawa because he never repented what he did."[17] I asked him once, as we sat in the sun after a session at the Naha District Court, "You really wanted to bring the Kokutai to Okinawa?" "Yeah," he said, "I thought it would be good for the community, and that in Yomitan we could have a Kokutai without the flag and show the rest of the country. I was wrong." Then he added, as if he had just made the discovery, "You know, it's *all rigged!*"

It had taken some time from the telling of the tales for the families to agree upon a way to memorialize the Chibichirigama dead. For it was an enormous step to take, from keeping a secret

---

[17]Chibana, *The Burned and Discarded Rising Sun*, p. 38.

for nearly forty years to commemorating it publicly: to lay bare the shame and grief attendant on communal suicide, to risk the return of old nightmares, and to make of this stuff something plastic, public, and permanent. The families decided that together with other members of the community, they would create a sculptural memorial with a representation of each person who died. They would work under the guidance of Okinawa-born sculptor Kinjō Minoru, for it was the experience some of them had had of watching Kinjō produce his *Mother-and-Child* sculpture for Nagasaki City's Peace Memorial Park that persuaded the still-hesitant families to embark on the project. Contributions came not only from every single household in the hamlet of Namihira, where Chibichirigama is located, but from various points around the country, including Minamata, the site of devastating mercury poisoning caused by corporate irresponsibility and compounded by government collusion. Shōichi reckons that several thousand people participated directly and indirectly in the building of the statues.

First came the task of cleaning the cave that had been shunned for so many years. The families and friends sorted through the bones and artifacts and removed most, but not all of them; they had decided to preserve in one corner signs of the routine of life in the cave and of its rude ending. It was a laborious task, impossible to complete perfectly—sifting through the soil, separating out the dry, splintered bones so that they would not have to commit the desecration of walking on them. What palpable relief it must have been, then, to handle the wet clay and to give new form to the dead. Grade-school children born decades after the war worked alongside the bereaved *obā*. This is the vital substance behind the sculpture's prosaic name, "Peace Memorial to Bind the Generations."

People began to travel from afar to see the memorial and to hear the story of the cave. But only months after the figures were unveiled, Shōichi burned the flag; and then the figures were smashed, leaving their wires exposed like entrails. As Higa Heishin, head of the Chibichirigama Association of Bereaved Families and senior member of the trio responsible for the telling of the story, put it, "It's as if the victims of the cave had been killed twice over."[18] The families covered the maimed figures with a blue plastic sheet and retreated into silence. Shōichi, for his part, visited each family with a letter of apology as soon as he was released from detention. He says they worried about his safety but admits that relations were strained because of the smashing. Some blamed the writer-artist Shimojima: if only he hadn't come and made them talk about what they'd always known was best kept quiet. Heishin, reflecting on those days, says that Shōichi seemed to lose confidence in what he had done. His mother quit going to her music lessons; his father stayed home from croquet, the passion of the elderly throughout Japan. It especially grieved Shōichi to see his father, a spirited teacher of that "mean game," confining himself to the care of his grand-children. They were engaging in a form of "self-restraint," taking responsibility for the disturbance their son had caused.

To create an awkward moment is a sin in Japan; to cause disruption puts one beyond the pale. In a small community like Yomitanson, it was commonsensical to deplore Shōichi's act, especially in light of the aftermath. Naturally, his parents felt apologetic for the trouble he was causing the mayor, his former teacher, as well as for bringing the hamlet under right-wing siege. No memorial service was held at the cave on April 2, 1988. In fact, the police warned Higa Heishin against observing the oc-casion on the grounds that they couldn't guarantee the villagers' safety. Though I didn't realize its import at the time, it was while my friends and I sat in amiable conversation with Shōichi in the Combat Hut on that peaceful March day in 1989 that a message

---

[18]Quoted in Shimojima Tetsurō "Kowasareta Zō no Shīto ga Toriharawareta Hi: Chibi-chirigama 1989nen Shigatsu Futsuka" (The Day the Sheet Was Removed from the Broken Statues: Chibichirigama April 2, 1989), *Sekai*, no. 529 (July, 1989), p. 330.

arrived from Heishin (who had written it out with brush in his beautiful hand but who insisted that it be reproduced by word processor) for Shōichi to copy and distribute to the families. It called on them to gather at the cave on April 2: to cut the grass and clean the surroundings, to mourn the dead and pray for their repose, and above all, to renew their resolve to honor their sacrifice by telling of their own hopes for peace in spite of the grave shock they had recently suffered. This was the beginning of the healing of the breach between Shōichi and the villagers.

I can't find a way to get Shōichi to talk about how his business and politics might come together. Like many people, he defines politics narrowly. I remind him of the passages in his book describing how he had initially disliked the idea of going into business, the fruitless shuffle of things and money; of how he gradually discovered the central place of a general store in the life of a small community, whereupon he began to feel responsibility for the items he stocked and the information he offered. He continues to pride himself on running a good store. He wants it to be a place where people can shop comfortably regardless of their views. He maintains his old routine, out of the house by five or five-thirty to stock up for the day, with pricing taking up the rest of the morning. The afternoons are for other activities, now more various and taxing than ever. Ten o'clock is closing time for the shop. After that, though, there are often more meetings—for planning musical performances and film showings, protests against U.S. paratroop exercises, and business ventures. On the last, he clasps his hands in frustration over the impossibility of Okinawans' ever amassing enough resources to contend with mainland capital. "We think of the resorts as new bases—one more place that's off-limits to us." And in fact, when the emperor died, the new high-rise hotel was the only place in Yomitanson beside the U.S. bases that displayed the Rising Sun.

I ask Shōichi if he thinks of himself as Japanese. "That question always gives me trouble. I always find myself hesitating." My fearless guide Toshiko jumps in to help him: she has decided for herself, after the example of "Mr. LeRoi Jones" (Imamu Baraka), whom she has read avidly in translation, to call herself a Ryukyuan-Japanese. "I never hesitate," she says. But Shōichi isn't entirely persuaded. "Well, when someone says to me, 'Are you Japanese?' I want to say, 'I'm Ryukyuan'; there's something that keeps me from saying I'm Japanese outright." "You're only Japanese from an administrative point of view," continues Toshiko. "I know," Shōichi agrees. "I could just go along with common sense and call myself Japanese. And I know, if people look at me from the outside, from Asia, I am Japanese, just like the ones who went to war against Asians. But inside Japan, I want to say, I'm different, at least, I'm not the same as the Yamato race."

Yamato is a common way for Okinawans, when speaking to each other, to refer to the large islands to the north of them. (Sometimes older people will ask tourists, "Are you from Japan?") Mainlanders are "Yamatunchu," and Okinawans themselves are "Uchinanchu." This logic inclines some progressive Okinawans in the direction of nativism, a glorification of Okinawan customs as a resource to counter the lure and corruption of mainland capital. Yet this enabling appeal to tradition, like all claims to ethnic distinction, runs the risk of promoting romantic delusion as well as of replicating the structure of domination and exclusion. I wonder if Shōichi is tempted by this path. In his written statement to the court, he refers to the president of the Japan Softball Association as a Yamatunchu. It is an economic expression of contempt for the man who, having forced the display of the Rising Sun at the Forest of Peace Park, turned around and tried to worship at the cave in spite of the presence of an *obā* who stood guard and said, "This is a private grave. Let him go to Mabuni." Mabuni is a national memorial park on the southern end of

Okinawa Island, dedicated to honoring noble sacrifices to the war effort.

Chibichirigama is a short ride from the Chibana home. My friends and I take steep, narrow steps—recently installed—from the road to get down to the mouth of the cave and then stoop to get in. Inside, Shōichi relieves the darkness by lighting small candles for each of us. We make our way carefully to the back. In spite of the painstaking cleaning, it is still difficult to walk without stepping on a bone somewhere. We come to the corner where buttons, dentures, cups and saucers, eyeglasses, and bones—a child's vertebra, for instance—have been gathered together. There, Shōichi stops and speaks to us. He has done this hundreds of times before, but he is neither perfunctory nor melo-dramatic. He presents a simple, sober account of what happened here. At the end, he asks us to blow out our candles so that we can feel the darkness and try to imagine the conduct of daily tasks, and then to envision the confusion and terror when some, but not all, decided it was time to die.

Outside, to the right of the entrance, spread over the disfigured memorial, is the blue plastic sheet, so incongruous amid the dark greens, grays, and browns of the surroundings. Two weeks later, when the families gather on the anniversary, it will be removed at Higa Heishin's initiative.

Shōichi wants to show us around the area, littered with traces of double military abuse, by Japanese and Americans. We drive by the hangars intended for kamikaze bombers, the ones that went unused because there were no planes left for Okinawa. Their dark, eery curves emerge suddenly from the sugarcane fields. The airstrips that had been built with the labor of approximately three thousand workers—men, women, and children—per day, sup-plemented by several hundred horse-drawn carts, had to be torn up by the same to prevent enemy use. Once the Americans landed in Yomitan, they rebuilt the strips in no time with the help of machinery and were soon flying bombers to mainland Japan, and several years later, to Korea.[19] Since then these facilities have been used for paratroop exercises, with the consequence that villagers have lost sleep, and schoolchildren instruction, from the deafening roar of helicopters hovering by day and night. Before reversion such exercises involved equipment transport and therefore more numerous and serious accidents, including the death of a ten-year-old girl who was crushed by a parachuted trailer while playing outside her house. Now only men, not machinery, fall from the skies. They, too, can miss their targets, and garbed for chemical warfare, they make terrifying specters.

Near the old hangars there is a *chūkonhi*, a stone marker whose shape is reminiscent of a Japanese army shell. It is the site of enshrinement of the brave souls who died in combat. *Chūkonhi* are condensed, localized forms of the prefectural Defense-of-the-Nation Shrines, which in turn represent Yasukuni Shrine in Tokyo. Yasukuni Shrine constitutes a curiously egalitarian space where all who perished in the defense of the fatherland, whether thieves, outcasts, or Okinawans, were granted enshrinement, and the mothers of those fallen men are honored as "mothers of Yasukuni." The hierarchy of *chūkonhi*/prefectural Defense-of-the-Nation Shrine/ Yasukuni Shrine reflected the transformation of shrine Shinto from a local religious phenomenon into a national politico-religious one, with the emperor at its apex, not mere sovereign but direct descendant of the supreme deity, the sun goddess Amaterasu, and as such legitimized to demand the ultimate sacrifice. Part of the surface of the Yomitan memorial was blown off by American bombing. Today, shell-scarred and solitary, it stands as a pathetically sinister relic of an imposed creed, mainland Shinto.

We drive by two massive concrete *torii*, the traditional entrance

---

[19]Arasaki, *Okinawa off the Tourist Course*, pp. 60–61.

marker for Shinto shrines. Just as shrines with *torii* were greeted with abhorrence in Singapore or Korea in the days of the Co-Prosperity Sphere, so their presence here reminds us of Okinawa's quasi-colonial treatment by Japan. But there is something peculiar about these *torii:* behind them is a barbed-wire fence and rows of institutional structures. I finally grasp that this is a gateway to a U.S. military base, called, of course, "Torii Station." Some military mind had come up with the idea of identifying this intelligence base with what it presumed were the symbols of the native religion. During the Battle of Okinawa, at least, Americans had known enough about Okinawa's history to appeal to the record of exploitation by the mainland in urging for a speedy surrender. Their appeal was of no avail, to be sure, since it was precisely because of that history that Okinawans were bent on proving themselves more loyal subjects than other Japanese.

For me, the sure touch, the idiot genius with which the *torii*, complete with circular emblems of Mount Fuji between the lintels, had been turned into a symbol of goodwill toward the Okinawan natives sparks dusty memories of a school song about blossoming cherry trees and the land of the rising sun. Someone had gone to the trouble of composing it for a school fated for an ephemeral existence on an American military base in Occupation Tokyo. I hated the song—it was one that most children would easily dismiss as "dumb"—but even more, I suffered from having to conform to my schoolmates' pronunciation of Japanese place names. The old abjection comes back as angry contempt when I read a sign announcing Torii Station's welcome to a new brigadier general and his wife. It hangs inside a kiosk-like structure with an ostentatiously Okinawan tiled roof crowned by *shīsā*, porcelain lions that guard the entrance to Okinawan homes. Since 1984 this base has been home to the Green Berets, who are more and more chosen from among Asian-Americans so that they can be inconspicuous for covert operations in this part of the world. Another sign, bilingual and unadorned against the barbed wire, announces: U.S. ARMY FACILITY/UNAUTHORIZED ENTRY PROHIBITED AND PUNISHABLE BY JAPANESE LAW.

Such signs as this one reveal the extremely qualified nature of Okinawa's return to Japan in 1972. Shōichi participated in the political struggles leading to that return. He doesn't renounce that movement even today. Between remaining under American military rule and "returning" to Japan, the choice was clear. "We wanted to return so that the Constitution would apply to us literally," as our guide Toshiko puts it. She uses the English word "literally" for emphasis. In Article 9 of the postwar Japanese constitution, the "Japanese people forever renounce war as a sovereign right of the nation and the threat or use of force as a means of settling international disputes." The application of Article 9 remains one of the unfulfilled promises of reversion. On the stark northernmost point of Okinawa Island there is a natural stone marker addressed to "friends throughout the nation and the world." This is an unusual monument, for it commemorates failure, not success. It repudiates all rejoicing in a reversion that betrayed Okinawan dreams for peace. It is the *struggle* for reversion, and not the reversion itself, that should be remembered.

The history of the American presence in Okinawa is a strange one. The prewar Japanese state had no interest in fostering higher education or in preserving indigenous Okinawan traditions or artifacts. It was the American Occupation that inaugurated what are today the Ryukyu National University and the Okinawa Prefectural Museum. I have even heard friends say that if it weren't for the American bases, which took the best beaches and made them off-limits to Okinawans, there would be no nature left on Okinawa Island itself. I have heard others say that as bad as the Americans were in pre-reversion days, the Japanese have been more impervious to Okinawan demands. And that echoes anecdotes about sympathetic *kāneru* (colonels) and handsome GIs whipping out combs from back pockets in the early postwar years. The geniality and playfulness of American boys have unmistakably contributed to the Okinawan imagination.

Even so: geniality serves the ends of deliberate domination. Yomitanson villagers are reminded of this when an MP fires shots, "accidentally" or "in warning" as one of them walks outside the fence.[20] The question of Okinawa versus Japan has been reconfigured by the American military presence, for if village workers, often with Shōichi's former teacher Mayor Yamauchi or his deputy at their head, demonstrate in protest against such episodes, it is the prefectural police, or the riot police with their shields who confront them. They are also Okinawans, but Okinawans now representing the interests of the Japanese government according to the terms of the U.S.–Japan Security Treaty. The ironies of modern Japanese history find concentrated expression in Yomitan.

On a late March evening the beaches of Yomitan are deserted. Shōichi wants us to see what "mainland capital" is doing to the area. We wander along the magnificent sweep of coral-strewn beach. Like so much else, land titles were lost in the war, and everyone claimed an extra few inches here and there. The result: the mainland corporations that have bought up this land with the intent of building resorts own not only the shoreline but some of the sea itself. A few years hence, we won't be strolling here to admire the great "tortoiseshell" tombs facing the expanse of sea.

These tombs are huge structures, large enough to have sheltered in life during wartime those whom they would house forever

---

[20]As occurred on April 4, 1983. Yomitanson Shokuin Rōdōkumiai [Yomitan Village Office Workers' Union], *Dokyumento: Fukki Go no Yomitansonmin no Tatakai* [Documents: The Postreversion Struggles of Yomitan Villagers] (Yomitanson: Yomitanson Shokuin Rōdōkumiai, 1983), p. 293.

in death. Hollowing them out had required enormous communal labor; now abandoned, they are overgrown with vines, and their entranceways, normally sealed with stone slabs, stand gaping open. The "tortoiseshell" name is suggested by their shape as seen from above, but people are also reminded of the belly of a pregnant woman. Thus the tomb becomes an economical representation of death as a return to the origins of life. The Okinawan valuation of life, Shōichi explains, means that suicides traditionally couldn't be buried in the tomb proper. The tombs were meant to hold the remains of whole clans or age-groups or other cohorts, and because cremation is a relatively new practice in Okinawa, bodies were left to decompose for a period of time within the tombs and then removed for bone washing by the women of the family. The washed bones were placed in elaborate urns, which were shelved inside the tomb. The urns have already been removed from the tombs sold to make way for hotels. Imagine selling the family tomb, says Shōichi.

Family and communal ties in Okinawa have endured to a degree unimaginable in Tokyo and are all the more constricting for being dependable. One branch of a family holding out against developers is subjected to unbearable pressure from the rest of the family and neighbors, as are landowners who don't wish to yield their property for military use. And so far, observes Shōichi regretfully, resort development is the only alternative to military bases that progressives have been able to propose as a revenue source.

Dusk deepens. We can barely make out the horizon on the one hand and the tombs receding into the hillside on the other. The children have their pockets full of coral. We pile back into the van, too tired to talk.

In Okinawa the sea is omnipresent. The way to the holy site of Sēfā Utaki leads through groves of twisted trees giving suddenly to a small clearing with towering slabs of rock, one leaning sharply against the other. In the angular shelter thus formed, the woman to become chief priestess, sister of the sovereign, sequestered herself for three days and nights. In the traces of such Ryukyuan practices Japanese scholars are fond of detecting evidence of brother-sister rule in their own more remote history. Directly across the way lies Kudaka Island, where the founding Ryukyuan deity first descended. The sound of the sea roars into the stone chamber, sweeps me into its swirl and up the soaring vault. Otherwise, it is absolutely silent.

Poet, scholar, chemistry teacher, and activist Takara Ben has brought me here with his six-year-old daughter and her friend. They have been showing me the sacred sites around the southern tip of Okinawa Island. This is where he grew up, and in the darkening light he can still conjure up the speed with which a boy would want to run an errand through these groves. Here and there lie wide, flat sticks of incense. Rocks, water, and trees are all that is needed for a sacred site in Okinawa. *Torii* are super-fluous.

The south of Okinawa Island is also dotted with war memorials. The remnants of the Japanese army, together with mobilized students, girls and boys, retreated here, sought refuge in caves, and encountered civilians. Sick or injured troops were injected with potassium cyanide and finished off with bayonets or swords if necessary. Those who still survived, who were released upon orders of disbandment into the rain of shellfire, found themselves on cliff tops with the sea below and the Americans behind.

One of the most beautiful memorials takes the form of a stone sphere set at the bottom of a large ring, on one side lengthening and solidifying to form a wall bearing the sign MONUMENT TO PEACE. And indeed, it is painfully peaceful there at the tip of Kyan Point, with the azure sea interrupted by the sphere and framed by the clean contours of the ring before spreading to the horizon. The explanatory sign insinuates the glorious end of the soldiers and of the ten thousand civilians whose remains were gathered here.

Not far from Kyan Point, on Mabuni Hill, is the huge national war memorial park that the *obā* outside Chibichirigama recommended to the president of the Japan Softball Association. In Mabuni it is as if the nation's prefectures had vied with one another to design the most splendid, costly memorials to their dead. The tour buses disgorge their passengers. They dutifully buy flowers, find the pertinent memorial, bow, get themselves photographed, buy a souvenir or two and finally an ice cream cone if the day is hot, for in Okinawa, the U.S. military presence has also meant the availability of American-style ice cream— that is, one with a high fat content.

But almost no one stops at the Okinawa Prefectural Peace Memorial Museum, perhaps deliberately situated beneath the memorial-studded hill. There, it is still possible to find documentation of the several dimensions of the war, to see the multiple implements of compulsory suicide, and finally, in a darkened room, to read page after page of oral history to learn that even Japanese soldiers didn't die shouting banzai to the emperor. If they had the strength, they called out to their mothers or their wives or their sweethearts.

All projects dedicated to the world of darkness seem obligated to admit a ray of light in the form of evidence of an inextinguishable human spirit. Here, it comes almost as an afterthought at the end of the museum, in a corner devoted to the POW camps formed as more and more Okinawans surrendered. There is the extraordinarily elaborate wedding dress stitched from parachute fabric; and samples of the ubiquitous *sanshin*, the traditional Okinawan three-stringed instrument, rigged out of empty cans and field cot frames, said to have filled the camps with song and dance even in those dazed, desperate days. But this corner in no way attenuates the force of so many words on death and dying. Museum goers who spend time in the oral history room stagger out of the darkness and sink into benches. I overhear a young man confessing to his companion, "I'm no good at places like this."

Memorial hill is blindingly bright. Here, the dead have been silenced by noble formulas carved into gaudy stones. As I stand in the sun, the voices locked in my skull from the dark museum room burst out and release their agony into the air. In Mabuni the wind over the dazzling sea is heavy with the shrieks of the dying.

All over Okinawa elderly women sit before altars with pictures of husbands young and handsome enough to be their grandsons. How can one say to them, your husband died a dog's death? Yet without the arduous exchange that would be provoked by such words, the bereaved are twice duped: this time, into accepting the shoddy redemption offered by the state in the form of stones carved with ornate language in addition to the naked cash provided survivors. The only way not to let those deaths be wasted is to acknowledge how those lives were squandered.

Yet it is precisely here in the south where losses were the greatest, where, a taxi driver told me, every time you saw a tree with ripe fruit you could bet there was a rotting corpse underneath, that there is most support for the government's version of war death. That account relies on the rhetoric of sacrifice by noble spirits, a rhetoric that found its culmination in some of the writings of the late novelist Mishima Yukio. This conjuncture of massive suffering and willing acceptance of government explanations is hardly distinctive of Okinawa; it also pertains among the bereaved in Nagasaki and Hiroshima, and indeed, throughout Japan.

Camouflage gear reminiscent of Vietnam, along with miniature weapons and the ubiquitous ice cream, are the staple of souvenir shops lining the way to the most popular spot of all, the Princess Lily Memorial. This commemorates the 194 teachers and girls aged fifteen to nineteen who died while mobilized as students of two elite girls' high schools. Their school magazines were called *The Young Princess* and *The White Lily*. The image of young girls nursing wounded soldiers only to die themselves—by the standard combination of American fire and self-administered hand grenades—has proved irresistible to the popular imagination and has bred an unholy industry capitalizing on the not-so-subliminal association of chastity and patriotism. This memorial is never without flowers—a roadside vendor does a brisk business—and neighborhood enterprises, including a cactus park down the road featuring black figures in a Wild West setting, have profitably adopted the Lily name.

Toshiko is a graduate of one of the schools, older by two or three years than the ill-fated group. I persuade her to take me to the new museum next to the memorial, opened, it is said, precisely to counter the lurid commercialism. Snortingly skeptical, she nonetheless accommodates me. She has brought a red rose, and we stop first at the memorial. Tossing it on the pile of wilting flowers, she speaks, as if face-to-face: "Here I am. I was a few years ahead of you in school. I brought you a rose. I grew it myself." Her tone is, as usual, brisk and matter-of-fact, her "you" intimate.

So there is Toshiko's way of remembering the dead by direct address. And there is Shōichi's. He can and does tell the *obā* of Chibichirigama that what happened in the cave was in part retribution for the Okinawan role in Japanese aggression in Asia.

Late June in Yomitanson. The monsoon has left Okinawa and will never get to Hokkaido. The two places live a different rhythm from the rest of the archipelago. Once the monsoon has broken, the days are uncompromisingly hot, and Okinawans are resourceful with remedies for enduring the heat ranging from concoctions featuring bitter gourd to more than usually serious drinking. In the potter Mabui's house in Yomitan, the nights are comfortable. It is a dilapidated farmhouse that she has made exquisitely habitable by adding floors, walls, doors, windows, and ceilings, mostly by herself, as pieces abandoned by others in favor of new synthetic materials presented themselves on her walks. The roof leaks during typhoons, but that doesn't matter, she points out, if there really isn't anything to get hurt. In the morning light Mabui's living room becomes a quiet celebration of the possibilities of wood and vine: wide floorboards smooth from wear, wisteria rug, bamboo blinds. Colors come from muted Indian and Tibetan fabrics.

Mabui is an Okinawan beauty. Raised by a grandfather from the age of four, she is versed in herbal and maritime lore. Virtually everything growing around the kiln in her garden is edible and medicinal. Except for a group of tombs, her house is isolated. She doesn't mind. "Mabui," her Okinawan name, as she calls it, means "spirit."

She has never belonged to a movement before, but she has become an active member of the Yomitanson Committee for Peace. I first met her at a meeting of Chibana supporters in the cramped upstairs of an Okinawan bar in Tokyo. They had gathered in part to prepare for the resumption of the Chibana trial after six months of "self-restraint." Actually, for the two ongoing Chibana trials: one for Shōichi, of course, and another for Chibana Moriyasu, no relation but a fellow member of the Yomitanson Committee for Peace. Moriyasu, a melon farmer, was charged with obstructing police efforts to apprehend Shōichi after the flag burning—ludicrously enough, given that Shōichi himself was asked to wait before turning himself in because his arrest warrant wasn't ready.

The discussion that night in Tokyo reflected the tensions within movements such as this one. First of all, those who are drawn to such activities are naturally the opinionated and assertive minority in a society that passionately believes in the advantages of being genuinely opinionless if possible and unassertive if not.

Moreover, the Chibana defense team consists of lawyers from Tokyo, Osaka, and Okinawa. This not only poses daunting financial and logistical burdens but more delicate challenges as well. The Osaka team is the most aggressive in proposing strategy. But it has been observed that Okinawan movements become dominated by mainlanders, for Okinawa is as seductive to progressive intellectuals as it is to corporate and military concerns. The contrast it still offers to the frenetic yet jaded urban Yamato culture can unwittingly prompt a version of colonial behavior: an eroticized attraction on the one hand and scornful impatience on the other. The Osaka attorneys try to defer to Okinawan initiative. But the local attorneys are comparatively young and overburdened by cases involving U.S. military bases, and they seem more comfortable deferring to their experienced mainland counterparts. To coordinate these elements through what could easily be a ten-year court struggle requires a staggering amount of tact, faith, and feasting. This Mabui understands exquisitely. Her generosity is immense.

It survives, perhaps is intensified by the staggering heat of her kiln under a cloudless summer sky. It is the same blue sky of the travel posters, but instead of the blue sea punctuated with the bikini-clad young from Tokyo, there is the variegated texture with muted tones of an herb garden through which Mabui moves, dressed for work in cotton pants and shirt, with a scarf holding her waist-long hair on top of her head, away from sweating brow and torso. She goes through three complete changes a day when she is firing. She has just finished preparing a shipment for Osaka and offers to accompany me to Shōichi's house, where his mother has agreed to see me during Shōtarō's nap. Shōtarō is the son born during Shōichi's detention. He is asleep, as promised, and Mikiyo the daughter is in day care. Since the flag burning, senior and junior Chibanas have lived together. Holes in the sliding doors immediately indicate the presence of young children: they come from the same poking and shredding my young cousins, and my own son after them, performed in our grandmother's house. Unrepaired, these doors suggest a shared practical good-humored tolerance.

Now, almost two years after the event, a certain normalcy has returned to this household, although Mrs. Chibana and her daughter-in-law Yōko are quick to speculate, with a mixture of resignation and gaiety, about what life will be like without the trial—"Maybe we'll get all those letters answered!" Mr. Chibana has been back at croquet for some time now, and Mrs. Chibana resumed her music lessons after one year. She took up *sanshin* (the three-stringed instrument) first, then returned to her other groups gradually. Her friends wanted her back sooner, but she hadn't felt free—all those groups involved dancing, she adds by way of explanation. So, I learn, in this sort of community, a woman taking responsibility for her grown son's antisocial behavior finds playing a musical instrument more acceptable than dancing.

Yōko, who worked for six years as a nurse in Tokyo, doesn't have the extensive communal involvements of either her in-laws or her husband. She belongs to one age-group *moai*, or mutual financial assistance association, just so that she'll have some friends when she's her mother-in-law's age. Her mother-in-law, whom she refers to as *Obāchan*, "Grandma," is now in the old folks' group, having retired from the women's group at the prescribed age of sixty. Yōko hasn't entered the women's group yet because she doesn't have any ties with the other members and she doesn't think it would be fun. Most of her age-group don't understand her situation, and she doesn't feel like initiating conversation about it. Yōko worries that *Obāchan* worries that she doesn't have any friends coming over. She thinks her life is full enough for the moment.

Shōichi's, on the other hand, is too full. Both women are anxious about his health. They think he won't be able to play a mean game of croquet like his father when he's that age. He seems to have a blessedly easygoing streak, I counter. "Ah, you don't see what he's really like," says Mrs. Chibana. "He's always tired. There're stresses in the family, at the store, in the support group that don't show on the outside. He's asked to make appearances everywhere. But he always tries to get all the morning chores done before he runs off to the airport. Sometimes he misses his flights just because some group has turned up, asking him to guide them to the cave. They're joking about firing the president over at the store."

Even so, this is preferable to the long strain that set in after the right-wing invasion of the village and the smashing of the memorial. "*Ojīchan* [Grandpa] said he would never forgive Shō-ichi," says Yōko. "He told me to tell him not to expect any cooperation from him," adds Mrs. Chibana. "But when the book came out, *Ojīchan* read it right away. His age-group began to read it, too. We put two hundred copies by the check-out at the supermarket and they sold really well."

"*Ojīchan* still thinks he shouldn't have burned the flag. I've wondered, too, why he had to be the one to do it. But I don't think he did anything wrong." Yōko refers to her husband in the old-fashioned mode as *Otōsan,* "Father." After Shōtarō's birth, she had wanted to come straight back from the hospital, but everyone thought she should stay with her own parents until things calmed down. "The neighbors used to look in on me. I thought it was a little strange, but I didn't realize until my parents told me that everybody thought I was going to leave him." Yōko laughs in recollection. It was not just the uninvolved and the elderly who speculated in that vein. Mabui and one other member had been designated by the Committee for Peace to talk to Yōko in case she was thinking of divorcing Shōichi.

His mother still has misgivings. "If only he hadn't burned the flag. But I know that's why the movement's spread around the country. I shouldn't have sent him off to university. You should have seen him before then, he was such a good boy." He must

have shown early signs of leadership, for the other children in
the neighborhood used to wait for Shōichi until he was ready to
leave and then follow him to school. "He didn't do anything
wrong," she continues. "Sometimes I feel like saying so out loud
to everybody at New Year's parties and all the other get-togethers."
It is only when I listen to this last comment on tape back in
Tokyo that I catch the sob in her voice. Mrs. Chibana, like the
rest of her family, is a handsome, unaffected person accustomed
to conducting herself with confidence.

Mrs. Chibana still thinks her son shouldn't speak out of turn
at his trial. Yōko also used to wonder if this wasn't rude of him,
but his supporters have assured her otherwise. "I can't really tell
what's going on, so I go by how Father's behaving."

Mrs. Chibana won't go to the courthouse, but she insists that
Yōko go. "She worries about me, wants to stay home, but I tell
her to go, that I'll do what I can here." That has meant, for
instance, cooking for all the supporters who gather for the trial.
Mrs. Chibana used to make sea-grass tempura, but that can't be
prepared in advance, so she has settled on noodles in broth,
Okinawa-style. There are usually about sixty who come, and she
has enough bowls for all of them. "I don't know if I'll make it
to the end of the trial. I'm just going to do what I can."

We have been talking long enough to run over Shōtarō's nap-
time. He sleeps in a basket suspended from the ceiling, and Mabui
keeps him content for another half hour by pulling on the rope
and rocking him gently. When he has had enough of that, his
grandfather steps in, puts on a record, and starts doing hand
movements with him to the music. This is a seventy-year-old
who had just lifted a motorcycle single-handedly onto a pickup
truck so that it can go in for repairs. He begins his day at six,
seven days a week, by cleaning up the supermarket.

Mr. Chibana is equally good with his granddaughter, who
suffers from a congenital brain disorder. Yōko remembers how
sad she was that their eyes never met while she was nursing her.

Mikiyo is only now learning to call out to her father, but she has been utterly attached to *Ojīchan* and still likes to fall asleep with him. Yōko and Shōichi have taken her to be treated by specialists on the mainland, and Shōichi converses knowledgeably about her condition. They are all much happier now that she is in a day-care facility where she is treated much the same as other children, and they have been able to see her progress in a matter of months. They are awaiting the birth of a third child. I have never met so capacious a family.

I am coming to recognize that Chibana Shōichi should not be understood simply as an exceptional individual, an entrepreneur who suddenly took the extraordinary step of burning the flag. The qualities that make so many people, including me, respond to him as to a "born" leader were nurtured by a particular family situated in a distinctive community. The shape of that community, in turn, owes a great deal to the direction of Mayor Yamauchi Tokushin, Shōichi's high school history teacher.

The village office is not far from the church where Shōichi and Yōko, whose mother is Christian, were married. A large billboard next to the main gate displays the text of Article 9, the war-renunciation clause, of the Constitution. At the bottom right are cartoon figures of a Japanese soldier pointing a rifle at a group of children and elderly men and women, with balloons containing the words "Commit collective suicide" and "The young and old are holding us back!" It is difficult to imagine such an entranceway to a bureaucratic agency anywhere else in the country.

Mayor Yamauchi is necessarily a supple politician. As the mere head of a village, he has had to take on both the Japanese national government and the United States armed forces, which he has done with astounding success. The fifteen years of his administration have seen the construction of a village welfare center on the edge of an American base and the completion of village athletic facilities, including the luxurious Forest of Peace Stadium, within Yomitanson Auxiliary Airfield. American commanders complain that these lands were "provided" to U.S. forces by the Japanese government. Yamauchi retorts that the land was not the Japanese government's to provide. It was plundered, first by the Japanese military, and then by the American. And, as Yamauchi has lectured to less-than-appreciative American commanders, it was his study of American democracy that taught him the importance of respecting local rights.

Yamauchi wanted the first village athletic facilities to be built on the finest site in Yomitan, at a spot where there would always be ocean breezes. Such a site, a survey concluded, existed within the airfield, coincidentally the exact location where the Americans were preparing to construct a PC3 antenna. Ingenious tactics of negotiation and protest (such as the mayor's waiting for hours for days on end just to catch American commanders as they stepped out of meetings to go to the men's room) failed to persuade the Americans to change their plans. Then Yamauchi got wind of plans to dispatch Japanese riot police, a sure provocation to violence. He decided to appeal directly to Jimmy Carter, "the person vested with supreme responsibility for the American people," as he puts it, to halt construction of the antenna. After sending out the letter—in Japanese ("Why would a Japanese compose a document in horizontal writing to begin with?")—he held a press conference to disclose the text of his message, which was widely reprinted in both local and national newspapers. The riot police did not appear. Instead, the mayor was roundly scolded by telephone from Tokyo for meddling in foreign affairs. He says he responded by asking, "Is foreign policy the exclusive business of the national government? If so, think of all the times I've been to the American bases, the consulates and the embassy, the [Japanese] Defense Facilities Administration, when nobody would listen. The American people are guaranteed the right to pursue happiness by their Constitution. Aren't the people of Yomitanson entitled to pursue their own happiness?" He says that Tokyo retorted with "Thanks to what you did with that press conference and all, we couldn't even send out the riot police."

The response from Carter was slow in coming. In fact, the mayor had just decided to send a sample of Yomitan weaving to Rosalynn with a request that she put in a good word with her husband when word came from the local base that not only would work on the antenna be discontinued, but prior construction would be removed. The mayor had the athletic field rushed to completion for a fall opening. For the ceremonies he invited the American commander and his wife as the guests of honor. He knew this would incense the villagers, as well as the young members of the village office workers' union. So he told them that for the opening event, he was planning a footrace in which the top three officials of Yomitan would run against the top three officers from the U.S. base, and that moreover, he intended to win. Which he did. Yamauchi Tokushin cannot possibly be taller than my mother, who is four feet ten. "I knew the Americans would come in their heavy leather shoes. I was going to wear my spikes." He adds, eyeing me pointedly, "It was for show. American soldiers like that sort of thing, you know." He thinks it gave him maneuvering room. "You see, of all sports events, nothing brings people out like track. I could say to the Americans if they came back asking for more land (which they did), 'Did you see all our young people out there? If they started to protest, I wouldn't be able to hold them back.' "

It took another five years of struggle against the American military and the Japanese government before the Forest of Peace Stadium could be built. After initially encouraging village employees to participate in the communal protest against paratroops exercises (sending up giant kites, parking cars, or singing and dancing to Okinawan tunes on the runways), the mayor changed strategies, withdrew his staff, and negotiated successfully, though controversially, for the construction of a baseball park for joint

U.S.–Japanese use within the auxiliary airfield, right near the paratrooper training field. During that campaign he spent hours on research to produce a letter two yards long in which he rehearsed the history of the United States, "the source of the democracy that has given us our hopes and our dreams"; reviewed the work of Gandhi, Tagore, and Nehru; and finally, reminded the American diplomat to whom it was addressed that when Admiral Perry stopped in Yomitan in 1853 before sailing on to Tokyo, the villagers had provided him with eggs, chicken, and cucumber. He was not, he made clear, requesting repayment of a 130-year-old debt. He was pleading his case, drawing on the examples he respected most in the hope of receiving diplomatic assistance to gain the right to construct the Forest of Peace Stadium within the grounds of an American base.

The stadium was built. The softball games of the National Athletic Meet were held. Shōichi burned the flag and was indicted. Paratroop exercises have intensified.

Mabui recalls running into Tokushin during paratroop exercises as protestors experimented with strange, distracting sounds. The drawback to this technique was that the noise bothered the villagers as much as the American paratroopers. The mayor asked Mabui if she had any suggestions, and she came up with the idea of sending up electronically controlled toy airplanes.

Yomitanson, with a population of thirty thousand, is entitled to incorporate as a city. It remains a village by choice of its inhabitants. The artist Shimojima Tetsurō goes so far as to say that perhaps, in all Japan, Yomitanson alone has attempted to realize the democracy that the end of the war was to have brought the entire nation.

Yamauchi Tokushin walks a tightrope between the United States armed forces and the Japanese national government. His ambitions push him to the brink: don't just build an athletic facility inside an American base, but put it next to the paratrooper training field, then host an event for the National Athletic Meet.

He thought he could do it with impunity, that is, distinguish between Kokutai and *kokutai*—liberate the body in sport from the body politic. Was it hubris? He uses the word "earthquake" to describe the forces that overwhelmed him, that forced him to promise the Rising Sun on the eve of the games. If only he had had more time. "But we didn't sing the anthem. And we put up the anti-nuclear flag alongside."

"Shōichi expressed our feelings for us," he says. "People say it's inconsistent for us to have waved the Rising Sun in the reversion struggle and to be rejecting it now. In those days we were protesting the abuse of human rights by Americans. In any age, the people have a right to protest oppression. It's resistance that's important. Go on passively accepting the flag and the anthem today. It should be obvious, what's down the road. These are choices that we as citizens of modern Japan must make. That's what Shōichi was doing, because even though he belongs to the postwar generation, he learned the lesson of Chibichirigama. Now he and I are in the positions of defendant and plaintiff. But he'll go on asserting his civil rights. And for my part, as representative of this village, I'll pursue the Rising Sun issue to the end. I'll fight its imposition. I think we'll both act in ways that will bear the scrutiny of history, and that our paths will meet."

I tell him that I had frankly grown critical of him inasmuch as it was his bringing charges against Shōichi that gave the state the opportunity to stage a trial whereby the Rising Sun could be established as the official flag of Japan. He responds that he had always thought of the trial as a means by which Shōichi's act could become more than an incident. I ask him about the just-announced U.S. Supreme Court decision in *Texas v. Gregory Lee Johnson*, in which Johnson's burning of the American flag was determined to be protected speech. The mayor is silent for a moment, then says, "Given the state of the Japanese courts today, it is possible that Chibana Shōichi's act will not be properly evaluated. But history will prove him right."

The mayor has his eye on the history of the future. I cannot help hoping that that history, in Yomitan, will claim among its agents the survivors of the cave. I have hesitated to meet them. Unlike Shōichi, who belongs to their community, and Shimojima Tetsurō, who has devoted years of his life to recording them, I don't think I have the right to hear their stories. And, I suppose, I am afraid to hear them directly, even though I've read them over and over in Shimojima's writings. A young television producer I meet in Nagasaki tells me that in interviewing victims of the A-bomb, she has been moved to interrupt her subjects: if it hurts you so much to remember, please stop; I am not worthy of asking you to tell me.

But I am also driven, perhaps by an atavistic impulse to *see* human beings who have survived extremities. Shōichi arranges for me to meet Higa Heishin, head of the families' association, and two women, Chibana Kamado and Yogi Toshi. Mabui drives Toshiko and me to the Heishin home. Mrs. Heishin is dressed in black, preparing to attend a funeral. I remember the announcement of a death in the community from a loudspeaker on a civic center truck breaking the silence of Mabui's neighborhood early that morning. The details complete each other, suggesting one more way in which this community is bound together, sustaining and constricting its members.

Higa Heishin supposes that he heads the association of the bereaved because all the others are women, and because he lost fifteen close relatives. Shimojima has written that as part of his basic training in Korea, Heishin, along with others, had spent three months practicing with his sword on straw figures. At the end of this training period, his commander strapped the old Chinese who had been working for the division onto the straw figure and ordered the men to thrust into his heart. When the men hesitated, the commander lopped off the old man's head to make the assignment easier. Thereafter, each time the division approached a new village, the men beheaded the guide who had brought them.[21] I'd like to ask Mr. Higa about those days, see what shape he gives to them, listen for his accents to find out if and how he relates those experiences on the continent to the Chibichirigama episode that he worked so hard to unearth. I make several forays, but they are parried. I suspect that this soft-spoken gentleman wouldn't—and why should he?—be comfortable recounting those experiences to a woman, even a foreign one.

So instead I find out how he learned of the deaths of his relatives. The first night he spent with his parents after demobilization, his uncle appeared to him in a dream. He began to sob in his sleep, which prompted his parents to awaken him. Heishin demanded to know what had happened in his absence and was told that all those relatives were dead. There were mumblings about smoke inhalation, but no other details. And after that, a wall of silence went up, unassailable for thirty-eight years.

Meeting him, I am puzzled that he should have held so firmly to the resolve to overcome that silence. Maybe I am obtuse to a passion that seems, finally, like a wordless obstinacy. The detail of the dream, which he repeats, alerts me to an unexpected sensibility in the man. He also uses an interesting word, *hana-shikiru*, meaning "to say completely," "to tell everything," to explain why the survivors gathered in groups of twos and threes once they decided to talk. A person couldn't tell it all by himself, thinks Mr. Higa.

Mr. Higa belongs to the majority holding that Shōichi should not have burned the flag. True, he worries about the recent prominence of the flag in schools, something that has happened without people quite noticing it. But he has a sense of limits, and he thinks that Yomitan resisted to the extent possible and

---

[21]Shimojima Tetsurō, "The Day the Sheet Was Removed," pp. 352–53.

that it was time to give in. Like most members of the families' association, he wants to see the statues restored, even though Shimojima and others are arguing that the damage inflicted by the rightist youths needs to be preserved as much as the record of wartime violence. The parents of one of the youths convicted of smashing the statues have come to see Mr. Higa to apologize, to express regret that they had not taught their son about the war, and to offer payment for restoration. It was refused.

We look at some of Mr. Higa's picture albums. He belongs to a group that recently erected a memorial to their fallen comrades in Thailand. The Rising Sun is conspicuous. I cannot bring myself to say anything. Mabui and Toshiko are also silent. I tell Mr. Higa about *Texas v. Gregory Lee Johnson*. He takes it in quietly, and I cannot tell what he thinks. Toshiko, by contrast, says, half-accusingly (to me) and encouragingly (to him), "You see? You're always criticizing America, but that's why I prefer it to Japan." Mr. Higa finally says, "Have you told Shōichi yet?"

This I am able to do while he drives me in one or the other of the two battered vans that he maneuvers with reckless expertise on the narrow, hilly roads of Yomitan. The news of the U.S. Supreme Court decision obviously excites him. I save for the end the mayor's parting words on Japanese justice and his prophecy of Shōichi's vindication by history. Shōichi all but stops the van and half turns toward me, hands still on steering wheel. When he finally speaks, it is only to ask, "Did he really say that?"

Shōichi takes time off from the supermarket to introduce me to some of the old women survivors of the cave. Listening to him talk with the *obā*, I grow dialect-hungry: it suddenly feels lonely to be confined to standard Japanese, a language produced in the course of a centralizing, rationalizing history. Even its less formal locutions don't convey the intimacy that dialect seems to offer.

From Yogi Toshi I learn new details: what it was like to have a baby in diapers in the cave, for instance. Mrs. Yogi washed the dishes in a small stream just outside the entrance, which was protected by an overhang, but the clothes and diapers down-stream, hanging them out to dry on branches. That was in late March of 1945, when she could no longer go home after dark to prepare meals for ten, the size of her extended family minus the men. Before that, she had come to the cave only during the most severe air raids. Getting there was hard because she had a five-year-old, a five-month old, and a severely asthmatic mother-in-law in her charge. Grandma often had to sit down to catch her breath even if they could hear the bombers approaching. Then Mrs. Yogi would have to carry both her baby and her mother-in-law on her back. Why didn't she end up dead on April 2? She says she was prepared to die, but her five-year-old boy said no, he wanted to grow up so that he could kill the Americans. "I thought that made sense, so I said to Grandma, 'This is war, so no holding grudges, okay?' and left the cave." Her mother-in-law, along with her nieces, ended up coming out half an hour later. They had a single kimono cord around their necks, but they had changed their minds. What does Mrs. Yogi think of the flag today? "The Rising Sun? I wouldn't mind if it were a symbol of peace, if everybody around the world thought so, too."

In describing life in the cave, Mrs. Yogi refers to Chibana Kamado, who was known as *bāchīgua* or "auntie" because of her good nature. *Gua* is the diminutive suffix Okinawans apply with promiscuous affection to everything from a cup of coffee to an island. I remember Chibana Kamado's story more vividly than any of the others. She was one of the four women who put out the first fire in the cave. On April 2, as smoke filled the cave, she groped toward the entrance with her baby daughter in her arms and a six-year-old son hanging on to her clothes. Just as they were about to step into the daylight, her son stumbled over a body and let go; her daughter seemed on the verge of suffocating, so she pressed forward. The daughter lived, thanks to a piece of sugarcane that an American soldier stuck in her mouth as soon as he saw her. Kamado went back to find her son, but the smoke blocked her path. I remember Shōichi telling me about the first time he tried to take her back to the cave. She patted the walls and burst into sobs of "I'm sorry, I'm sorry."

At seventy-one, Chibana Kamado has an unforgettable face covered with deep, dark brown wrinkles. Her small frame carries no flesh. She single-handedly grows and harvests enough sugarcane to deliver seven truckloads. When I meet her, she is relaxing from her bath after a day in the fields. The three of them, she and Shōichi and her husband, a vigorous ninety-year-old, talk amiably about the mosquitoes at the cramped apartment where they are staying while they await completion of a new home to be shared with a son and grandchildren. This is her third husband. Her second, by whom she has several children, is dead. She never sought survivors' benefits for her daughter because regulations required her to temporarily declare the children by her second husband illegitimate. Chibana Kamado has never reproached Shōichi for the consequences of the flag burning. She seems to have vast resources of humor. I cannot ask her anything, except, do you ever forget? No, she says. I have dreams. I never forget.

My parting image of Shōichi has him standing in a park near Naha courthouse, microphone in hand, addressing a rally after hearings on melon farmer Chibana Moriyasu's case. It is a colorful assembly, with the huge banners characteristic of Japanese demonstrations of any kind and a fair number of masked figures, the remnants of a faction of the student movement of the late sixties and early seventies. (I learn that a rival faction is accusing Shōichi of being a government collaborator who was only trying to make trouble for the progressive Yamauchi administration.) Shōichi offers an incisive analysis of the morning's proceedings in the courtroom and its implications for future struggle. Everyone listens intently in the blistering heat while he speaks. I juxtapose this sunlit Shōichi with the one standing in the dark to tell the story of Chibichirigama.

Since that telling, I have had the chance to hear another compulsory-suicide story, this one told by a woman, also of Shōichi's generation and mine. She has heard from her mother about how her grandmother insisted that her husband slit the throats of his family with his razor. The only son died, and the daughters lost consciousness but were saved by American soldiers, and the wife lived out her years with a tube inserted in her throat. She never forgave her husband for the death of their son. What struck me was the granddaughter's abiding anger, not only at the circumstance of war and the ethos that both compelled and permitted such action, but most especially at her own family for having participated, for having submitted to their own victimization. No doubt it is Shōichi's blessing that his family was not involved in compulsory suicide, that it is in part this distance that makes possible his extraordinary sympathy, which allows him to urge the survivors to acknowledge their own complicity as Okinawans in Japanese aggression.

From that sympathy emanates the faith that impels Shōichi to awaken his people and through them, all of Japan, to their historical responsibilities—an improbable project in the face of common sense, produced by government, business, perennially unsuccessful opposition parties, and, above all, the solidity of everyday life in a successful society. Shōichi's efforts are fraught with contradiction. Necessarily so, for he continues to be an aspiring member of that successful society. Yet thus far he has not overcome, or perhaps, been abandoned by, his innocence, sustaining an ethical imagination that allows him to recount the past as if in the first person so as to earn the right to address the future.

I struggle back to Tokyo freighted with memories and gifts from the Naha market, a labyrinth of shops with pickled scallions, dried sardines, tender fish cakes, fresh-fried doughnuts, linen and cotton jackets, pajamas, aprons, pottery, flowers. Premodern ecstasy. Nothing is packaged: from moth-repelling herbs to brown envelopes, goods are simply bundled. The taxi driver from the airport in Tokyo is surprisingly expert about the best route home for me. He asks where I have been, and when I tell him, he says the fish must have been good. I say yes, and ask where he is from. Niigata, in northern Japan. The fish there is fabulous, he says. You don't feel like eating sashimi in Tokyo for a while once you've been home. But home is too expensive to visit much. In fact, he hardly ever does it anymore, he can't afford the going-home gifts. So he does it covertly, packing the family in the cab and staying at business hotels, the high-rise equivalent of motels in space-hungry Japan.

My grandmother exclaims over the breadth and thickness of the seaweed I have brought back. It is an instant reminder of her birthplace at the opposite end of the archipelago. Sixty-five years after leaving Hokkaido, she has never stopped yearning for it. Fingering the luxurious seaweed, my grandmother thinks, by analogy, what a good place Okinawa must be. She considers another souvenir, Mayor Yamauchi's 1989 policy statement to the Yomitanson village assembly, and sighs with envy. She doesn't often come across politicians willing to address issues of peace and justice so forthrightly. A product of the northern frontier, notoriously frail in the heat, my grandmother will never visit Okinawa. But it has begun to take root in her imagination, through its suffering and its bounty.

II

YAMAGUCHI

AN ORDINARY WOMAN

ON JUNE 1, 1988, a historic 14–1 verdict of the Supreme Court of Japan, overturning the decisions of two lower courts, pronounced the termination in failure of a widow's fifteen-year contest of the legality of state participation in the Shinto enshrinement of her deceased husband. I read about the case in the *New York Times*. Enshrinement, more technically apotheosis (*gōshi* in Japanese, also not an everyday word), here means conferring the status of a Shinto deity upon a deceased person. No doubt an unreflectingly modern, Westernized part of myself was embarrassed at being confronted with such signs of atavism in my homeland. But it was a different sense of historical futility that more immediately swept over me. To think that a widow could not prevent the state from turning her deceased husband into an object of veneration, and that this denial would be cynically ratified by the highest judicial body of the land, filled me with rage and despair.

The significance of the suit brought by Mrs. Nakaya Yasuko lies beyond the merely legal: the case reflects the incommensurateness of judicial capability and judicial will with the challenges she issued to Japanese militarism, to the Japanese treatment of religious minorities, and to the situation of women in Japanese society.

Mrs. Nakaya, with her small size, round face, and ready smile—even moments after defeat in the Supreme Court—seems, disarmingly, the very essence of ordinary middle-aged womanhood. This quality has been much insisted upon by the media. Those who are sympathetic to her tacitly invoke her pleasing ordinariness: how inappropriate for the state to exercise its power against such a harmless (almost: such an insignificant) presence. Those who find her offensive, on the other hand, feel duped by her appearance: what business does she have defying communal values, looking the way she does? Her opponents come closer to the mark, for if there is one thing that distinguishes Mrs. Nakaya, it is her unfailing penchant for seeing abstract repression in daily acts, a capacity for feeling the tyranny of common sense. And she is remarkable, too, for the way in which her insights and passions find release in her own expressive but plain language.

Moments after I am introduced to her at a crowded publication party for one of her attorneys, Mrs. Nakaya tells me that she is concerned about her son, who is preparing to get married. He was six at the time of Mr. Nakaya's death and has chosen in adulthood to live in the northern city where his father died. She worries that he is insufficiently free, that he is too attuned to the desires of those around him. Such directness is startling. Middle-class Japanese women normally are not forthcoming with strangers, and in any case they would never brood over their grown sons' conformity. Nor can this candor be explained away by the festive occasion. Some time later, when I talk to her by telephone to make arrangements to visit her, Mrs. Nakaya asks me to spend one night at her house. I tell her I am delighted, but knowing she has a demanding job as a cook at a municipal day-care center, I am worried about tiring her. She reassures me that I will not be in her way, she will not do anything special for me. She adds, with sincerity, that she does not understand Japanese life very well.

Mrs. Nakaya's husband Takafumi was a member of the Self-Defense Force of Japan. He joined when it was still the National Police Reserve, which was established at the initiative of Douglas MacArthur in response to the outbreak of the Korean War. Article 9 of the Japanese Constitution, which was also shaped by MacArthur, states that

> . . . the Japanese people forever renounce war as a sovereign right of the nation and the threat or use of force as means of settling international disputes.
>
> In order to accomplish the aim of the preceding paragraph, land, sea, and air forces, as well as other war potential, will never be maintained. The right of belligerency of the state will not be recognized.

In 1954 the National Police Reserve was converted into Land, Air, and Maritime Self-Defense Forces, whose existence allegedly does not violate this article. In terms of gross measurements of ground troops, ships, and task planes, Japan's military strength now ranks sixth in the world.[1]

Nakaya Takafumi was killed in 1968 in a traffic accident while on the job as a member of the Self-Defense Force in Morioka in northern Japan. Three years later, the Self-Defense Force branch in Takafumi's native Yamaguchi Prefecture, together with the prefectural Veterans' Association (a private organization established to "bridge the gap" between the public and the SDF) initiated proceedings to enshrine his spirit in the local (prefectural)

---

[1]Defense Agency, *White Paper on Defense*, 1988, cited in Foreign Press Center, *Facts and Figures of Japan* (Tokyo: Foreign Press Center/Japan: 1989), p. 25.

Defense-of-the-Nation Shrine. His widow, a Christian, registered her unequivocal objection to these plans. Nevertheless, she eventually received a communication from the shrine in which her husband's name appeared with the title *mikoto*, indicating that he had become a deity. In consultation with her minister, Mrs. Nakaya filed suit in 1973 against the Yamaguchi Prefectural Branch of the Self-Defense Force and the Veterans' Association. She charged them with violation of the constitutional provision for separation of religion and state as well as violation of her religious rights. Fifteen years later, overturning substantial recognition of these claims at the district-court and high-court levels, the Supreme Court ruled in favor of the defendants.

Not long after the publication party, Mrs. Nakaya's supporters gathered for a different sort of occasion: the first anniversary of the Supreme Court defeat. Several members of her legal team (a mixture of Christians and non-Christians), constitutional scholars, writers, and Mrs. Nakaya herself were on hand to address the assembly. The first part of the evening was taken up with a slide show dramatizing the events that led up to the long courtroom struggle.

The line drawings began with the ominous appearance of an SDF agent at the small Nakaya apartment in January of 1968. I had read several versions of this narrative, but to see it translated into images in a darkened room with other sympathizers produced a new tension, perhaps precisely because the plot was known. I dreaded the unfolding of the sequence, how the agent would tell Mrs. Nakaya that her husband "seemed" to have been "involved" in a traffic accident. How, after a drive several hours long, after passing by the site of the accident, she would arrive with her son Takaharu at the recruitment station where her husband had been temporarily assigned, able to come home only on weekends. Where, at the insistence of the agents accompanying her, she

would have to leave her first-grader even though he said he wanted
to come with her, and proceed by herself to the hospital. Where,
unwarned, she would be led to the mortuary—or, in the Japanese
terminology, "room for the repose of souls"—to find her husband's body laid out naked under a blanket, a faint film of blood
still visible on his face. At the sight of which she would wish she
had brought pajamas and so would ask if she might go out to
buy some. To which she would be told that it was late, meaning
she should retire to the inn where a room had been prepared for
her. And obedient, she would go, though only after removing
her own coat and placing it on her husband's body.

She would still have to silence the son who wanted to see
Father no-matter-what with promises of tomorrow. But like most
parents' tomorrows, this one would fail to materialize, for Father's
body was already in a coffin awaiting transport back to Morioka,
where a company funeral would be held as soon as the Nakaya
family could get there from Yamaguchi, remote enough in the
days before the bullet train. The only thing Mrs. Nakaya could
do was knit furiously through her solitude to finish the matching
sweaters intended for her husband's weekend return, for his cremation instead.[2]

The presentations after the slide show could not rouse the
audience. This gathering was neither a political rally nor a religious meeting, and as critical as the fate of freedom of worship
might be, a reasoned discussion of that issue by like-minded
intellectuals failed to replenish communal energy. The publication party, on the other hand, with young girls describing the
importance of Mrs. Nakaya's trial for them even if they were not
Christian; with appeals by other defendants and plaintiffs engaged
in trials of conscience concerning separation of religion and state
or discriminatory fingerprinting; and finally, with hymn singing

---

[2]I am indebted most of all to Tanaka Nobumasa's account in his *Jieitai Yo, Otto o Kaise!*
[Give Me Back My Husband, O Self-Defense Force] (Tokyo: Gendai Kyōyō Bunko,
1988), pp. 18–26.

by all, Christian or not, had managed to produce a certain cohesion, a modest determination to pursue the long struggle. I recognized that I would have to overcome an instinctive resistance in order to properly apprehend the importance of Mrs. Nakaya's Christianity. It was, after all, the basis not only for this gathering but for the courtroom battle itself.

The very existence of Christianity in Japan had once been an irritating sign of my own inauthenticity. When I was a kindergartener in an American base school, the only bathrooms were in the chapel, at some remove from the classroom and deserted enough to make my footsteps produce solitary echoes on a weekday morning. My father was not a churchgoer, and so the chapel, and especially its bathrooms, became a new version of an America faintly enticing in its mystery but also forbidding and best avoided unless necessary. When I was in fifth grade, a plump, soft-spoken teacher from a Boston suburb added, along with the intrigue of her accent, the ritual mumbling of the Lord's Prayer, which seemed awkward and no more but no less objectionable than pledging allegiance to the flag. Later, when I was transferred to a private American school, all my friends turned out to be the daughters of missionaries. They weren't as well off as the children of diplomatic or corporate fathers by whom we were surrounded, but in spite of, or probably because of, their "mission box" clothing, they had a distinctive pride. Perhaps it was a precocious understanding of the futility of her father's mission that made one of my friends regularly refer to Japanese as "the heathen."

For my part, I had always been embarrassed by the Japanese infatuation first with Christmas, which in the fifties and early sixties found expression in male carousing on Christmas Eve, expiated on Christmas Day through the purchase of gaudily butter-cream-choked cakes for their families; and then with Christian weddings. (I have heard of an American graduate student who supported himself nicely in Tokyo by playing the part of a minister at a wedding hall.) But the missionary girls were not much help in providing an alternative vision. At the time of JFK's assassination, one of them observed that if he didn't know any better than to put himself in an open-top car, he deserved what he got. She belonged to a group of missionaries' children who abstained from folk dancing for gym on rainy days and ostentatiously said grace in the school cafeteria. The gap between her piety and the sheer malice of her historical assessment overwhelmed me. Her faith was too alien for any tools of understanding then in my possession.

At home, my grandmother's younger sister's daughters were inexplicably Catholic. They went to prestigious schools where their cousins, my mother and her sisters, wouldn't have dreamed of seeking admission. The oldest of them even took orders. My aunt-in-Nagasaki took me to see her because, as she said, once our cousin entered God's House, she would never come out again. As it turned out, the cousin fell ill and left God's House to return to her parents' not long after. Going back almost to the beginning, after my father attempted to kidnap me as a baby, it was Christian ladies associated with my mother's and aunt's Methodist mission school who interceded, entirely unsatisfactorily from my mother's point of view, since the burden of their message was that she should accept and endure my father.

This mission school in its prewar incarnation had retained pale vestiges of the progressive aspects of late-nineteenth-century Japanese Protestantism. Some of the finest leaders of the early socialist and labor movements were of this background. My grandmother had chosen the school for her two older daughters when they finished sixth grade on the grounds that they were not intellectually distinguished enough for public schools of the first order, and she preferred this school to comparable ones because it was modern. (She herself, though coming from the hinterland of Hokkaido, had graduated from a celebrated public school for girls, but during those first years of life in Tokyo she had developed an unfortunate addiction to movies featuring Dorothy and Lillian Gish and Richard Barthelmess, for which she paid with marriage to my grandfather.) My mother loved going to that school. The two or possibly even three friends she gained in spite of an obdurately retiring nature; the young American women sent by the mission from whom she acquired not only a passable ear for English but an exotic command of its grammar; the secret pleasure of chapel and hymns, and a bookstore on the way home with a ravishing selection of Christmas cards (each of which she devoured with her gaze before choosing a few for a closer, more rapturous inspection, which she then respectfully replaced since there was no one to send them to)—all of this made for a luxuriously textured life compared to many adolescences spent in the stark militarism of the 1930s.

Her skills in English won her the dubious reward of marriage to my father, a misstep redeemed only by the presence of her grandchildren, in accordance with the dominant narrative of my family, whereby generations of unfortunate marriages are redeemed by the promise of the youngest children at hand. There is another dimension to the devoted instruction my mother received in English, however, represented by an anecdote she is fond of repeating. After Pearl Harbor my grandparents could no longer peddle pictures of American and European movie stars. The linguistic war effort consisted in part of a vigorous production of neologisms to replace loan words for the tools, activities, and sensations that contact with Western cultures had brought. It also meant a cessation of foreign-language instruction. In my mother's school a teacher of Japanese grammar and literature told the young women, "We are entering an age when it will no longer be possible for you to pursue your English studies. But it will not last forever, and there will come a time when it will be important for young people to know other languages. In the days to come, do not forget what you have already learned."

In recent decades, entry into my mother's alma mater has become astonishingly competitive. What had been emancipatory in her generation has degenerated into the merely fashionable after a cynical detour in the sixties and seventies, when Christian trappings became a selling point with parents anxious to deter their offspring from campus activism. Today, these trappings are accentuated to produce an aura of romantic sophistication, referring, in this instance, to something resembling American preppy culture. Perhaps it is distaste for this enthusiasm, as well as the privilege with which it is associated, that has unfairly infected my views of the 1 percent of the Japanese population who call themselves Christian.

The vicissitudes of Japanese Christians, specifically the valuation of the cultural, political, and economic implications of their foreign faith, extend back to their earliest days. The largely favorable reception accorded the Jesuits in the sixteenth century, with the concomitant flourishing of Portuguese commerce, was complicated by the arrival of Dutch and English traders and the introduction of Protestantism in the early seventeenth century. Not long thereafter Christianity was proscribed altogether, and Japan embarked upon its period of isolation. The principal site of Christian martyrdom was the port city of Nagasaki, which, through the efforts of Portuguese traders and Jesuit missionaries, had become a center for Catholicism in the sixteenth century. It has continued in this role to this day. It was in Nagasaki that hidden communities of the faithful persevered for two and a half centuries after intense persecution made it impossible for them to practice their faith openly. The "Hidden Christians" who announced themselves to the world in the years following Commodore Perry's arrival were premature in doing so, for they continued to risk exile, torture, and execution for some two decades thereafter.

Some of those hapless Hidden Christians were sent from Nagasaki to Tsuwano in Shimane Prefecture and Hagi in neighboring Yamaguchi Prefecture, where both Mrs. Nakaya and her late husband grew up. These are beautiful towns, the principal tourist attractions of a region forming part of the cradle of the Meiji Restoration of 1868, in which the shogun was removed and the emperor plucked from centuries of obscurity and placed at the pinnacle of a modern state apparatus with a refurbished, militant Shinto to serve as glue and propellant. It wasn't by accident that Tsuwano became a site of martyrdom at such a late date: recalcitrant Christians were sent there because of the presence of a nativist scholar who was confident that he could make them recant the barbarous foreign faith and recover their essential Japaneseness. When persuasion by other means proved unsatisfactorily slow, he resorted to several modes of torture, including exposure to the snowy cold of the area, in dramatic antithesis to the boiling in sulfur springs practiced in Nagasaki two centuries earlier.

The theorists and activists of the Restoration, so many of whom came from this region, summarized their claims to legitimacy with the slogan "Revere the emperor, expel the barbarians." "Barbarians" here means "foreigners." (It is of course one of the ironies of history that a movement with such an inception should have inaugurated a period of Japanese saturation in Western modernity. Tsuwano itself was not only the site of belated Christian persecution but the home to several eminent figures of the Japanese enlightenment.) Many Christians were influential for several decades in this process until it yielded to a deadly nationalism and the persecution of a suspect foreign faith once again.

Yamaguchi Prefecture is also the birthplace of several prime ministers from the Meiji period on down to the brothers Kishi Nobusuke and Sato Eisaku in the postwar years. The elder, Kishi, who was instrumental in the military-economic development of Manchuria before the war, was arrested as a Class A war criminal but went unindicted. After the San Francisco Peace Treaty he became prominent for his pro-U.S., anticommunist activities.

As the prime minister who presided over the controversial renewal
of the U.S.–Japan Security Treaty of 1960, he was a vigorous
proponent for the revision of Article 9 of the Constitution, the
"no-war clause." His brother Sato, who also exerted himself on
behalf of the United States, in his case by supporting the American role in Vietnam, attracted notoriety in some circles for the
Nobel Peace Prize which he received in 1974. In short, this
region, the home of prominent nationalists and conservative theorists and politicians for over a century and a half, is inhospitable
to Christian dissidence.

Yamaguchi, where Mrs. Nakaya returned, having no choice
after her husband's death, is the westernmost prefecture on the
island of Honshu. I have never traveled so far on the bullet train
and in fact, have not been west of Kyoto at all in nearly fifteen
years. I note features new to me on the bullet train: an electronic
board above the door to each car that flashes the weather, headlines, and, for a touch of thrill, the diminishing number of
kilometers to the next station once the train is approximately
eight minutes away. This electronic dramatization of speed seems
little appreciated, since most of the jaded passengers have drunk
themselves into a stupor. Also novel to me is a synthesized female
voice announcing the major stops in English. My stop, Ogōri,
for instance, adjacent to Yamaguchi City, goes unnoted by this
voice, no doubt on the reasonable assumption that it is still
beyond the reaches of the new internationalism. (The detail of
St. Francis Xavier's sixteenth-century visit to the region during
his campaign to evangelize in Japan has yet to be amplified and
reformulated so as to warrant Ogōri's mention in the itinerary.)
The journey is scenically dull. The Pacific coastline had been
well traveled for centuries, but it was the arrival of the bullet
train in the mid-sixties that achieved the obliteration of the picturesque. I tell myself it is probably less destructive than com-

parable air traffic over this terrain. But the fare is equally if not more expensive than plane fare, and I speculate grimly about the additional nuclear power plants built on this crowded, earthquake-prone land in order to maintain what is, after all, an awesomely efficient system. When the train skims by the Seto Inland Sea, just after Hiroshima, I gasp: admittedly, it has been decades since the train window here offered an enchanting ink painting of perfectly poised islands, but I hadn't expected, or remembered to expect, the phantasmagoria of Gary, Indiana, with its spherical and cylindrical tanks accentuated by billowing smoke and shooting flames at any hour of the day or night. I had forgotten all those newspaper articles from twenty years ago, worrying about generations of children not knowing that water should be colored blue instead of the red they had begun to apply in their depictions of the Inland Sea. This would have been during the same years when the Cuyahoga River, which empties into Lake Erie, was deemed a fire hazard.

Soon even the bullet train, traveling at speeds of up to 170 miles per hour, will seem quaint. By the end of the century, there is to be a magnetic levitation train (known as the "maglev" train in the science-fiction-like spirit of capitalist fantasy) running west from Tokyo at speeds of over 300 miles per hour, supported by yet more nuclear plants and high-tension wires discharging electromagnetic radiation. At such velocity will a steady stream of pretty young women still move down the aisles with heavy carts selling beer, snacks, Chinese and Japanese box lunches, sandwiches, and specialty foods from the region just whizzed through to busy travelers who didn't have time to buy presents for those they left behind or those they are going to see?

The bullet train and the projected maglev train represent the technological prowess of what was until recently the operation called the Kokutetsu, or the Japan National Railways (JNR). The Japan National Railways has been denationalized into several regional companies. By good fortune the abstraction of this process is removed for me by Mr. Urabe, the husband of a close friend that Mrs. Nakaya has asked to meet me at the station. It is highly unusual for a Japanese man to be free to meet someone, not job-related, at 6 p.m. at the train station. Until recently Mr. Urabe was a veteran conductor for the Yamaguchi line of the JNR, but now he works nonstandard hours as a guard at a prefectural athletic facility. For him and thousands of others around the country, denationalization signaled the beginning of sustained harassment designed to achieve a substantial reduction of the work force together with the dismantling of what had been one of the most important unions in the country. (Japanese labor is now being reorganized into one massive unit, a development my friends worry will spell an end to the labor movement altogether.) Mr. Urabe chose early retirement. He admits that his present job is neither stimulating nor meaningful although he enjoys the opportunity of talking with young people. Deprivation of his career has not robbed him of dignity, for being an avid fisher, an accomplished calligrapher, and a serious churchgoer, he is conscious of the advantages of peculiar work hours. Indeed, his nonstandard schedule even when he was a conductor freed his wife to attend the Nakaya trials and to undertake other activities prompted by that experience.

Mrs. Nakaya lives in Yuda, in the outskirts of Yamaguchi City. Yuda is an old hot-springs town, and though there are several ostentatiously renovated hotels, most of the inns lining the main street are still invitingly dark, wooden structures. By the time we arrive at Mrs. Nakaya's house, she and Mrs. Urabe have finished preparing a feast of several kinds of fish, shrimp, sushi, salad, and soup. I am greeted at the same doorway where, twenty years ago, a Self-Defense Force agent appeared to request the papers of the late Nakaya Takafumi in preparation for apotheosis at the prefectural Defense-of-the-Nation Shrine.

Mrs. Nakaya laughs at herself as she says, "You know, I'm a lucky woman to be able to keep saying my husband this, my husband that all these years. It's thanks to the trial. If it weren't for that, I probably would have forgotten him a long time ago." It is also through the trial that the friendship with Mrs. Urabe developed.

Although the Urabes and Mrs. Nakaya belong to different churches, they are in the same district and consequently became acquainted through such activities as the church study group on the Yasukuni Shrine problem. Yasukuni was established to enshrine the souls of loyalists who died in the Meiji Restoration; it went on to include imperial subjects who died in later wars. From its location in the heart of Tokyo, Yasukuni radiates the logic whereby the war dead are transformed into guardian deities of the nation (a logic whereby, half a century ago, the living were persuaded to die *in order to* become guardian deities) through a network of prefectural Defense-of-the-Nation Shrines that duplicate the apotheosis, and finally, most locally, through the stone markers called *chūkonhi*, such as the one in Yomitan in Okinawa.

Marking as it did the apex of the cult of death on behalf of the Japanese Empire, Yasukuni was stripped of its privileged status by the Occupation authorities. Their vigilance, however, was short-lived as American dedication to the cause of democracy in Japan was diverted by the onset of the Cold War, the establishment of the People's Republic of China, and the outbreak of the Korean War. American interests dictated the nurturance of a healthy anticommunist ally in Japan.

Japanese interest in reviving the official character of Yasukuni Shrine was already apparent by the mid-fifties, and it has taken increasingly insistent form since. Beginning in the late 1960s, the Liberal Democratic Party sponsored a series of legislative measures aimed at establishing government funding for the shrine. This in turn prompted the mobilization of opposition by diverse progressive and religious groups nationwide, including the church study group in Yamaguchi.

Mrs. Urabe grew up as a colonial child in Korea whose father died in the war and whose mother had to return to Japan alone with her children. About 1960, Mrs. Urabe was notified that her father had been granted posthumous honors, including enshrinement at Yasukuni. Although she was dubious, especially when she learned that the costs associated with the procedure were being assumed by the local government, she did not protest. When she heard of Mrs. Nakaya's suit, therefore, she instantly recognized that someone else was assuming a task she herself had been unwilling to confront. "Not everyone is qualified to bring such a suit," as she puts it, by which she seems to mean a combination of circumstance and character. From the beginning she went to every Nakaya hearing she could, but once, when the court was meeting in Tokyo, she stayed home for reasons of time and expense. That single omission made her understand that for Mrs. Nakaya herself, the trial was a constant preoccupation, one she couldn't cast off at the end of a session. Mrs. Urabe resolved then to accompany Mrs. Nakaya to every session and to all rallies, whether in Hiroshima (the high court) or in Tokyo (the Supreme Court).

Mrs. Urabe points to the Yamaguchi Shin'ai Church's confession of war guilt in 1967 as another motive for her dedication to the Nakaya trial. This was part of a belated admission by the United Church of Christ in Japan (an organization of Protestant churches dating from 1941, established to enhance state control and surveillance of Christians) of complicity with the government's wartime position, which dictated that state Shinto was not a religion and that Christians, like other imperial subjects, could and should participate in civilian ritual such as bowing in the direction of the Imperial Palace and offering thanks to the heroic spirits of Yasukuni. The confession asked the forgiveness of God and of the people of the world, especially of Asia, for the sins perpetrated by Japan with the support of its Christian citizens. Although it is generally acknowledged that by the late 1930s it was impossible for any Japanese to engage in dissident activities and remain free, it has been a source of deep chagrin for some Christians that their faith was not more strenuously defended. (Only the Jehovah's Witnesses refused all compromise.) This record should not, however, cancel out such modest but compelling examples of resistance as the story of a minister's son who put pebbles in his shoe on shrine worship days at school so that when the other children were making their deep bows, he "in fact" would be removing a pebble.[3]

Mrs. Urabe's initial response to the church confession was incomprehension. After all, she had been a child during the war years. She could not be held responsible. If anything, she was a victim, a child made fun of by others for being fatherless. "You know how kids are. If you didn't have a father, they thought you probably weren't even eating white rice." Mrs. Nakaya agrees, in measured tones. "Yes, there is a tendency to discriminate against fatherless households in Japan." I am instantly reminded of all the times I was rebuked for my manners, begged to study harder, and threatened with the prospect of juvenile delinquency by my harried mother and grandmother, all because I was growing up without a father. The phrase "People will say" is never far from the lips of the mothers of such children. Uttered at the child's every failing, actual or imagined, it is an urgent plea already weighted with bitter resignation.

As a child Mrs. Urabe was inwardly proud—her father had not died in just any way, he had died in battle. Then one day, well into adulthood, she came upon a picture in a book entitled *Journey to China*[4] of a man with his Japanese sword poised over its victim's neck. It was a poor reproduction, but she became convinced the soldier was her father. The turmoil stirred by that photograph, a dismay so sickening she couldn't tell anyone, was reinforced by a talk given by a minister who had been in the

---

[3]Letter to *Asahi Shimbun*, August 26, 1975, cited in Tanaka, *Give Me Back My Husband*, p. 99.
[4]Honda Katsuichi, *Chūgoku no Tabi* (Tokyo: Asahi Shimbunsha, 1972).

Philippines during the war. On this night when we are gathered
for a fine meal, Mrs. Urabe will not recount the details; canni-
balism is what I imagine. Even though she subsequently confirmed that at least the man in the photograph was not her father,
and even though she had no evidence that her father had engaged
in any of the acts described by the minister, her victim's innocence and confidence were forever shattered. This, too, prepared
her to become a stalwart companion throughout the sixteen years
of the Nakaya trial.

Mrs. Urabe had a job through the trial years, but since it was
with the church, she enjoyed a certain flexibility. Her husband
reminds her that their two children were still young and that
moreover, the trial had coincided with a movement Mrs. Urabe
herself launched on behalf of children like their daughter who
had received quasi-permanent muscular injury from injections
in infancy or early childhood. (Injections used to be the staple
of Japanese medical practice: certainly in my childhood no one
felt that a trip to the doctor, whether for a cold or a stomachache,
was complete without an injection.) Mrs. Urabe attributes that
endeavor to her experience of the Nakaya trial: without witnessing
Mrs. Nakaya's protest against state intrusion into her life, she
would neither have thought to question medical authority nor to
have mobilized a community of fellow victims.

In sum Mrs. Urabe was busy outside the home, and it was
Mr. Urabe who, extraordinarily enough, managed the household
while he worked as a conductor. It is evident that these circumstances fostered an unusual friendship between these two proper
middle-aged women, a friendship without the conventional supports of theater going, tea sipping with French pastry, or the
occasional hot-springs excursion. It is an intensely serious but
not solemn friendship. Mrs. Nakaya, paying tribute to her friend's
steadfastness, describes herself as a person who has always needed
a keeper. At which Mrs. Urabe laughs her magnificent, rolling
laugh and retorts, what, I've become your keeper now?

It is Mrs. Nakaya's turn to share her stories. Her body, suffused with the energy of memory, bursts through the carapace of matronly propriety, and her pleasantly husky voice recovers the intonation of interlocuters—most often in dialect—from conversations conducted decades ago. What she remembers from the discussions and activities provoked by the church's war guilt confession and anti-Yasukuni activism crystallizes as "A Tale of Mothers."

The first bill calling for government sponsorship of Yasukuni Shrine was introduced in 1969. In the Yamaguchi Shin'ai Church, it was the Reverend Hayashi Kenji, then pastor, who organized study sessions to point out the dangers of the bill. Among the people in their twenties, thirties, and forties who belonged to the study group was one Mrs. Watanabe Takano, then eighty years old. Mrs. Watanabe's two sons had both died, the first in infancy, the second as a twenty-one-year-old in 1944. A quarter of a century later, she began to call herself a "stupid mother" who had killed her son out of ignorance. Mrs. Nakaya remembers, "That was the way she put it. She didn't literally talk about war guilt, but that's what she was taking on, wasn't it? Taking responsibility for herself, her own past." The state had killed her son, but so had she. If she had known what war was, if she hadn't let herself be fooled by the trickery of Yasukuni, she would have hidden her son and saved him. It was no consolation, indeed it was an affront, to have him deified at Yasukuni. She didn't want future generations of mothers to be duped and mobilized as she had been. Not everyone agreed with Mrs. Watanabe even in the distinctive congregation tutored by Reverend Hayashi. One woman objected that she, too, had lost a son in the war, but that he was giving her presents to this day. She was referring to the survivors' benefits that she received thanks to his sacrifice.

Coming to understand the past in these terms only intensified

Mrs. Watanabe's sense of loss. She required action—expiatory action—of herself. At Reverend Hayashi's suggestion, she began to collect signatures for a petition to protest state funding for Yasukuni. Using a baby carriage to support her spare frame, doubled over from years of farm work, she positioned herself at the bus stop on the main road in Yuda, stopping passengers as they got off. When she saw the bus going the opposite direction pulling in, she hobbled over the busy street with the baby carriage so as not to let any precious signatures slip away. People spat on her, called her a traitor, accused her of doing it for money. There were members of her church who found her unsightly and embarrassing. Mrs. Watanabe paid no heed. In three years she collected 30,000 signatures in a conservative city with a population of 110,000.

In those days Mrs. Nakaya was struggling with her first job as an insurance agent. The sight of Mrs. Watanabe and her baby carriage triggered an old memory of another mother. As an elementary school child, Mrs. Nakaya had passed by a cemetery for the war dead every day on her way to and from school. And every day, she saw a mother offering water at the graves of her two sons who had died as suicide pilots. The gravestones provided by the state for soldiers who died in combat were instantly recognizable by their pointed tops. At school she heard this mother praised along with her sons, and she and her classmates were taught to send off new conscripts with the words, "Brave soldiers, please go do your best, and we will do our best at home." The child Nakaya Yasuko was obedient, but when she thought of the noble mother sacrificing for her country, she hungered for the mother who had died when she herself was only six. It was the recollection of this yearning that focused the recently widowed Nakaya Yasuko's vision of Mrs. Watanabe as a woman who was translating her unappeased longing for a lost son into an act of affirmation.

* * *

Indeed, it is the image of the mother—her mother—that has guided Mrs. Nakaya's labors. Her mother, Ogawa Sadako, I think of as Sadako I to distinguish her from her stepmother, Sadako II. There is, of course, no possibility of confusion for Mrs. Nakaya herself, though she says, in response to my American, psychologizing question, that as a child she was on the whole pleased and hopeful to learn that her new mother had the same name as her real mother.

Sadako I died before Pearl Harbor, so she was not directly connected to the war. Rather, her mother was "a victim of the patriarchal family system," asserts Mrs. Nakaya, immediately chuckling over her academic pronouncement. Sadako I was originally married to Mrs. Nakaya's uncle, her father's brother. Mrs. Nakaya's father was the third son; her mother's first husband was the oldest. After the birth of a first child, a boy, the uncle died. Sadako I returned to her natal home, leaving behind her son in the Ogawa house. "Returned" and "leaving behind" are imprecise. It was also a "being sent back" and a "having to leave behind" her son who was, after all, the family heir. Misfortune visited the Ogawa house not long thereafter: the second son committed suicide, forcing the third son, Mrs. Nakaya's father, into unanticipated prominence. His life to that point had contrasted embarrassingly with his name, Hidesaburō, or "Excellent Third Boy," to indulge in Hiawatha-like translation. The Nakayas thought of bringing the dead son's wife back into the household. Sadako I was extremely reluctant. Her first experience as an Ogawa bride had shown her the tyrannical nature of her father-in-law, known as *Jīsama*, reducible to "Honorable Grandfather." Still, she ended up consenting, mostly on the grounds that she would be reunited with her son. Her mother, even as she pushed her daughter into the second marriage, understood her misery and took the unprecedented step of dressing her a second time in white bridal kimono.

Sadako I had four daughters by Hidesaburō. The Ogawas were a busy household, juggling rice cultivation and a series of entrepreneurial ventures. At various times, and on occasion simultaneously, they made soy sauce, processed shrimp, refined rice, and ran a cargo service on a boat that *Jīsama* had bought for his son in the perennial hope of turning him into a business success. Even today, the Ogawa house is one narrow road away from the ocean. At the peak of the shrimp season, two huge cauldrons were fired on the beach for boiling the shrimp before they were set out to dry. That was one of Sadako's tasks.

"My mother was always working in the water, wearing huge boots, hands all cracked and bleeding. There used to be a black ointment that people put on the tip of a medal rod and heated up over the hibachi until it was red-hot and then they'd put it right into the crack. It was a painful cure." I don't know if Mrs. Nakaya has ever had this done to her. Most of what she knows about her mother has been gleaned secondhand and carefully stored up over the years. On the day Sadako I died of cerebral hemorrhage, Hidesaburō was away on his boat. "She kept complaining about the heat even though it was the middle of winter and she was working outside. Her blood pressure must have been up." Sadako had taken time from her work to attend a school meeting for her son, where she collapsed. She was thirty-eight.

Some of this history Mrs. Nakaya learned when she came with her young son to the Nakaya house as the widow of Takafumi. It was the complicated interrelationship of her own family, the Ogawas, with her husband's, the Nakayas, that made it possible for her to garner precious information about her own history. For instance, there was her stepmother-in-law, whose mother was aunt and confidante to Sadako I. Through this elderly woman Mrs. Nakaya acquired tangible evidence of her mother's unhappiness in marriage: "Your mother didn't want to worry her own mother, so she used to come to our house to cry. She persevered, though, for the sake of her children." Mrs. Nakaya says she loved that grandmother, a kindly woman, overwhelmingly capable in the way that women of the Meiji period are reputed to have been. She could do anything, and she served her family resolutely. "She was what everyone thinks of as an admirable woman. She believed wives were meant to serve the households they married into. What she didn't say was that it killed my mother. She just said that I was my mother's daughter, and if she could endure her situation, I could mine in the Nakaya household."

As Mrs. Nakaya eventually learned, this woman had given more pointed expression to her notion of woman's role to her own daughter Fumiko, that is, Mrs. Nakaya's stepmother-in-law. Fumiko had also suffered during her initiation into the Nakaya household. It was a second marriage for her, following a divorce in which she, too, had had to leave behind two children whom she would seek out furtively over the years. After she married into the Nakaya family, Fumiko came home so often to cry that her mother, thinking this would only hurt her daughter's position in her new household, told her the next time she wanted to come home, she should first throw herself into the Sabagawa River, which flowed between the Nakaya house and Fumiko's natal home.

To think, given this background, that a stepmother-in-law would be sympathetic to a newly widowed daughter-in-law is to conjure up a more imaginative narrative, in which ordinary individuals are able to make daringly generous choices, than history customarily provides. Fumiko—that is, Mrs. Nakaya senior—having been (lovingly?) rebuffed by her own mother, settled into the regimen of fulfilling her husband's demands, which increasingly meant shielding the world and his abrasive personality from each other. Mrs. Nakaya junior had no illusions about receiving a sympathetic welcome at her in-laws' house. She and her young son had already spent some time there to save expenses while Takafumi was in a training program in the Self-Defense Force. Then, even though she was pressed into service in the maintenance of an extensive and socially prominent household, to which her son Takaharu, as oldest grandson, was heir presumptive, she had been made to pay for her keep. After Takafumi's death, widow and son were kept in the smallest room in the house. Once again, Mrs. Nakaya found herself working in the house throughout her waking hours. There was no time to mourn, no time to plan, and most devastatingly, no one to confide in. "I felt as if my head would burst," she recalls. In spite of the dark, complicated space of the house, she was always watched and could not go anywhere on her own, especially to church, which was what she craved. "I thought I would die if I stayed in that house, and then my son would end up being yet another motherless child."

She presented her wish to leave the household as a formal request to her father-in-law. He refused, no doubt for reasons of pride but also because he shrewdly recognized that she represented a long-term source of income, what with insurance payouts and possible compensation from the Self-Defense Force. Mrs. Nakaya insisted. A family conference was convened. It was decided that she should be allowed to work outside the home if she wished.

In those days there were three gardeners in the Nakaya employ, and she confided in one who had made sympathetic remarks after the family conference ("If I'd been your dad, I'd never have let you stay here") and arranged for him to pick up and deliver her bags. After the conference she and her son had been moved to her in-laws' room, and they, in a display of perverse humility, now occupied the cramped room to which she had first been assigned. She did not want to leave without some token of her husband. The forty-nine days during which the ashes of the deceased are customarily kept in the home had not yet lapsed. Thanks to the television show her father-in-law was watching and the miraculous silence of the normally agitated dog, she was able to creep into the Buddhist altar room and remove Takafumi's picture and some of his bones without detection. (In the course of the trial, her father-in-law would accuse her of having stolen them.) She awoke her son and slipped out of the house.

Freedom meant that Mrs. Nakaya could pursue her life as a Christian in earnest, and that she would have to find a job. The Reverend Hayashi, who had baptized her in the restless, unhappy years of her early womanhood, was then the minister of Yamaguchi Shin'ai Church. At the time, in addition to his ministry, he was engaged in an exhausting, solitary effort to prove the innocence of a man convicted of murdering six people in 1954. It wasn't until 1972, in a celebrated reversal, that this man was declared innocent. The majority of the congregation were dubious of their minister's involvement in what seemed to them to be nonreligious matters. For Mrs. Nakaya the minister's activities provided a first exposure to a political and social world extending beyond her all-consuming domestic travails. Her curiosity was provoked, and she eagerly absorbed what Reverend Hayashi had to say about human rights and the Japanese criminal justice system.

The Self-Defense Force, which had been so active in observing her husband's death, had little interest in contributing to his bereaved family's life. Even today, Japanese want ads discriminate explicitly on the basis of age and sex. Mrs. Nakaya was then thirty-five, without previous experience, seeking employment in a nonindustrial provincial city. Reverend Hayashi found her a position with an insurance company. She was hesitant, not being confident of her capabilities, but she had not much choice. She bought a scooter in order to cover her territory. There was a stretch of road, she says, where there weren't any lights, and she relished speeding along at night, alone with her thoughts. It is one of my favorite images of her: a middle-aged woman not five feet tall, helmeted, astride her scooter.

The job itself caused her anguish. "I wasn't much of a success. I was assigned a territory that included the town where I grew up. So I would call on my friends and sit with them over a cup of tea." She did meet strangers, though, in her capacity as bill collector. "Back in those days, I didn't know there were all kinds of people living in Yuda." What she means is that she didn't know the range of financial circumstance and the stories that went with them in the small hot-springs town. "One of the people in the territory was a grandmother who was supporting a grandson. She worked during the day as a maid in one of the inns. The grandson got some sort of office job as soon as he finished junior high school. The insurance company was running a campaign to get everybody's sales up. So, someone in my company told this grandmother that she should upgrade her policy." Mrs. Nakaya says she was no expert but she understood enough to know that this was unnecessary and inappropriate for the grandmother and her grandson, and told them as much. Eventually, she was summoned by her supervisor. She announced that she would be happy to resign. When he started hinting abut the approaching bonus season, she said she didn't care about that, but that she would reserve the right to write in to the local newspaper about company practices. "I didn't know I was going to say that." After all these years, Mrs. Nakaya still seems surprised with herself.

Her next position was equally disagreeable, but through that employer she heard about the modest house where she lives comfortably today as well as the plot of land where she gardens avidly. Food was taking on an unexpected and growing importance. Producing it alerted her to the effects of chemical fertilizers and pesticides; preparing it for others, in what was to become a lifelong career as a cook at municipal institutions, developed her sensitivity not only to the dietary but to the social and political

dimensions of meals; preparing it for herself revivified the plea-
sures of regional cooking, the tastes of her childhood; sharing it
widely gave her a certain commonality with her neighbors, coun-
tering her strangeness—the effects of her being "that trial person,"
as she was referred to from time to time.

Her first job as a municipal cook was with the "Garden of
Felicitous Longevity," an institution that in America would be
called a nursing home. The hours were arduous and unpleasant.
A staff of six, three cooks and three "dormitory mothers," were
charged with the care of fifty elderly residents. Mrs. Nakaya
discovered that even a six-person staff could be stratified, with
the cooks unmistakably subordinate to the caregivers. This division naturally muted perceptions of their common exploitation:
overtime work, for instance, was frequently demanded but not
remunerated. Overnights came up three or four times a month.
This was a special hardship for Mrs. Nakaya, whose son was still
in grade school. She tried to organize her coworkers to improve
their collective lot but met with unyielding refusal. The "dormitory mothers" were used to being bribed by the residents; they
assured her that she would soon get used to it herself. Mrs. Nakaya
was also disturbed about the care provided the residents. She
campaigned for a professional dietitian, again to no avail, and
ended up taking time off to enroll in courses herself.

Along with the nutritional quality of the meals, the rituals
enforced when they were served troubled her. The elderly were
made to bow and offer their thanks to the gods and buddhas every
day. Mrs. Nakaya was both offended by the sight of the elderly
being led off as children to devotions deemed good for them and
infuriated that it was the state, in the form of a municipal institution, imposing such practices.

From the Garden of Felicitous Longevity Mrs. Nakaya went
on to cook at a series of schools. By then she was well into the
trial. To become involved in a lawsuit in Japan is to risk becoming
the sort of person who is whispered about. As a young woman

lawyer told me, she never accepted job discrimination cases, regardless of the merits, unless she was confident that the clients were prepared for complete social ostracism. (She wasn't encouraging about divorce, either, but she had found that women who went through with divorces tended to be profoundly gratified in spite of the devastating costs.) Nakaya Yasuko has managed to survive the trial years without looking or behaving like a pariah. The preparation of meals for large numbers—all the chopping and the stirring—makes for a sense of amiable companionship, even allowing for occasional forays into the dangerous realm of issues. Mrs. Nakaya has become a shrewd and generous conversationalist.

But she is firm. One summer, the director of the day-care center where she was working brought in a homemade implement for a pool-safety ceremony at the beginning of swimming season. It consisted of a bamboo rod with diamond-shaped pieces of white paper attached to one end. Anyone seeing it would think of a Shinto purification rite, and the director waved it over the poolside, just as a shrine priest would. To Mrs. Nakaya's objections, the director responded, "What can you possibly find wrong with such a modest ceremony? All I care about is the children's safety." To which Mrs. Nakaya responded that if that were the case, wouldn't everyone be better off with a discussion of water safety?

To take an unpopular stance (such as objecting to an updated version of folk custom) is bad enough, but to assert it as a right (freedom of religion guaranteed by the constitutional separation of religion and state) makes things much worse. People greet such arguments wih suspicion, and understandably so. The recognition of rights compels a community to countenance uncustomary behavior. Where the understanding of custom is broadly and intensely shared, or rather, purported to be so, as is the case in Japan, to assert a difference of view in the form of a right is at the very least to create awkwardness. It is preferable simply to do or not to do something and hope that it will either escape notice or be deliberately ignored.

For example, it is still commonplace for women scholars to be required to use their husbands' names at their schools, including private institutions, even if they often publish under their own names. Recently, a librarian at a national institution sued to win the right to use her own name. A friend of mine, a literature scholar at a different national institution, was asked by a senior colleague whether she had been publishing under her own name. (She of course used her husband's name in her capacity as instructor.) Since by chance she hadn't written in any of the publications of her home institution that year, he decided that he didn't have to "mention" her in his report. The suit had triggered a survey by the Education Ministry ostensibly to gather information on current practice. My friend's response was, "I wish that librarian hadn't gone to court. She's made it harder for all of us."

Mrs. Nakaya's son Takaharu was a sixth-grader when charges were filed against the Self-Defense Force and the Veterans' Association. That unleashed a barrage of threats and vituperation by mail and by telephone. Often enough young Takaharu, at home alone while his mother worked, took the calls. I have only seen a sampling of the most recent letters, those that came in after the Supreme Court decision. It is unnerving to handle pages filled with such concentrated hatred; the malice burns my fingertips. These letters are wide-ranging in style, by which I mean orthography and calligraphy as well as diction, but they tend to be more schematic in argument and sentiment than the letters of support.

One letter consists of defaced copies of Mrs. Nakaya's pictures from newspapers, with captions such as "You are possessed by the spirit of death! You are not a woman! You are a human demon on this earth!" The "you" here, *omae,* is the "you" applied

by brothers and sisters to younger siblings, old-fashioned em-
ployers to employees, upperclassmen to their juniors, police to
suspects, husbands to wives. If I add "people to animals" to this
list, it might convey the ambiguity of this second-person pronoun,
an unabashedly hierarchical "you" suggesting affectionate intimacy at one end of the spectrum and brute hatred on the other,
as in this instance. The back of the envelope identifies the sender
as a woman. On the face, after the name of the addressee, the
customary honorific suffix -*sama*, uniform for Mr., Mrs., or Miss
(here, historic contingency makes Japanese seem advanced in the
symbolics of gender politics over many Indo-European languages), is missing. In a language so intent upon social discrimination, it is jarring to find a woman writing so crudely and
attaching her name to it—or to put it more cautiously, to find
someone writing as a woman in such terms.

Other letters are addressed to "Nakaya Yasuko-sama" in splendid brushwork, with such parenthetical additions as "the trial
person." Several return addresses identify the sender as "An Angry
Old Woman" or simply "An Old Woman." A number of these
letters are subliterate. This is startling in a society where proper
execution of Chinese characters has been equated with not only
intellectual but moral worth, an ideology mobilized to produce
a statistically stunning literacy in the postwar decades, thus contributing the sense that traditional virtues underpin economic
might. There are occasional glimmerings of wit, such as the one
addressed to "Nakaya Yasuko-san" (the plain, as distinguished
from the honorific, suffix for Mr., Mrs., or Miss) with the *san*
written with a homonym meaning "to scatter."

Overwhelmingly, though, a dreary sameness pervades the
imagination of loathing: "If you don't like the verdict, get out!
Go to a 'Christian country,' a foreign country"; "You aren't Jew-
ish by any chance, are you?"; "Hairy barbarian!"; "Get off Japanese soil, unclean thing!" There are also epithets new to me,
like the ones suggesting that Mrs. Nakaya is an untouchable, a

Burakumin. A number of writers lecture her on the true spirit of Christianity and denounce her distortion of the kind intentions of those who arranged for her husband's enshrinement. Many letter writers, not knowing that in order to bring suit at all, Mrs. Nakaya was required to claim damages, accuse her of having been motivated by greed. There is envy for her status as the widow of a public servant, and frequent reminders of her support by taxpayers' money, together with rebukes for wasting the same on lengthy litigation. The charges are contradictory, the sources of fury discontinuous. Yet the logic of unhappiness is unmistakable: these are the shrill cries issuing from spoiled lives, a still-uncomprehended waste, experienced now as heavy tedium or unredeemed despair. Again and again there is outrage over Mrs. Nakaya's rejection of her husband's enshrinement in Yasukuni or in the prefectural Defense-of-the-Nation Shrine: have you no feeling for those of us who lost husbands, brothers, and sons, whose only consolation lies in the knowledge that they will be honored in perpetuity by the nation?

Former Prime Minister Nakasone understood this perfectly; as he declared in 1985, "It is fitting that the people express their gratitude to the nation's martyrs, else who would offer his life for his country?"

It wasn't only strangers whose diffuse frustrations, annoyances, and tragedies were crystallized by Mrs. Nakaya's refusal of her husband's enshrinement. Her father-in-law, Nakaya Yukitsugu, announced his gratitude for the enshrinement as soon as her objections became known. His son, he declared, had joined the Self-Defense Force precisely so that he could die and become a "guardian demon" for his country. He testified that Takafumi had quit his job with city hall to seek a more worthwhile position, one which, in the event of his death, would earn him enshrinement at the Defense-of-the-Nation Shrine. This was quite literally imposs[...] [in]asmuch as wha[t...] [Tak]afumi [...] [jo]ined was the National Police R[ese]rve and not the a[...] [t] inexis[...] Self-Defense Force. During their nine years of marria[g]e, Takat[um]i never once intimated to Yasuko that he thought about his o[w]n death, let alone that he entertained hopes for enshrinement. What made his father concoct—as became evident during the trial—such a statement? The need to express his own political convictions? The desire for revenge against an unwelcome daughter-in-law who had robbed him of a favorite grandson? The attempt to reclaim in death a son with whom he had never been at ease in life?

In the course of fifteen years of trial Nakaya Yasuko became skilled at juxtaposing public abstractions, historical and political as well as legal, with the details of private life. She had to grapple with contending formulations of her case within the ranks of her own supporters. The family schism suggested to some of them that the trial should address the issue of a "wife's freedom of worship." In the Nakaya case, pitting widow against father-in-law would have dramatized historic inequities. Japanese women were only enfranchised after World War II. Even today divorced women must wait six months before remarrying, whereas a man can enter a new union immediately. (When Reverend Hayashi decided to pursue Mrs. Nakaya's case as a constitutional matter in the courts, an attorney asked her if she had any plans for remarriage: not that it mattered to him, of course, but there wouldn't be a case if she did.[5]) Public high schools restrict admission for girls. Employment quotas are explicit. Against this background, it would not be surprising if religious freedom for women were found to be more restricted than it is for men. I have met wives who refrain from converting to Christianity, at least in the lifetime of their in-laws. It is often the wife's d[uty to] tend the family Buddhist altar—a go[od] [e]xan[ple]

---

[5]Tanaka, *Give Me Back My Husband*, p. 171.

fication with the sacred—in this case, the dead—can still be a form of bondage for certain of the living, namely, married women.

However the historical record might substantiate the particular risk incurred by married women in Japan of having their religious (as well as other) rights violated, the argument for a legal guarantee of freedom of worship specific to married women raises qualms because it undermines the importance of insisting on religious rights for all citizens. Moreover, it distracts from the principle of separation of religion and state. Article 20 of the Japanese Constitution reads,

> Freedom of religion is guaranteed to all. No religious organization shall receive any privileges from the State, nor exercise any political authority.
> No person shall be compelled to take part in any religious act, celebration, rite or practice.
> The State and its organs shall refrain from religious education or any other religious activity.

Another strategy that was considered by Mrs. Nakaya's supporters and then dropped, though contentiously, was to name the Yamaguchi prefectural Defense-of-the-Nation Shrine as a codefendant along with the Yamaguchi prefectural branch of the Self-Defense Force and the Veterans' Association. This course was rejected on the grounds that it would in effect pit one religion, the plaintiff's Christianity, against another, the defendants' Shinto, with the state being asked to validate one over the other. There was an analogous risk with the notion of "the wife's freedom of worship," in which the state would have been asked to weigh Mrs. Nakaya's wish to memorialize Takafumi in Christian services against his father's wish to have him memorialized as a national hero in a Shinto shrine.

The discussion of rights as we commonly understand them emerges from the eighteenth-century modernity of the West and was not introduced in Japan until the late nineteenth century. There, it has never been bolstered in the popular imagination— as wayward as that has been in Europe or North America—by historic markers equivalent to the American Revolution or the French Revolution. In Japan there is always the inclination to pose the question, is it another consequence of Western domination that we have to argue the separation of religion and state in the first place? The postwar Constitution, the product of the American Occupation, is for conservative Japanese a grating symbol of the unmanning of their nation. They, along with many bereaved families, argue that their government leaders not only should be free but should be obligated to worship those who gave their lives for the nation. There is still no habit of appealing, justifiably or not, to a notion of rights in making an argument in Japan, as there is in the United States. This surely accounts to some degree for the vaunted nonlitigiousness of the Japanese, a tendency that has its repressive as well as its beneficial aspects. Nor is there any structural provision comparable to the so-called checks and balances of the American system or a substantial tradition of judicial autonomy.

In lieu of addressing the issues, leaders and officials at times attempt to resolve conflicts through a cynical deployment of symbols. Then–Prime Minister Nakasone produced a memorable example on the occasion of his official visit to Yasukuni Shrine on August 15, 1985. Prior to that visit, because of the controversy plaguing first the repeated efforts to secure state sponsorship of the shrine and then the increasingly official-seeming visits by cabinet ministers on that charged August date, Nakasone had declined to specify whether his visits were public or private— almost as if in mimicry of the American policy of neither affirming nor denying the presence of nuclear weapons on vessels calling on Japanese ports. On those earlier occasions Nakasone had followed the established procedure for formal shrine worship by offering a sprig of the sacred *sakaki* tree, bowing twice, clapping twice, and finally bowing once more. In 1985, however, when he explicitly visited as prime minister, he offered flowers purchased with public funds and bowed once.[6] This "new style" of worship was presumably designed to circumvent objections based on Section 3 of Article 20 forbidding religious activity by the state and its agents. This will not come as a shock to those who know that the Japanese government's response to protests against the fingerprinting of resident aliens, especially the Koreans who had been conscripted before the war or their children and grandchildren who know no home other than Japan, was to offer a colorless ink and a new plastic cover for the alien registration card, designed to cover the invisible fingerprint with a paulownia seal.

The insistent gestures of cabinet members paying tribute at Yasukuni Shrine, or the new educational directives mandating use of the flag and anthem may seem quaint, if not baffling, when set against the slick images of postmodern Tokyo purveyed the world over. Yet these gestures are directed at reinforcing the ruthless discipline underlying that slickness, a sort of psychic quality control. It is a mode of control that, for the moment, at least, relies on an unsurpassable regimen of commodity gratification combined with artificial austerity of a traditional cast that makes more unsubtle instruments of repression superfluous.

In such times the presence of courageous minorities becomes especially precious. To the uncertain extent that rights mean something more, or other, than the right to make a profit, their formulation and defense depends upon the protest of abused minorities. Particularly in a society where everyone seems suc-

---

[6]Murakami Shigeyoshi, *Yasukuni Jinja: 1869–1945–1985* [Yasukuni Shrine], Iwanami Booklet no. 57 (Tokyo: Iwanami Shoten, 1986), p. 2.

The last section focuses on Mayor Motoshima Hiroshi's endeavor through 1988-1990 with free speech, the death of the emperor, and far-right conservatives in Japan. As the emperor lay dying in December 1988, Motoshima was asked to give a statement. A conservative who had just broken with the Liberal Democratic Party, Motoshima declared that the emperor held responsibility for the war, but that he had since been assigned to be an emblem of the post-War constitution. He never wavered from this position, despite huge conservative criticism and death threats. Motoshima pointed out that he had once been an educator in the army and had to tell people that the emperor was greater than their own life, which he believed a falsehood, and that his post-War right to free speech protected him to say as much. He received so many complaints and threats that eventually he published the letters as a book. In the summer of 1990, an attempt was made on his life, which he survived with debilitating injuries.

The three essays written within the novel demonstrate a variety of "fault lines" that can be seen throughout Japan. Many, if not all, of these "fault lines" are connected to the existence of an "Emperor System" that completely dominates Japan. Within the pages, there is also fierce opposition to ending the "emperor system," from the government, right-wing extremists, and society in general. The novel further demonstrates how individual Japanese are refusing to partake in the system anymore and are paying a high price for their opposition; this can definitely be seen throughout the stories about Chibana Shouichi and Mrs. Nakaya. In Chibana's story, Field explains how there is a major segment of people whom still believe in the "emperor system," however, she later states that those same people are being forced to conform to the system, through social pressure, threats, and violence. In Mrs. Nakaya's story, I believe that we see a fault between the separation between church and state, as the Japanese government uses her situation to reinforce the system that she felt was unjust, and restricted her religious beliefs. Lastly, within the essay about Mayor Motoshima's, we again see how elements within Japanese society will stop at nothing to maintain the "emperor system." However, we do see growing dissatisfaction amongst the people in this instance as well. The

First and foremost, the Yamaguchi prefectural branch of the Self-Defense Force, by cooperating with the Veterans' Association in seeking the enshrinement of deceased members of the former, violated Article 20, Section 3 of the Constitution, which bars the state from religious activity. In so doing, Mrs. Nakaya's attorneys argued, the state also violated her "religious human rights": even though she was not compelled to participate in shrine worship, the continual observance by an agent of the state of her husband's death in a religious practice not her own disturbed her religious peace of mind.

The Yamaguchi District Court and the Hiroshima High Court substantially admitted these claims although they did not order the Veterans' Association to annul the enshrinement since it had already asked the shrine to do so. (The shrine refused.) How did the Supreme Court go about overturning these findings? Contrary to normal practice, it reexamined the facts as determined by the lower courts and found that the application for enshrinement was in effect the sole act of the private Veterans' Association. According to the justices, the state was therefore not culpable.

Evidence introduced during the district court proceedings had emphasized the extent to which the prefectural Self-Defense Force rather than the shrine or the Veterans' Association had taken the initiative in preparing for the apotheosis of SDF members who died on the job in peacetime to supplement the customary practice of enshrining those who had died in combat. A letter of inquiry from the Yamaguchi SDF to prefectural counterparts in Kyushu, where the new practice was widely established, along with encouraging responses to the same, comprise what came to be known as the "secret documents" of the trial. These were delivered by an insider from within the SDF to Reverend Hayashi. (This is one of several heroes encountered by Reverend Hayashi who must go forever unsung.) The importance of the documents is underscored by the fact that both the Yamaguchi SDF and the Kyushu branches tried to deny their ex-mayor falls victim of the faulted system, just like the other characters within the story, as he is left to deal with harsh criticism and even assassination attempts, for simply speaking his mind.   3

Overall, I would have to agree with what Norma Field is saying because she is very knowledgeable on the subject, and provides a variety of different reasoning surrounding her philosophies. Her use of having three separate stories explaining a different set of faults within the "emperor system" only strengthens the argument she is attempting to make, which I believe is the idea that the system has deeper faults in its foundation than we realize.

that the SDF had "cooperated" with the Veterans' Association in the process leading to enshrinement. It had then to be determined whether such cooperation amounted to religious activity as prohibited by the Constitution: "The State and its organs shall refrain from religious education or any other religious activity." As read by these justices, this clause does not preclude every sort of religious activity. This is where the Nakaya decision becomes enormously influential, for the justices had to define the criteria for distinguishing permissible from impermissible religious activity by the state and it organs. The following points for consideration were recommended: (1) the site of the religious activity; (2) the assessment of ordinary citizens as to the religious character of the activity; (3) the presence or absence of religious intent and the intensity thereof in the agents of the activity; and (4) the effect of the activity on ordinary citizens. The justices sought an "objective judgment" consonant with socially accepted views. And, in the Nakaya case, they concluded that the cooperation of the SDF with the efforts of the shrine and the Veterans' Association was only indirectly religious, and that the intent of such cooperation, leading to apotheosis, was not religious since the goal was to elevate the social status of the SDF and to promote the men's "fighting spirit." It seems not to have given pause to the

---

[7]Tanaka, *Give Me Back My Husband*, p. 124.

justices to be acknowledging the mobilization of religion to promote the cause of one organ of the state. To buttress their conclusions, and no doubt as a precaution against future suits, they
added that the separation of religion and state stipulated in Article
20 was not meant to guarantee the religous freedom of an individual as such, but to specify activities prohibited to the state
and its agents.[8]

The Supreme Court was utterly disinclined to explore the
somewhat novel notion of "religious human rights." First, the
application for apotheosis was found to be the exclusive act of
the private Veterans' Association; second, the cooperation of the
SDF in this effort was deemed not to constitute religious activity
by virtue of intent, effect, or social common sense; finally, application for apotheosis was determined to be fundamentally distinct from enactment of apotheosis, and since the state was
involved only in the former, demonstrably nonreligious act, it
could in no way be construed as having infringed on Mrs. Nakaya's religious rights.

Ironically, the court adopted precisely the interpretation that
the Nakaya legal team had sought to avoid. Once the state had
been extricated from the charge of participating in a religious
activity, the issue resolved into a conflict between the religious
freedoms of private individuals wherein, of course, the state could
not interfere. The guarantee of religious freedom required that
everyone be tolerant of the religious practices of others so long
as they did not interfere with the pursuit of one's own faith.
Specifically, it was a freedom guaranteed to all "to make someone
the object of one's faith, or to memorialize or to seek the tran-
quillity of soul of someone according to the practices of one's
own faith."[9] This observation prompted one of my more ingenious friends to hope that left-wing radicals would have sufficient

---

[8]*Jurisuto* (Jurist Note) no. 912 (July 1, 1988), p. 133.
[9]Ibid., p. 134.

imagination to invoke the spirit of the emperor for their own purposes since, as he put it, "the Supreme Court says it's okay."

Even in a society accustomed to court decisions consonant with government wishes, the Nakaya decision, with only one dissenting opinion, met with considerable skepticism. Mrs. Nakaya herself, by the time she turned to the press and her supporters, was ready with her famous smile.

It is worth remembering that the road to victory was suprisingly difficult for Mrs. Nakaya's opponents. What was at stake for them? One of the items included in the "secret documents" offered to Reverend Hayashi was the response of the Fukuoka prefectural branch of the SDF in 1971 to the inquiries of the Yamaguchi branch. It contained this revealing observation:

> It being indisputable that the bereaved families of [members of] the former army are dying out, no plausible future can be envisioned for the Defense-of-the-Nation Shrines without the enshrinement of SDF members.

A historical speculation supports this course of action:

> In the case of the former army, what gave the men the courage to leap to the charge on the battlefield was the united support of civilians ["the citizens behind the guns"]. In that sense we are in agreement with the policy of enshrining SDF members."[10]

For many years after the war there were expeditions to the Pacific islands to retrieve the remains of Japanese soldiers. The possibility of identification meant the possibility of new names and therefore souls for enshrinement in Yasukuni and the Defense-of-the-Nation Shrines. Now there are fewer such expeditions, and be-

---

[10]Quoted in Tanaka, *Give Me Back My Husband*, pp. 126–27.

reaved family members, the audience for memorial rites, are themselves dying out. The lengthening decades of postwar peace have deprived the state of raw material for such ritual occasion. And in the creation and sustenance of an ethos, nothing is as economical as ritual.

It isn't accidental that the religious character of such ritual is ambiguous. As is frequently observed, surveys of Japanese religious affiliation produce totals twice the size of the population. There are predictable responses to these familiar results: either an embarrassed "we Japanese must seem primitive to Westerners" or a defiant "we're different from them and it's senseless to apply the same yardstick." The statistics aren't surprising in a society in which the major religions have practiced a division of labor— Shinto for birth and marriage (with the popular option of Christianity for the latter) and Buddhism for funerals. Such habits produce a tolerance that contains its own intolerance, for an exclusive faith such as Christianity necessarily seems aberrant and at best, gracelessly rigid. The adjective *keppeki*, "fastidious" or "squeamish," has been tellingly applied to Mrs. Nakaya. Having exculpated the state, the majority opinion more than once urges Mrs. Nakaya to be "tolerant" of the religious preferences of her in-laws and the practices of the Defense-of-the-Nation Shrine.

The elaborate denial of the religious nature of SDF activity reads as a peculiar transmutation into legal terms of a postwar version of Shinto as not so much religion but folk custom. One might fairly ask, what's the difference? Rather than argue the distinction, it is important to point out its usefulness as a strategy for dismissing quibbles over the relationship of state and religion. The "new form" of worship demonstrated by Mr. Nakasone at Yasukuni (flowers and one bow) is a striking example. For all its contortions, the Supreme Court decision is a revealing confirmation of the social and political truisms of contemporary Japan: don't be different; don't waste energy fighting in the courts against political strategies masquerading as common sense; understand that the religion of Japan is Japaneseness, which is best practiced in daily life. Cultivated to the point of invisibility by daily practice, this religion is resistant to challenge even in its more concentrated, obtrusive forms as manifested at Yasukuni or the Defense-of-the-Nation Shrines.

Yamaguchi City is easily explored on bicycle, even from Mrs. Nakaya's house in Yuda. One morning I borrowed her bicycle—she prefers her motor scooter—and headed out for the Defense-of-the-Nation Shrine. It made sense to go by myself, of course, but only later did it occur to me that I should have taken greater care in parking Mrs. Nakaya's bicycle, since her name and address are painted on it. All Japanese bicycles are identified in this way, and Japanese policemen are fanatical in the pursuit of stolen bicycles. I suppose it is possible to envy a society that so occupies its police force, but it strikes me as more of an extension of the family registry check: the yearly or so visit by the local policeman to see who is living in every household in his district to match it up against the registry, which means that my grandmother has had to justify my presence off and on over the years. There is always some bantering, in which requests to report irregularities are slipped in along with tips for warding off robbers.

As luck would have it, for I am not adept at finding my way in strange cities, in Yamaguchi Prefecture the Defense-of-the-Nation Shrine and the Self-Defense Force headquarters are next to each other, with the former overlooking—protecting—the training grounds of the latter. The shrine is of plain, dark wood, low and graceful. I learn that it is a style developed for Defense-of-the-Nation Shrines. To my eye, it differs only in scale from all the shrines that still dot the Japanese landscape, hidden in groves in the countryside and in cities ever so modestly, but still sequestered enough to be inviting for children's play. There is such a shrine in my grandparents' neighborhood, where, about the time chrysanthemums go on display, the dry, sweet scent of burning leaves and the purple trail of dusk-festooning smoke announce quintessential autumn. This is where my aunt-in-Nagasaki showed me the dazzling magic of festivals at nighttime, where I take my own children now and run into friends on school patrols, prowling lantern-eyed in search of wayward youths.

The timeless air of shrines comes from their rootedness in locality. This, to be sure, contains its own potential oppressiveness: do I want to be in the care of a tutelary deity just because I happen to have been born in his territory (and therefore have to contribute, as if it were a matter of course, to festival expenses, grounds maintenance, etc.)? And, in fact, this informal conjuncture of the civic and the religious is an echo of official policy from the days of state Shinto, when countless small shrines were abolished, or rather, merged with larger ones representing whole administrative units in the interest of bureaucratic coherence and efficient surveillance. Still, the local, tutelary shrines existing today should be distinguished from the modern ones established to honor specific historic figures as well as from Yasukuni and the Defense-of-the-Nation Shrines.

The Yamaguchi prefectural Defense-of-the-Nation Shrine was built in 1941 in compliance with a 1939 directive whereby each prefecture was to have one official Defense-of-the-Nation Shrine. The title on the pamphlet for visitors refers to it as a "shrine for revered spirits." According to this document, there are 52,099 "pillars" (deities are traditionally counted as "pillars") of revered spirits enshrined here, including 45 pillars of SDF agents (as of 1985). The "merit" of these deities is expounded as follows:

> It was for no other cause than the security of the **Japanese nation and peace on earth** that the enshrined deities offered their prayers in the form of the ultimate sacrifice during the wretchedness of war.

This means that through the families that they left behind, they will watch over the **supplications for household safety and health** of all citizens along with the sound development of their descendants as they are born. . . .

Those who live in the present should not forget that they are receiving the protection of the shrine deities and should pay their respects in a thankful spirit.

Not surprisingly, the brochure is written in the language of the Greater East Asia War, as World War II is often called by Japanese who have not given up on a certain claim to its legitimacy. Here is the brochure's description of a "Memorial to the Heroic Martyrs of the War Crimes Trial":

Exalts the illustrious memory and comforts the souls of the martyrs from Yamaguchi Prefecture who were executed, committed suicide, or died in prison, their innocence unrecognized, due to the one-sided trial conducted by the victorious nations of the Greater East Asia War.

I ask at the shrine office whether anyone is available to show me around. A priest steps out right away, willing to answer my questions at length. He tells me that the carving on this memorial is in the hand of the late Prime Minister Kishi, a native son who somehow managed to escape indictment as a Class A war criminal even though he was arrested as such. I ask him about the large shell and propeller ornamenting the base of the flagpole, which the pamphlet states was built in commemoration of the enshrinement of SDF agents. Oh, those are nothing, he says. That propeller might even be from an old American plane.

There is a structure distinguished by black *torii* gates off to the side of the main building. That, it turns out, is where the enshrinement ceremony begins. At 8 p.m. the spirits to be deified are summoned by name, transferred onto branches of the sacred *sakaki* tree, and borne in a palanquin reserved for this purpose to the main shrine structure, where the *sakaki* will be kept and worshiped in perpetuity. The *sakaki* is a species of evergreen that has traditionally been regarded as sacred, its shiny-topped leaves thought to sympathetically attract deities to alight on them. In the enshrinement ceremony the branch becomes the deity incarnate; other shrines may use other objects of veneration, such as mirrors or swords. Even though the *sakaki* will deteriorate in time, according to my guide it is never disposed of. The deity names are recorded in a book. The importance of the name suggests that these spirits have a dual, or perhaps a divided, existence, contained both in their names and in privileged objects.

The form of this ceremony follows the practices observed during the mass enshrinement ceremonies held at Yasukuni Shrine during the Pacific War and its prelude. These were broadcast live by radio throughout the empire. On one such occasion, on April 25, 1933, when 1,711 pillars were enshrined, the announcer dramatized the psychology of the bereaved families in attendance:

> Ah, their forms as they departed for the plains of Manchuria to cries of "Banzai," those courageous forms still flitting before our eyes, dear father, husband, son, grandson. Four thousand families clasp their hands intently and bow faces wet with tears to the ground in reverence for this wondrous occasion of a ceremony observed by the entire nation, an august ritual whereby these deities settle in repose. It is impossible to convey to you in words the sight of these families overcome by tears of joy as they reverently behold the passage of the palanquin.

By 1941, it was becoming difficult to keep up with the accelerated death rate. It is even said that announcers had to maneuver their microphones to block out sobs and cries of "Murderer!" and "Give me back my son!" from the assembled families.[11]

None of this comes up in the short history of enshrinement

---

[11]Murakami, *Yasukuni Shrine*, p. 29; text of broadcast, p. 25.

that my guide offers. I ask about the Nakaya case. My guide is familiar with it. He sees it as a question of the shrine's rights as opposed to Mrs. Nakaya's. Souls exist on different planes. A soul in Shinto is no more to be compared with a soul in Christianity than apples with oranges. He doesn't wish to be rude, but perhaps it is a sign of weakness in her faith that she objects so strenuously to Shinto enshrinement?

I wonder how he regards phenomena such as Mr. Nakasone's new style of worship. Frankly, he finds it laughable. Why go to such lengths to deny a religious act? So far, I have picked my way carefully through this conversation, generally pleased with my interlocuter's candor. But the next turn surprises me with its familiar crude reasoning: Shinto is not really a religion as such. That is why discussions about separation of church and state are beside the point. "*Chāchi*," he repeats, to emphasize the foreignness. It is almost as if *chāchi*, that is, Christianity, exhausted the notion of religion. Shinto is something else, he continues, folk custom, perhaps. The Japanese have long tolerated and adopted multiple religions. Some people have criticized this, but isn't it really a sign of wisdom, the kind of wisdom that comes from daily life? We might call it a Japanese wisdom, which allows people to live together harmoniously. Gingerly I venture, how about state Shinto? To be sure, there were excesses, he replies, but in a different period of history. And how about your close relationship with the Self-Defense Force? We want to protect our country, everyone in it. That is surely natural? My guide uses the familiar, somewhat homey word *kuni* for "country," artfully erasing connotations of statehood.

Our exchange has been polite. I thank him and tell him I will make another tour by myself. It is a weekday morning, and the grounds are deserted. I notice a stone memorial to Yamaguchi youths belonging to a Manchurian-Mongolian expedition whose "dreams of settling the frontier were dashed . . . on August 15, 1945. . . who had to bury their bones in an alien soil." Are these young spirits appeased by shrine memorial rites? Have they been cajoled into the role of benevolent guardians? Fifty-two thousand spirits are gathered here, their lives cut short by war. And more are invited to join each year. How can this be a place of repose?

Nakaya Takafumi continues to be enshrined at the Yamaguchi prefectural Defense-of-the-Nation Shrine. Mrs. Nakaya says it doesn't bother her anymore. Over the years, she has painstakingly pursued the meaning of the arduous legal effort and has come to summarize the trial as a protest against the state's use of her husband's death.

Such a bald statement occludes the specific and intimate labor of thought exacted by the trial—the cost at which she acquired the skill of juxtaposing public abstraction and private detail. That it was hard for her to "keep up" with the support movement that also provided the financial resources for sixteen years of legal battle is one of her more oblique, polite phrasings. In part she has in mind the intellectuality of her supporters, but she is also referring to a skepticism many of them shared with her critics: namely, hadn't she known about the Self-Defense Force to begin with? Having married a man who belonged to the SDF, what business did she have rejecting what came with the territory? Such doubts had flitted through my own mind when I first learned of her case. I didn't know then, for instance, that the SDF was an accessible employer for second and third sons from poor families in Kyushu, even ones who had only finished junior high school. I confess this to Mrs. Nakaya, and she says that she, too, has learned to be careful to distinguish the Self-Defense Force from its members when she speaks.

Had she been wrong to marry Takafumi in the first place? The question preoccupied her for several years. I don't think she ever seriously answered in the affirmative. Still, she desperately wanted a release from the convergence of private loss and public conflict.

The circle of brooding—if the Self-Defense Force was uncon-stitutional, then her husband's career was wrong, which made the marriage wrong, but the marriage had felt true—became unbearable. She decided that her most important task was to persist in the role of plaintiff, and to do that she could not press herself too hard. Mrs. Nakaya now says of her husband, "He has been used," "He has served." She means it affirmatively, in a sense undreamed of by the Self-Defense Force, the Veterans' Assocation, and the Defense-of-the-Nation Shrine. Slowly and circuitously, Mrs. Nakaya reclaimed her husband's death from their notion of use and service, reclaimed it not only for herself, but for an imagined community embracing unborn generations. In so doing, she not only absorbed the question of the validity of her marriage, but transcended her misery over the literal fact of enshrinement.

The members—they wouldn't necessarily know themselves as such—of the community mobilized by the trial wrote to Mrs. Nakaya in great numbers after the Supreme Court verdict. One teenage girl thought that if she was married to someone she loved and he died, she'd want the funeral to be in the religion of her choosing. Her friend wondered why society should bother with a Constitution that didn't count. A woman office worker wanted to remind Mrs. Nakaya of all those sympathizers who wouldn't have the courage to express their support; she herself, though, was determined to bring up the subject at her workplace. A housewife, reflecting on her thirty years of marriage "spent with-out knowing anything or thinking deeply about anything," en-closed a stamped, self-addressed envelope so that Mrs. Nakaya could explain why she was not content to let her husband be enshrined so long as she could go on memorializing him as a Christian. A seventy-seven-year-old man wrote in a postscript, "This verdict corroborates the fact that the tendency to elevate men and to denigrate women remains an ineradicably powerful force in Japanese society today." A young woman studying law saw "the contradiction of Japan" exemplified by the Nakaya trial: namely, the Japanese "attempt to establish a democratic, liberal state in the postwar era even while retaining the emperor cult." Surmising quite sensibly that her own chances of career advancement in the legal profession were limited given her mother's activism in citizens' movements, she said she was trying to take courage from Mrs. Nakaya's example. A young man who was eight years old when the Nakaya trial began, who of course knew nothing about it until quite recently, exclaimed, "How tired you must be after fifteen long years," and thanked her for persisting in her "fruitless struggle" because it had protected his generation from being dragged away as soldiers and allowed them to live in peace instead.

I suspect such effusiveness has made Mrs. Nakaya laugh in embarrassment. The courtroom and the church, or even her various workplaces, have never been Mrs. Nakaya's only spheres of action. She takes her opportunities where she finds them. At the bank, for instance, where stacks of preprinted forms with the year given in the reign-name form rather than as 19—— are usually filled out as stipulated by obedient citizens. The reign-name law of 1979, yet another of those surprisingly unsubtle, reactionary measures in an age of dazzling prosperity, made official what had previously been customary, namely that dates should employ the current emperor's reign name. For example, Hirohito, posthumously known as Emperor Showa, died in the sixty-fourth year of Showa. An image replayed over and over on television two or three nights after Hirohito's death showed rubber-stamp makers working around the clock to engrave stamps that would simultaneously cross out "Showa" and print "Heisei," the new reign name. Sovereignty may reside with the people, but time is measured by the lives of emperors.

On one of her visits to the bank during the year the reign-name law was passed, Mrs. Nakaya used a ballpoint pen to cross out the bank's printed designation of "Showa 54" and wrote in

"1979." The teller refused to accept it. An old lady standing nearby tried to smooth things over, saying it didn't make much difference either way. Mrs. Nakaya simply stated that she could not use the reign name. After consultation with her supervisors, the teller agreed to proceed with Mrs. Nakaya's transaction.

Part of the reason Mrs. Nakaya can make such gestures without becoming an outcast has to do with the "plump, calm appearance" that surprises almost everyone who sees her newspaper pictures. This surprise is another confirmation of the normative Japanese assessment of dissent: anyone, especially any woman, who would take the state to court must look *obviously* (perhaps *racially*) different. Mrs. Nakaya looks reassuringly ordinary, and her flourishing garden provides a wide basis for uncontroversial exchange.

Mrs. Nakaya knows her garden so well that when she gets there after work at the day-care center, she stays well into the night, saving the tasks for which she needs no light until the end. Then she loads up her harvest on the back of her scooter and distributes it to friends and acquaintances on the way home. Nothing goes to waste, including the seedling carrots pulled out for thinning—*mabiki*, it is called, the same word used for infanticide in periods of food scarcity. When she gets home late after making her rounds, she can park her scooter in the garage and step right into the shower without tracking mud through her house—all her own design.

Where she acquired her farming expertise I don't know. It may have been at home. Her family still grows quite a bit of rice, and her stepmother, Sadako II, keeps a vegetable garden. I am eager to visit the house, the site of dimly remembered and therefore mythic happiness followed by concentrated misery, ingredients that nourished the rebellious strength necessary to become a "trial person" as well as the generosity by which she has remained a plausible neighbor and coworker. Mrs. Nakaya also wants me to see the house and meet Sadako II. My presence gives her an excuse for a rare visit. She chuckles gleefully as she speculates about how the neighborhood will buzz with news that *Yassa* (a sort of dialect diminutive) who started a trial was now taking up with foreigners. The house is but a stone's throw from the sea where her family earned so much of its livelihood, and Mrs. Nakaya gaily reels off the names of shellfish she used to gather on the beach.

By contrast with the dazzling sea and the verdant June rice before the monsoon, the Ogawa home is cool and dark. I have to climb to get up from the slate floor of the entryway over the threshold to the first room, and I am taller than most Japanese. Was there at one time a stepping-stone that hinted at greater hospitality? I have never been in such a house, at least one that isn't a museum. This one is about seventy years old, and I see how the house in which I was born and raised was a sadly diminished, urban version of the Japanese dwelling. We proceed from one tatami-matted room to the next. This arrangement accommodated the business dealings of the men: the progress of negotiations was marked by increased proximity to the inner sanctum, just as it was in warlord castles of earlier centuries. We settle down to be served tea and sweets by Sadako II in the room farthest from the entry.

Beyond the red-carpeted hallway, the garden is a small-scale version of the gardens on all the postcards designed to convey Japaneseness to the world. Its magnificence gives us a civilized topic of conversation. When we turn to the subject of her farm work (continuing our aimless politeness, making admiring noises for all the work she continues to do), Sadako II becomes animated. Ah, when it's spring and she knows the *warabi* is coming up in the hills, nothing can hold her back, not even an aching back. *Warabi* is a kind of bracken much appreciated when lightly pickled or stewed, a good example of how nature has been combed to make Japanese cooking what it is. Sadako II is bone thin, her back ramrod straight in spite of years of work in the fields. Her face is finely wrinkled, the skin stretched taut, and her eyes have been reduced to slits, as if they were no longer interested in or willing to admit much of the world. But now Sadako II half turns toward her stepdaughter, and gesturing in her direction, says, "People like what they grew up with. If they're from the ocean, they like the things of the ocean. I'm from the mountains, so I like the things of the mountains." A smile relaxes the skin on her lower face, and I think, she isn't just a wicked stepmother. Later, Mrs. Nakaya says that Sadako II was herself a stepdaughter who left home and went off to Manchuria to earn her independence.

Next to this set of rooms overlooking the garden is another set consigned to the perpetual darkness of the rear of the house: the altar room, the kitchen, and the other workrooms. The first of these contains a Buddhist altar dedicated to ancestral souls, as well as a Shinto altar for family deities. The former extends from floor to ceiling, a size that has me gawking, for I am accustomed to the portable cabinet size fitted into urban corners. The latter is a high shelf. Mrs. Nakaya is surprised to find that the customary spot for pictures of the emperor and empress is empty—waiting for the new set, she suspects. She also recalls a picture of the "Three Heroic Human Bullets" that hung next to them. It usefully memorialized the courage of three Burakumin (outcastes) in the Shanghai Incident, the precursors of those Okinawan adolescents who strapped bombs on their backs and charged into American tanks in World War II. Evidently a popular scene framed and displayed in many homes, it has a more durable incarnation as one facet of a bronze lantern at Yasukuni Shrine.

As we take our leave, I try to picture the house with all its wooden shutters drawn. That was how Nakaya Yasuko regularly found it on her return from school between first and fourth grades, after her mother died and before the new Sadako came. She remembers how the distance from the altar room, an obligatory prebreakfast stop, to the kitchen was fraught with terror; how she would clap before the Shinto altar and strike the bell loudly at the Buddhist altar to make sure it would be heard in the kitchen before racing on. I remember the nighttime scariness of the very short hallway leading to the bathroom in the house where I was born. The terror was concentrated in a mirror, and once I was tall enough I had to be mindful not to accidentally catch my reflection. Now, confined as many of us are to light, efficient spaces, I think nostalgically of houses with eerie recesses; but that longing presumes a menace contained by the presence of grandmothers and unmarried aunts who had time to chide and comfort young children.

From the Ogawa house we drive on to Mrs. Nakaya's elementary school. She knows exactly where the *hōanden*, the structure housing the sacred imperial portraits, used to be located. She demonstrates how the boys and girls marched in separate lines to the school gate, where they had to halt abruptly and bow in the direction of the *hōanden*. The portraits themselves were brought out by the principal only on special days, when the children had to come in their holiday clothes.

Farm work was a compulsory part of the curriculum. The children had to clear fields and cultivate a version of victory gardens, here known more urgently as "decisive battle plots." The battle theme was prominent throughout the school day. I have a photograph of Mrs. Nakaya framed by her old school buildings. Her face is upturned, and her pointed finger is about to inscribe an arc against the summer sky. She wants to demonstrate the spray from a sinking American battleship hit by a Japanese bomber. This was the subject of many of her drawings in the third grade, when she had a kind woman teacher whom she was especially anxious to please. Moreover, she dedicated herself to learning the difficult Chinese characters for such terms as "destroyer," "bombing mission," "machine gun," and "warship" for the coveted privilege of being asked to write them on the blackboard.

From the school, we drive by the roadside cemetery where Yasuko saw the patriotic mother, but we cannot find the gravestones with the right name among the many pointed ones. We head on to the Nakaya house, first crossing the river where Nakaya Fumiko, the present mistress, was told by her own mother to drown herself before she thought to come home again.

The Nakaya house is awesomely walled and multiply gated. As Mrs. Nakaya says to Fumiko, her stepmother-in-law, "You know, the Ogawa house is really the house of a merchant family, so I thought our American visitor should also see the Nakaya house which is more of a—what shall we call it?—an official's, a bureaucrat's house." The main part of the house is a hundred years old, with newer additions dating back seventy years or so. They have just had the gardener in—the days of live-in gardeners seem to be past—and even that cost seventeen hundred dollars, Mrs. Nakaya Fumiko tells us in her soft, slow manner. The Buddhist altar here cost about seventy thousand dollars—with discount. Its shininess overwhelms the room and makes the black-and-white portraits of Takafumi, another brother who died mysteriously, and other departed family members look shabby and forlorn.

We manage to have a tour of the rooms before we sit down to be joined by Mrs. Nakaya senior. Nakaya Yasuko wants us to witness her course of escape, to imagine how she made her way into the altar room for part of Takafumi's remains, how the dog didn't bark, how old man Nakaya was watching television, how she left her bag for the friendly gardener to pick up; and later, when we are driving again, to note where the gardener delivered the bag. I am taken aback by the grip that the details of the night still have on her.

We chitchat more easily with Mrs. Nakaya senior than we did with Sadako II. Forgiveness for the deficiencies of a stepmother-in-law seems to come more readily than for those of a stepmother. Mrs. Nakaya senior, who is related to Nakaya Yasuko by birth (being her grandaunt's daughter) as well as by marriage, offers hostessly explanations of the antiques placed around us. The house is evidently quite a repository. Many pieces, we learn later, were sold off by one or another son enraged by their father, whose portrait gazes commandingly at us from two rooms away. We agree that he looks much younger than his eighty-five years. That prompts Mrs. Nakaya senior to reminisce about his last seizure and to reiterate how glad she is to have been able to nurse him to the end.

We leave by the imposing front gate, just beyond which a bamboo grove is being thinned out. I think of the relief my grandmother always feels after the gardener has been in to prune and trim in her own modest garden. She breathes easier, she says, and I see why.

The last stop is at Uncle and Aunt Sugii's. These are the only Nakaya relations that Takafumi and Yasuko were close to. Uncle Sugii is dead now, but Aunt Sugii still lives at the house where Mrs. Nakaya sought refuge with the young Takaharu. I refer to her as the "featherbed aunt," because that was the tangible sign of hospitality with which she greeted the pair on that February night. Mrs. Nakaya tries the name on her and happily pronounces it a success: "I think it pleased her." The featherbed aunt is the only person we have met today for pleasure as well as for information.

The term *jikka*, referring to a wife's parental home, continues to have currency throughout Japan, in urban as well as rural areas. It literally means "true," as in "original," "home," and if a woman is speaking of her natal home, she always uses this term. Legal truth, however, is otherwise, for at marriage a woman's name is struck from her father's family register and added to her husband's (except in those cases when the groom is adopted into the wife's family). This is one reason why it is so difficult for a woman to use her own name legally after marriage. At any rate, the return to her "true home" doesn't take place very often for most women, and there is a correspondingly inviting ring to the term.

The day's visits made clear just how homeless Mrs. Nakaya was left by her husband's death. The small apartment they had occupied in faraway Morioka was the first place where she had ever felt her steps quicken as she approached. She knew then that she had grasped what she had always craved, perfectly ordinary happiness. Her "true home" was tainted by her birth mother's suffering and death, her grandfather's tyranny, and her father's ineffectualness, especially in compensating for her stepmother's chilling competence. (Even now, her adult recognition that Sadako II as a stepdaughter might have suffered similarly cannot salve her anger over a haunted, hungry childhood.) "Why can't you be like the others?" was the question constantly posed Yasuko in the unhelpful manner of busy adults confronted with a child recalcitrant from loneliness. She couldn't, and by early womanhood she found herself wondering if the institution in her neighborhood known as the mental hospital might not be the sort of place intended for people like her. She was unsuccessful at working outside the home, but there was no place for her at home, either. When Sadako II bought her a sewing machine, she took it as a sign, much like talk of marriage, that she was being hurried out of the house. It was in that period that she had her first encounters with Christianity, which gave her glimmerings of community, and not too long thereafter she met and consented to marry Takafumi. "My steps quickened when I turned homeward," she repeats.

The repetition underscores Mrs. Nakaya's passion for and estrangement from ordinary happiness. If only she could, she would have been like the others: this was what made that old question so cruel and so futile. Her unyielding quest for ordinary happiness no doubt accounts for her sensitivity to the forces, both brute and subtle, that undermine it. This is what enables her to link her childhood privations with state intrusion into her widowhood, what allows her to understand that the state can take the form not only of the Self-Defense Force, the Veterans' Association, or the Defense-of-the-Nation Shrine; but also a father-in-law, a grandfather (one's mother's father-in-law, after all), a stepmother-in-law's mother (who teaches that wives are born to serve), an old woman at the bank who advises not to fuss over dates, co-workers who are discomfited by the presence of a "trial person" in their midst, scores of strangers who are baffled or even angered by an ordinary Japanese widow objecting to what are evidently commonsensical Japanese propositions.

Yet Mrs. Nakaya's unquenchable yearning for ordinary happiness makes her seem enough like these same citizens to cause some of them to hesitate before rejecting her outright. Perhaps her appeals touch forgotten wounds, revive longings dulled by the apparatuses serving to maintain the discipline of daily life. The possibility of such awakening is of course as important as— indeed, is intimately connected to—expanding commitment to constitutional principles such as separation of religion and state or renunciation of war. The "wisdom of daily life," the phrase offered by the priest at the Defense-of-the-Nation Shrine as a description of Japanese religious tolerance, is purposefully banal. It could also be a description of the regimen imposed on, and usually embraced by, schoolchildren, mothers, husbands, and fathers. In certain circumstances the "wisdom of daily life" sends young men to their deaths as their womenfolk cheer them on. Against such Japanese wisdom the ordinary happiness Mrs. Nakaya seeks is critical and utopian.

My last morning in Yamaguchi is a Sunday, and I plan to go to Mrs. Nakaya's church. Early sunlight floods my spacious room at the A-bomb Victims' Hall, also known more neutrally as Yuda

Hot Springs, where Mrs. Nakaya likes to have guests stay. Ya-maguchi Prefecture adjoins Hiroshima Prefecture on the east and therefore has a sizable population of bomb victims. The hot-spring bath opens at seven in the morning, and there are at least a half-dozen early-morning bathers joining me in the women's section. Some are grandmothers, and there is pleasantly hectic negotiating to send grandchildren in with grandfathers through cracked doors. Some of the bathers already know each other, others are meeting for the first time; but they quickly settle into conversation about which family members are bomb victims. The hall offers comfortable accommodations at reasonable rates, the therapy of hot springs, and an atmosphere of mutuality for victims and their families. Its rooms are also used for the psy-chological detoxification of teenagers retrieved by their families from Sun Myung Moon's Unification Church.

Mrs. Nakaya was to come by on her motor scooter and take my suitcase to the church, but I decide to head on by bus. The walk from the bus stop to the church borders a river running through the northern part of the city. The banks are lined with cherry trees, and everyone regrets that the firefly season has just passed. The morning is so lovely and the path filled with so many traces of my childhood now vanished from Tokyo—dark, inviting hallways glimpsed through sliding doors, of course, but even wooden trash boxes—that I miss the church the first time in spite of the unsubtlety of its modest spire against the roofline of old houses. The church building is more than eighty years old. It is as fine as in the pictures, but close up the paint is peeling, making it shabby within its splendid frame.

There is a category of Japanese institution where shoes must still be removed. It includes schools, temples, and churches. I meet Mrs. Yabuki, the minister's wife. She is a hearty young woman, mother of three children, of whom the oldest is just five; and the church organist. She begins playing when twenty or so have assembled in the spacious sanctuary. The lesson for the day is Matthew 12:1–14. The Pharisees charge Jesus with violating the Sabbath when his disciples pluck ears of corn to ease their hunger and he himself heals the withered hand of a man inside a synagogue. The sermon is entitled "Jesus Who Ruptures Destructive Common Sense" and is dedicated to the subject of rest: how commonsensical it has become in Japan to minimize the need for rest, and the guilt attendant in claiming it. I know that a pattern has been recently recognized and dignified as a syndrome, namely, the "sudden-death-from-overwork syndrome." Such a diagnosis can now serve as a legal basis for demanding compensation from the employer, although the parameters are excruciatingly narrow. Sudden-death-from-overwork syndrome is a designation applied to men in the latter half of their thirties through their early fifties who literally drop dead. Their widows are stunned to realize that the companies that made so much of their husbands' fidelity in life are apparently uninterested in their death. (Corporate Japan, which purifies its robots and memorializes its dead laboratory animals, has yet to develop an equivalent to enshrinement for its foot soldiers.) Reverend Yabuki fears the intensified mechanization of human beings that he is convinced is the consequence of the Japanese work ethic. He even uses an anecdote I had shared with him about my daughter, who, early in her kindergarten experience in Tokyo, was "told on" by her classmates because she began to draw as soon as the teacher handed her a sheet of paper instead of waiting for the signal for the whole class to begin.

At collection time the plate is filled with some thousand-yen bills (about seven dollars) but also with ten-yen coins, showing me again how wrong I had been to categorize Japanese Christians as a snobbishly well-to-do lot.

The activity planned after the service is weeding the church grounds. As is invariably the case in Japan, some people have taken complete responsibility for preparing for the activity. There is a variety of tools in sufficient number and work gloves for everybody.

This is a good time to chat. Mrs. Nakaya introduces me to a socially prominent man's wife, who forbears from converting out of deference to her mother-in-law, a war widow and firm believer in her husband's sacrifice. She is concerned about her daughter's recent decision to become a dental hygienist; she has asked her daughter if she isn't underrating her own capabilities. The daughter has retorted that it is perfectly respectable to take care of people's mouths. The mother admits to a suppressed elitism, and Mrs. Nakaya offers a similar experience she had with her own son.

The mother says she and her daughter have consulted Reverend Yabuki on this matter. They are lucky, and this anecdote makes me wonder whom most Japanese turn to for such consultation. The overwhelming majority of the traditional clergy, Buddhist and Shinto, see their roles as celebrants of weddings, funerals, and a handful of other life-cycle commemorations (the more successful being entrepreneurs of the same) and do not seem even remotely available for consultation on existential matters. Psychotherapy in any of its forms has never taken. Or where it has, in a clinical setting, it has adopted the standard Japanese "two-minute examination" format whereby the patient waits for two hours, is seen for two minutes, and is sent home with medication. Schoolteachers are concerned with students' academic performance and with fitting them into appropriate ranks for efficient sorting. Add to this the absentee father, and the plight of the mother struggling with her child's future becomes Sisyphean, the exalted hilltop here being lifetime employment with a corporate giant. The most readily available resources to a mother consist of her fellow mothers, who are at least partly her competitors, and a staggering amount of commercially generated, stupefyingly detailed information on how to administer her child's life for maximizing potential. Japanese society in its educational pursuits offers a pitilessly thorough realization of American aspirations.

Conversation continues over noodles—a free bowl for me, as is customary for the first-time visitor. The post-service interlude has been so amiable that I have forgotten how resistant this congregation has been to political activism, and am even surprised to learn that Mrs. Nakaya has been attending only one service a month here. So this welcoming bustle is the warm face of weariness with "social problems" and inclination toward the "church [as] salon," as Mrs. Urabe put it at our first meeting. Some of the congregation accused Mrs. Nakaya of conceit, just as they had Reverend Hayashi, for imposing her problems upon them. Though they apologized, Mrs. Nakaya isn't persuaded that it's a question of apology and forgiveness; she wants to see what more they're willing to do. In the meanwhile, she has developed a skepticism about the church. After all, she reasons, it might be just another institution.

Once the bowls are washed and everyone disperses, Mrs. Nakaya and I wait outside before going on to a discussion group. She gives advice on fertilizers to Mrs. Yabuki, who has just begun a vegetable garden next to the large, Japanese-style rectory and the burial urn repository. The latter is a white stucco boxlike structure where Mrs. Nakaya's portion of her husband's remains have been deposited. Given that the most common form of burial is in temple graveyards, Japanese Christians, like other Japanese faced with a rapidly aging population, have yet to resolve the problem of appropriate burial. I have seen several sizes of ceramic urns with crosses, made in the famous kilns of Hagi. Mrs. Nakaya herself has two such Hagi ware urns, one of which she keeps in her kitchen for miso, the fermented soybean paste that is the staple of Japanese cooking. Why shouldn't she get some use out of it now, she says. Her son will frown when I tell him this. He thinks it's another example of her tendency to excessive self-assertion. I associate it with that same penchant for unsentimental scrutiny that at once compels her to acknowledge the financial benefits of her husband's death and also prevents her from being mollified with mere apologies.

The afternoon discussion session on the Nakaya case is to be held in the Urabes' church in Ogōri, the town where the bullet train stops. Mrs. Urabe was to have led the discussion, but Mr. Urabe's sister has just died, and so Reverend Yabuki must take her place. I don't recognize any of the faces from the Yamaguchi church in this sedate gathering. It is excruciatingly difficult to get anyone to talk. A distinguished-looking man begins and another follows. It takes several rounds before a woman's voice breaks the earnest monotony. The topic she broaches is the familiar one of what to do with the informal town organizations affiliated with local shrines that always come around asking for festival donations. To raise it as an issue with one's neighbors is to create awkwardness, and the woman's husband has told her to remain silent. Now, more voices, slow and hesitant, join in. I have a chance to sense, and even to confirm, the anti-SDF elitism that Mrs. Nakaya had to face, although here it emerges as a bias that the speaker describes himself as having overcome, this being one of the gains of the trial for him. I am sorry not to be able to follow the surfacing richness of the discussion, for I must catch my bullet train back to Tokyo. As I rise from my seat, Reverend Yabuki asks me how Americans might respond to enshrinement of the sort practiced on Nakaya Takafumi. I've no confidence speaking for Americans, but I say, purely speculatively, that I think there would be considerable sympathy for Mrs. Nakaya—not out of any fastidiousness for the principle of separation of church and state, but out of a sense of identity with her for being a Christian. I can't quite bring myself to say, for it seems rude even though I am speaking to Japanese Christians, "because most Americans would find Shinto enshrinement primitive and bizarre."

One month later, I find myself seated opposite Nakaya Takaharu at a restaurant in the northeastern citry of Morioka in Iwate Prefecture. For most of the evening we are the only diners. Takaharu came here for college and returned after graduate school for a hospital position as a clinical psychologist. Why? Because this is the only place where he has felt safe.

I am startled by the candor of Nakaya Yasuko's son. I suppose it's the suggestion of vulnerability that is most surprising in an adult Japanese male. As we talk, I have a growing sense of being treated to a rare pleasure. For Nakaya Takaharu's training has made him introspective and articulate, but in a society where psychology has yet to provide the clichés of thought, his speech is fresh and decidedly unnarcissistic.

Morioka is the city of his parents' married life and his father's death. He has only two memories of his father, one of being scolded by him, the other of playing with him near their apartment. "But I can only see him up to the neck. There's no expression, no voice to attach to him." Of his father's death, he remembers vividly the sound of the stone pounding the nails into the coffin.

The trial seemed to him like a fight between relatives. He resents the SDF and the Veterans' Association for having involved his father's family and most of all, for having robbed him of his father. That was the effect of the enshrinement on him, and he thinks that if the case had been focused in that way—had been centered on the child—it might have won broader support in a place like Japan. At one point, in his teens, he was told by his grandfather that he had to choose between him and his mother. Thereafter he, the favorite grandson, resisted seeing his grandfather even though his mother actually encouraged him to visit regularly. He was further shocked when the opposing side suggested in the course of the trial that his parents actually hadn't gotten along, that they might even have gotten divorced. Still, he has no bad memories of his grandfather. He was invited to his grandfather's funeral. His mother was not.

As for himself, he never wants to have anything to do with legal battles. No, that isn't precise enough: he isn't averse to having recourse to the courts as along as it doesn't involve relatives. He is deeply skeptical of movements. He stands aloof because he worries that he might be used. He claims he is a compromiser. In any situation, he decides what his position is, then selects a point of compromise with the world. I tell him how his mother and the director of the day-care center had words over the purification ceremony. He shakes his head. He would not have confronted the director but would have talked to the children later about water safety. He thinks his mother may have grown self-centered through the years of trial, but he quickly acknowledges that he lacks her courage. Would he resist, for example, if he found that psychology was being used as a tool by the state? Only to the extent of talking to others so that they would be forewarned. No, he does not have his mother's courage, he emphasizes.

He shares a memory of his mother crying. It was after he had been caught shoplifting, and his teacher called her in. The teacher had apparently delivered a "naturally-there-are-problems-with-fatherless-children" speech. After his mother came home, he heard her sobbing, but he didn't say anything to her, nor she to him. Not long after that, she moved them so that he could attend a different junior high school.

He knows nothing about fathers. He is about to get married, and he wonders what he will do as a father. He has never even sought what Americans would call a father figure. His mentor is a woman psychology professor from his college days, whom he has introduced neither to his mother nor to his fiancée. He keeps asking his fiancée what she thinks—about anything. He is beginning to see her ordinariness. But he is a person who can't even choose clothes for himself. Confronted with stacks of shirts at a store, he is helpless. He is utterly without criteria for preferring one over another.

He thinks of his mother as being inarticulate. Surprised, I supply him with counterexamples, and he seems to be persuaded. I tell him she may be moving away from the church, which he also finds good. He is a regular churchgoer, though he hasn't been baptized. The more I refer to the trial, the more I realize how little mother and son have talked to each other about the dominant event of their lives. For all the resistance he displays to his mother's mode of life, he is very like her in sheer stubbornness and, moveover, thoroughly informed on the same issues that preoccupy her. I can't help remarking on the resemblance. He doesn't protest. Upon my return to Tokyo, I will receive a courteous letter from him explaining how, in spite of his exhaustion at work the following day, he was glad to have had a stranger hear him out on these matters for the first time in his life.

Takaharu wonders if I have any time before I return to Tokyo the following day. I do, and I ask for suggestions. "You have a choice of two poets—Kenji and Takuboku." Miyazawa Kenji and Ishikawa Takuboku—two northern poets born late in the nineteenth century, to die of tuberculosis—like so many—in the twentieth. I've always been drawn to the concise lyricism of Takuboku in contrast to the opulent fantasies of Kenji, so I go to sleep in preparation for an early bus ride to Takuboku's home, Shibutami Village.

The bullet train ride northeast had been as disappointing as that southwest, perhaps more painfully so inasmuch as the desecration is more recent. Yet, once beyond the greedy reaches of that train, which will eventually transform this entire region into a suburb of Tokyo, this is still Tohoku, beautiful and poor, beautiful because poor. There are one- and two-car trains that traverse the countryside, cars with wood trim and straight-backed seats, charming no doubt because I am not riding them for twelve hours, with fans suspended from high ceilings and doors that must be opened by passengers—for conserving heat in winter in the snow country.

At Shibutami Village the air is clear; wildflowers bloom in profusion by the roadside, and the *uguisu*, most exquisite of warblers, sings here and there, leaving a quiver in the listener as upon the receipt of a rare gift. I know there is a famous poem marker—yes, poems as well as the war dead are memorialized in stone throughout Japan—and embark on a long walk through rice fields overlooked by the mountains so beloved of Takuboku. At twenty-four, long deprived of those mountains and but a scant two years before his death in faraway Tokyo, he put it plainly:

> Facing the mountains of home
> I have nothing to say;
> how grateful one is
> for the mountains of home.

The lofty stone marker I find on the plain beneath these mountains was put up ten years after Takuboku's death by unknown admirers. It was badly neglected during the war. Indeed, a grammar school teacher who copied one of his poems on the blackboard in Shibutami Village was fired the next day. Takuboku's passion for socialist ideals was obscured and indeed led to a partial oblivion in spite of his enormous popularity. It was not until after the war, nearly forty years after his death, that previously censored works were first published.

The schoolhouse where he was known as a prodigy (a "divine child"), to which he returned as a substitute teacher to support his mother, wife, and child at the age of twenty, still stands. He called himself the "finest substitute teacher in all Japan" and offered extra classes to high school and grammar school students, even providing lessons in English, something he thought necessary for a new nation. He eventually encouraged the high school students to go on strike for academic reform. He succeeded, was dismissed, and left the village forever. Many years later he was to reflect, "There're pains in my chest again today;/If I'm going to die/I would go home/to do it."

The walk back to the train station keeps me in sight of his mountains. I am delirious with the day, infused with the unspent energy of the young Takuboku. I wish I had someone to share it with. This is the closest I have come to my grandmother's native land. Her mother, whose beauty comforted—no, surely, tormented—soldiers when she saw them off at the train station as they left for the Russo-Japanese front, grew up in neighboring Aomori Prefecture. She would have been Takuboku's contemporary. Daughter of a well-to-do draper, she studied the violin and became a schoolteacher. I don't know if she had any knowledge of English, but she was interested in nutrition and European cuisine, and strict about hygiene when that was extravagantly laborious. When this great-grandmother died at thirty-nine of a heart attack brought on by the stresses of nursing my granduncle across the street through a bout of dysentery, my grandmother placed a can of MJB coffee in her coffin before cremation.

I pass a large sign put up by the youth group of the local agricultural cooperative: ABSOLUTELY PREVENT IMPORT LIBERALIZATION OF AGRICULTURAL PRODUCTS AND LIVESTOCK THAT WILL DESTROY JAPANESE AGRICULTURE. "Absolutely prevent," "import liberalization," and "destroy" are in red ink. Like most Japanese urban consumers and, coincidentally, would-be American exporters, I have blamed such people as the writers of this sign and their Liberal Democratic supporters for the absurd cost of Japanese foodstuffs. Today, I feel a new twinge. It is the raw sensation of farming as shaper of life and landscape. I can't help thinking that some rearrangement should be possible, must be made possible. Whom would it benefit for Takuboku's valley to be siliconed?

I'm drawn to the tensions of a man who was at once poet and socialist, cosmopolitan and intensely local. Such are the tensions, or the dual yearnings, of modernity. It's the privilege of poetry to conjoin the rational and the magical.

Nakaya Yasuko, who is intensely attached to the spoken word, nevertheless has two favorite texts. They are Article 20 of the Constitution and 1 Corinthians 10:13:

> No temptation has overtaken you that is not common to man.
> God is faithful, and he will not let you be tempted beyond
> your strength, but with the temptation will also provide the
> way of escape, that you may be able to endure it.

The two sustain each other, and at the same time each refers to a realm incommensurate with the other. Mrs. Nakaya doesn't cherish Article 20 only because it grants her the right to practice the faith described in Corinthians. Her struggle to claim Article 20 has nurtured a skepticism toward authority generally. For in her shorthand, the church, with its potentially oppressive hierarchy, in itself constitutes an emperor system. Nor does she confine the structure described as "the emperor system" to masculinity or patriarchy, as so many have done, for her memories make her as wary of the weight of matriarchy as of patriarchy. I can't help thinking that Mrs. Nakaya's embrace of both Article 20 and 1 Corinthians has begun to point her to a world containing each but extending beyond either. In the midst of another feast conjured out of bits of time and scraps of garden, she turns to Reverend Yabuki with affectionate politeness to say, "I know the fault is mine, that my reading is shallow. But I have begun to be bothered by the phrase 'God Our Father.' 'God the father of

Jesus' would not bother me. But when I hear 'God Our Father,' I wonder what has happened to the maternal."

Knowing how arduous beginnings are, or more to the point, how painfully uncertain that shapeless time before a beginning can be, I have been wondering how she will begin again now that the trial is over; how she will harness her habit of resistance and her passion for gardening. There are requests for speaking engagements; other trials with citizens and lawyers still insisting on taking the Constitution seriously; and most taxing of all, the unpredictable arena of daily life. I think hopefully, surely you have traveled too far to desist now; and wish: you who have such restless tenacity, may you and the community born of that lonely northern winter persist in your quests and find steady replenishment in new comrades.

III

NAGASAKI

THE MAYOR

WHILE THE SOVEREIGN LAY BLEEDING through the autumn of 1988, the public's appetite for "self-restraint" was whetted by the establishment by local governments and the Imperial Household Agency at the palace of facilities for the expression of wishes for a speedy recovery. Media coverage gave the impression of throngs awaiting their turn, rain or shine, to add their names and addresses to the registries. Legislative bodies—national, prefectural, and municipal—vied with one another to pass resolutions for His Majesty's recovery. In busy modern societies the doings of royalty normally attract attention only to the degree they can be framed as narratives of indiscretion, usually libidinous. The Japanese imperial family is notoriously uninteresting, or, as it has been put more favorably, they have not become "entertainers" like the British royal family. The extraordinary attention accorded Hirohito's collapse was therefore welcome to those who, from their continuing belief in the sanctity

of the imperial institution or their understanding of its usefulness
for their own ends, had been resigned to waning popular interest
in the imperial family. At the same time, given the history of
Hirohito's era, so starkly divided between the dark prewar and
the brilliant postwar for those old enough to remember or willing
to engage in modest reflection, it was essential that public discussion be limited to formulaic well-wishing.

Then, on December 7, 1988, during a regular session of the
Nagasaki City Assembly, a Communist Party representative asked
the mayor to comment on the municipal registry for imperial
well-wishers and the question of the emperor's war guilt. Sixty-
seven-year-old Motoshima Hitoshi, serving his third term as
mayor, responded as follows:

> Forty-three years have passed since the end of the war, and
> I think we have been able to reflect sufficiently on the nature
> of that war. From reading various materials from abroad as
> well as the writings of Japanese historians, and from my actual
> experiences in military service, where I was especially involved
> in educating the troops . . . I think that the emperor does bear
> responsibility for the war. However, by the will of the great
> majority of the Japanese people as well as of the Allied powers,
> he was released from having to take responsibility and became
> the symbol of the new Constitution. My interpretation is that
> we must adhere to that position.[1]

To reporters after the session, he added,

> It is clear from historical records that if the emperor, in response
> to the reports of his senior statesmen, had resolved to end the
> war earlier, there would have been no Battle of Okinawa, no
> nuclear attacks on Hiroshima and Nagasaki. I myself belonged
> to the education unit in the western division of the army, and

---

[1] From the Municipal Assembly records, quoted in Komichi Shobō, ed., *Nagasaki Shichō
e no 7300tsū no Tegami: Tennō no Sensō Sekinin o Megutte* [The 7300 Letters to the
Mayor of Nagasaki: On the Question of the Emperor's War Guilt] (Tokyo: 1989), p. 10.
All quotations from this book are from the first edition, published in May, cited as *Letters*.

Japan's record economic growth after World War II can be described as miraculous, as an industrial expansion of the speed and duration experienced by Japan during this time was unmatched throughout world history. In the short span of three decades, after the end of World War II, Japan went from being an economic basket case in the eyes of the world, an industry largely reduced to rubble by wartime bombing, to being one of the wealthiest nations on the planet, and a model success story of economic development. Because of this, numerous scholars have voiced their opinions on the matter, wondering how such an occurrence took place.

Scholars have many theories to explain why Japan was able to grow so quickly and for such a long period of time. Much attention has been given to the role of the powerful central government bureaucracy in the nation's economic rise. Civil servants in organizations such as the Ministry of International Trade and Industry, it has been argued, worked closely with the business community, charting strategic plans for economic development and skillfully guide the nation's industrial and financial advance. What has been called Japan's developmental state was helped by the countries rapid growth through the careful application of industrial policy to promote rising sectors such as automobiles, but also charting the decline of sectors like mining, and encourage the export economy. Other scholars have traced Japan's rapid growth to favorable international conditions, readily available technology, and open access to international markets. Some have emphasized Japanese trade policy, which protected the domestic market and combined it with aggressive export efforts. A few others have suggested that Japan got a "free ride" to prosperity by relying on the United States for its military defense during the tense decades of the Cold War.

the story irresistible. Once a member of the Liberal Democratic Party, now an independent backed by the LDP in the middle of

---

[2]*Asahi Shimbun*, December 8, 1988.

his third term as mayor; counsel to the prefectural association of the party of which he was once executive secretary; chairman of the municipal Rising Sun Society, which has as its executive the priest of the city's principal shrine—in short, a politician with impeccable conservative credentials—Motoshima Hitoshi was an implausible candidate for any "vanguard" role, as one city leader put it disapprovingly. Mayors were supposed to keep busy building highways and getting bullet train stops for their city. Mayor Motoshima was known to fly off to the United Nations to plead for nuclear disarmament. An LDP politician who had been his classmate in middle school observed, no doubt with the benefit of hindsight, that in fact he had been looking more and more like a mayor for Socialists and Communists.[3]

One conservative organization after another demanded that the mayor withdraw his statement, otherwise threatening noncooperation so long as he remained in office. When the city representatives to the prefectural legislature called on him, the mayor told them that retracting his words would be tantamount to death for him. Japanese publications quoting the mayor always add "political" in brackets before "death." No doubt that is accurate enough, but I prefer to leave it plain. After all, this was the response of a man who unexpectedly found himself faced with daily threats of *physical* death. The unexpectedness was accentuated by his evident unsuitability for heroism: small, droll, and soft-spoken, Motoshima Hitoshi is a man who makes his most powerful points indirectly and understatedly, with occasional traces of dialect; the impact of his words catches not only his audience but evidently the speaker himself, hidden behind his glasses, by surprise. Now, having to wager his life for his words, words which, when pressed, he describes as the mere expression of common sense, he skirts tragedy.

Three days after this first refusal to withdraw his statement, the mayor responded to a visitation from the prefectural party organization with these words: "Having come this far, I cannot betray my heart. But it is undeniable that I have caused you trouble, so I have prepared a statement of resignation although I do not know if you will be willing to accept it."[4] They were not. Instead, they chose the more humiliating path of dismissing him, emphasizing that they would make good on their threats of noncooperation on both the national and prefectural levels. An old classmate put it succinctly: "We'll make him remember who got him his job as mayor."[5] The Rising Sun Society added its denunciation and dismissal.

In the meanwhile, sporadic incidents lending credibility to the incessant, deafening threats of the extreme right meant that the mayor and his family had to be placed under twenty-four-hour police protection. His morning walks were replaced by sessions on a treadmill installed in the official mayoral residence, since he could no longer live in his own house. He attended Christmas and New Year's mass under heavy police escort. His diet became severely limited, epitomized by instant cup noodles for New Year's Eve instead of the traditional buckwheat noodles, and boxed lunches from a fast-food franchise for New Year's Day itself, the high point of the Japanese culinary year.

Even those who were demanding neither his death nor even his resignation were unforgiving of his timing, his tactlessness in seeming to cast blame on a dying monarch. The mayor was treated to the outrage that society directs at a member who has egregiously violated its common sense. To this he would say that he was sorry, but having been asked a question in the legislature, he had no choice but to answer honestly.

Despite the terror of the right-wing trucks, some citizens began to raise their voices in support. But politicians were slow to join

---

[4]*Letters*, p. 10.
[5]*Letters*, p. 11.

in. One of the first, possibly the first, was Mayor Yamauchi of Yomitanson, Okinawa, who declared on December 21 that the emperor had the single greatest responsibility for the war. Somewhat later, the governor of Saitama Prefecture supposed that Mayor Motoshima's statement had come from Nagasaki because of its A-bomb history. He thought the threats were wrongheaded and that "each person ought to have the freedom to state his own position." When asked for his own views, however, he replied, "It's a difficult matter, so I cannot say anything."[6] Late in January, the mayor of Hoya, a division of Tokyo, announced as soon as he was elected that he believed the emperor had some responsibility. Finally, Doi Takako, chairwoman of the Japan Socialist Party, in an extensive statement before the Japan Press Club, declared that the emperor's responsibility could not be denied since it was in his name that the war was begun, the population mobilized, human rights suppressed, and aggression against Asia initiated.[7] In the fall Doi had been denounced by feminist activists for signing her name at the registry for the emperor's recovery at the Imperial Palace; this time, she was roundly criticized by members of her own party for speaking out imprudently.

All this while, everyone was waiting to see if the mayor of Hiroshima would say anything in solidarity. He did not. Likewise, Prime Minister Takeshita managed to avoid taking a stance on the grounds that the Liberal Democratic Party prefectural association was "working on" the matter.

One month elapsed between the time of the Motoshima "statement" and Hirohito's death. That death had been so long in coming that on the one hand it was no longer expected, as if archaic belief and technology had conspired to confer a new variety of immortality on the body that knew both divinity and humanity. Yet, on the other hand, it was an obviously ersatz

---

[6]*Asahi Shimbun*, December 27, 1988.
[7]*Asahi Shimbun*, January 19, 1989.

Thinking back to a recent discussion we had in class, I feel as though the single most important factor in the economic success for Japan has a great deal to do with Article 9, and the nation's ability to rely upon the United States for military defense. Because of this luxury, Japan did not have to put a great deal of time and effort into their military, focusing their attention on other economic aspects within the nation. Likewise, Japan was not obligated to provide a large sum of finances to their military, allowing them to make money available in other areas of need throughout the country. The mixture of less time, effort, and finances needed for the Japanese military ultimately   2 provided Japan with economic flexibility for their nation, leading to the economic miracle.

In the end, Japan's rapid economic growth can be attributed to a variety of different factors, some more prominent than others, which will provide scholars with an ability to debate the topic for many years to come. Whether the economic miracle occurred from measure taken by Japan itself or because of certain pressures from outside nations, one thing is certain, Japan did something right along the way, as the speed and longevity of their expansion is something to marvel over. It is because of actions taken shortly after World War II that have turned Japan into an economic powerhouse in modern day, showing no signs of going back to their pre-war economic status.

and the outbreak of the Korean War, and later, the headiness of High Growth Economics all served to render the question of Hirohito's war guilt moot and eventually taboo. The upgraded, 1980s version of blamelessness, strategically calibrated to Japan's elevated status in the world, aimed at sealing the question forever.

Yet the question of war guilt festered at the heart of "self-restraint." And it was because he nicked that heart that the mayor of a city of 450,000 became a national and even an international figure. This can be variously confirmed, but I find poetically gratifying the unhesitating renunciation of self-restraint by ul-tranationalists, whose reasoning is elucidated in the call for Mayor

Motoshima's resignation by the Kyushu Conference of the All-Japan Patriots' Association issued on December 21, 1988. It opens with the declaration,

> To begin with, our land has been unified under the sacred authority of the emperor, and if we think about our long history and our traditions, then to pursue the emperor's responsibility for the war becomes the most frightful act of disrespect imaginable for a Japanese.[8]

As one writer put it, under the circumstances, even if Mayor Motoshima's mumbled utterance were not so

> heroic as a sayonara [game-winning] home run in the bottom of the ninth, we could call it a hit into right in what was shaping up to be a miserable no-hit, no-run defeat. The empathetic applause that greeted Player Motoshima when he unexpectedly found himself alone on base was the candid expression of postwar democracy, which didn't want to go down in a shutout.[9]

In the face of calls for retraction, apology, and resignation, the mayor surprised the nation not only by standing firm but by elaborating upon his words:

> I am not saying that the emperor alone was responsible for the war. There are many who are responsible, myself included. The current political conditions, however, are abnormal. . . . Freedom of speech cannot be restricted to certain times and places. . . . I don't think that the conclusions I have reached after more than forty-two years of study are wrong. "But it [the

---

[8]*Asahi Jānaru* Staff, "Nagasaki Shichō 'Tennō Sekinin' Hatsugen no Hamon" [Ripple Effects of the Mayor of Nagasaki's "Emperor's Responsibility" Statement], *Asahi Jānaru*, January 13, 1989, p. 17.

[9]Kamata Satoshi, "Nagasaki Shichō Motoshima Hitoshi-san: Senchūha Kurisuchan no Kodawari" [Mr. Motoshima Hitoshi, Mayor of Nagasaki: Scruples of a War-Generation Christian], *Aera*, July 18, 1989, p. 53.

earth] does move!" I have warm regard and esteem for the emperor as a symbol, but he still bears responsibility for the war. [10]

Borrowing the words attributed to Galileo after he recanted in the face of the Inquisition may seem hyperbolic, but it is a familiar tag in Japan, and its use here is a gauge of the charged atmosphere in Nagasaki.

On December 21, sixty-two right-wing groups in eighty-five vehicles moved into the city. The mayor appealed to the citizens:

> At this busy time in the closing days of the year, my statement has prompted traffic jams, noise, and terror, and has enormously affected citizen life. I believe, however, that freedom of speech is crucial and must be defended, so I ask you for your deepest understanding. [11]

Between the first sentence and the second one expects an apology. Its absence is eloquent. It suggests that the mayor's original, apparently unprepared statement issued from a constant reflection on a past he had never managed to banish despite the enticements brandished by postwar life. Still, it is important to preserve the contingency, the hardly inevitable character of the utterance: as the head of Nagasaki City, the mayor had been issuing major peace statements every August for ten years without once touching upon the emperor's role in the war. It was the force of the moment that impelled him to say what he had long believed and asserted privately. And contrary to his critics, the timing was exactly right: the banality enforced by taboo, whereby critical questions become matters of etiquette, is shattered precisely by the utterance of the unsayable.

In the wake of media exercises in flattering the dead in order to soothe, or rather, anesthetize the living, the mayor patiently and modestly refused their new portrait of the sovereign. After

---

[10]Press conference, December 12, 1988, quoted in *Letters*, p. 68.
[11]*Letters*, p. 68.

all, he noted, the emperor "was not a doll," and he was always informed. "If he were really a pacifist, he could have said to them [his ministers], think it over again, form a new cabinet. As some people have written me, what's the point of a fainthearted pacifist anyway?" He adds, characteristically, that his convictions do not derive solely from history books. He insists on returning to the moment of his having been *there*, when he taught his men to die; when he, too, became forever guilty. He sketches a reciprocity of understanding with the emperor:

> The emperor read the newspapers, he listened to the radio, he knew all about it [men dying in his name]. It was the "Imperial Army" after all. In those days, we understood each other, we and the emperor, not that we ever talked to each other; that's just how the war was conducted. Everyone knew that the emperor knew that the people thought they had to "die for the emperor."

The mayor is not recasting Japanese suffering by blaming the emperor instead of the Americans. In recent years he has taken every opportunity to refer to Japanese aggression in Asia and its consequences:

> Those people who were brought over here from Korea, their children and their grandchildren: according to a survey last year, there are about 600,000 of them. They grew up in Japan, they've been educated the same as Japanese, but we don't let them become civil servants, teachers, or policemen, we don't let them vote, and major corporations won't hire them. That's what Japanese are about.

He says it is a national obligation to reflect on the history of that aggression and on the atrocities committed in its pursuit:

> Of course, it can be said that Japan imitated the colonial policies of the European nations. Those were the wars you had

one hundred years ago. But I think it's wrong to accept what happened as inevitable. [12]

The six to seven weeks intervening between the emperor's death and his funeral saw the culmination of "self-restraint." Things could no longer be left to chance, that is, to the normal reluctance of most Japanese to attract attention. The Education Ministry sent notices to prefectural boards of education directing principals to take measures ensuring that their pupils understood the meaning of mourning and especially urging the observance of silent prayer. Hirohito died on Saturday, January 7, and schools reopened after winter vacation the following Monday. The evening news showed children in school after school bowing in silence, then practicing the Chinese characters of the new reign name. The nation was shown how, in the midst of sorrow, a harmonious transition was proceeding. I don't mean to suggest there was absolute uniformity—far from it, at least in terms of the skill with which principals presented a death at once bureaucratic and mystical, modern and archaic. The vocabulary alone was daunting; during the ensuing month most adults would be grappling with new words, including *taisō* for the funeral itself, and with Chinese characters they could not previously read that had been introduced for the intricacies of an imperial death.

Classrooms are sites for ensuring cooperation in the future. Police enforce it in the present. And in January and February of 1989 they were everywhere in the heart of Tokyo and in the neighborhood of the mausoleum being constructed. Roadblocks snarled traffic and already taut tempers. A fruit knife left in a car trunk could lead to detention and questioning. Dog walkers and schoolgirls on their customary routes were followed. Condominium managers were told to submit resident lists; personnel man-

---

[12] "Ripple Effects," *Asahi Jānaru*, p. 16.

agers, employee names and telephone numbers. Punk rock musicians sporting banners opposing the emperor system were routinely roughed up by the National Security Police.

Already shaken by financial scandal, Prime Minister Takeshita needed to stage a well-run spectacle before the world in order to salvage his domestic dignity. But caught between opposition forces insisting on adherence to the separation of religion and state stipulated in Article 20 of the Constitution and rightists insisting on a Shinto ceremony as guarantor of national self-respect, Takeshita could only look indecisive, and ultimately, foolish. Familiar arguments were rehearsed: on the one hand, Shinto wasn't a religion, and in any case the Supreme Court allowed for a certain degree of religion in public life, witness the Nakaya decision; on the other, Shinto was undeniably a religion and Article 20 existed precisely because of the abuses perpetrated in its name in the prewar era.

The debate took on a new absurdity as Takeshita proposed one solution after another which only exposed the contradictions more baldly. The private (imperial), religious ceremony and the public (state), secular ceremony were to be held at the same site sequentially. At first there was to be no *torii*, or Shinto gate. But clamorings from the right wing of his own party forced the prime minister to agree to a *torii*, along with sacred trees, which were to be removed before the start of the secular ceremony. An enormous set of curtains was to screen off the constitutionally troublesome portion of the proceedings, but it was eventually decided that the curtains should remain open throughout the religious ceremony. (No doubt the results pleased the foreign dignitaries who would otherwise have been deprived of their share of exotica.) All of these nervous gestures were succinctly captured in a newspaper cartoon showing Prime Minister Takeshita dressed half in business suit and half in Shinto priestly garb, with a miniature figure of athlete Florence Griffith Joyner in bicolored leotard at his head ("It's the Joyner look . . .") and a bottom caption reading "amalgamation of church and state!"[13]

The security precautions evidently paid off, since the foreign dignitaries were brought in and whisked home without mishap. There were more of them, we learned, than at JFK's, Tito's, or Brezhnev's funerals (in chronological order; the previous high scorer was Tito). As a matter of fact, there were 163 delegations, or rather 164, as the Foreign Ministry later admitted. The February 24 edition of the *New York Times* listed 164 delegations, including one headed by the consul general of South Africa. That was all right: the international date line, that emblem of human codification of cosmic time, made the twenty-fourth in New York the twenty-fifth in Tokyo, the day after the funeral, when it was too late for other African delegations to withdraw in protest.

Tokyo itself was quiet. All the young who could had gone skiing. Most others, finding the television funeral fare unbearable, unrelieved as it was even by commercials, had ransacked the shelves of rental video stores. (Commercials, of course, are not suppressed on such occasions merely because their content is inappropriate; it is their founding presumption, the egalitarian reduction of all things to a price, that must be effaced for the presentation of the absolute, such as the death of a once divine emperor.) The mayor of Nagasaki attended the funeral in spite of fresh death threats and censure from new supporters.

Perhaps the most eloquent, and certainly the most enduring, testimony to the force of the Motoshima "statement" is to be found in the more than 7,300 letters, postcards, and telegrams sent to the mayor from throughout Japan and overseas during a period of three months. Convinced that they were too important

---

[13]Kumita Ryū, *Tokyo Shimbun*, January 11, 1989.

to keep for himself, the mayor sought to have them published. The choice fell rather quickly to Komichi Shobō, a Tokyo company with a staff of four, including the president, Harada Naō, a man who broke off a successful career at a distinguished publishing house to start Komichi.

Mr. Harada, now in his early sixties, says that he himself was a right-winger at the end of the war. He was a teenager who, in his own dedication to the war effort, had not allowed himself to grieve over family losses. August 15, 1945, shattered his anticipation of actual military service, leaving him to contemplate the profoundly confusing spectacle of adults who only yesterday had said they were going to die for the emperor now proclaiming themselves believers in democracy. The teenager was not so flexible; he became all the more determined to fight the enemies of Japan. If there is a common denominator to the books published by Komichi, it would seem to be their resistance to various forms of common sense, a legacy of the adolescent Harada Naō's confrontation with a society that changed its common sense overnight.

The process of publication of the Motoshima letters is emblematic of the modus vivendi of this unusual press, whose name translates as "small path." To begin with, the proposal for publication came to Komichi via a reader. Komichi's readers constitute a far-flung community. *Komichi Communications,* a pamphlet inserted in the books, regularly carries letters from readers, some of whom even meet each other at an annual summer retreat. Those in the Tokyo area who can do so donate their time, thereby helping to maintain an impressive catalog out of all proportion to the size of the company. With the Motoshima letters, a core of readers gathered daily in the two-room office, often bringing their lunches so that they could settle down to reading, discussing, and evaluating the letters, with Mr. Harada making the final decision on the selection of some three hundred letters. Then came the arduous task of getting the writers' permission. Readers didn't volunteer their services for just the more glorious tasks; some of them cooked, others answered the telephone, while still others made photocopies and addressed envelopes. Friends and family members were recruited. Some even took days from their annual leave to keep up the momentum, which they did, day and night, Sundays and weekdays. The discussion session held as the first proofs were coming in, recorded and circulated as an issue of *Komichi Communications*, included students, free-lance writers, a photographer, a seamstress, a civil servant, a housewife, a designer, and a publisher. They are all named. (Contrary to usual publishing practice, however, when the book finally came out, the printer and binder went unnamed. Fearful of right-wing retribution, they also refused to speak to the press.)

Immediately after this discussion a telephone call came from Mayor Motoshima asking Komichi to delay publication. Two episodes of bullets in his mail and the ensuing need for intensified police protection had made the mayor anxious about disrupting municipal governance. There were severe signs of stress in his family. (His daughter and grandchild had had to visit him secretly after dark at New Year's. His wife had required hospitalization.) Above all, his campaign committee, which had seen him through several elections, was now adamantly opposed to publication on the grounds of threat to life. The committee had been difficult from the start, placing restrictions on the contents. Now, they were unyielding. Once again, after a period of anguished waiting and debate, a collective decision was reached by Komichi's staff and the working corps of readers. Indefinite postponement in the face of anonymous terror seemed unwise and incommensurate to the responsibility they had set for themselves, a responsibility they saw as not being identical with the mayor's. He had gone as far as he could for now; it was time for Komichi to push ahead together with the letter writers themselves. So once again, each writer was asked to give his or her consent on the basis of the changed circumstances. Some were no longer willing, indicating fear of retribution to the publisher, regret that the mayor was yielding to pressure, or concern that publication would no longer serve as an expression of support for him. Some letters of withdrawal pleaded domestic disturbances such as wives no longer speaking to husbands or no longer willing or able to speak at all.[14] Still, the overwhelming majority consented to have their letters published.

The project had received unusual publicity from the start. In April, NHK, the government-owned broadcasting corporation, aired a one-hour documentary in which some of the letters were read and several of their writers interviewed. In this selection the number of letters favorable to and critical of the mayor were neatly balanced; by Komichi's count, only 5 percent of the letters were critical. Even so, some observers said, for NHK this wasn't bad. From an American perspective, the notion of a television show featuring voice actors reading letters written by ordinary people, with the letters themselves filling the screen, is simply preposterous. Audience rating was so high as to warrant a repeated showing soon after. With reports of continued threats to the mayor, followed by his dissociation from publication, the book reached the ranks of the top twenty at one of Tokyo's largest bookstores in the first month of sales. The first edition went through six printings in as many weeks and sold 36,000 copies. (Proceeds have gone to a peace organization in Nagasaki.)

One principle governed the selection of the three hundred–odd letters printed in Komichi's book: namely, evidence that the writer's own history had compelled him or her to take a position on the Motoshima "statement." Mr. Harada says that even though

---

[14]*Letters*, p. 158.

Komichi did not evaluate the position itself, there was a tendency on the part of those who denounced the mayor to do so on the basis of abstractions such as "patriotism" or "loyalty to his Majesty."

The letters constitute a spontaneous history of the era by its participants, whose range is immediately apparent in the indications of age and occupation customarily supplied in the letters-to-the-editor genre in Japan. There is the immediate contrast between those who lived the war and those who came of age after it; but the thicket of Chinese characters and now-remote honorifics with which the former revive their memories suggests a history of expression that not only reflects obvious changes in educational practices but also hints at the subterranean shifts in sensibility and social relationships that have taken place over the past half century. A dying emperor and a mayor threatened with death for having taken that emperor's life seriously stirred dusty memories and breathed urgency into textbook knowledge.

The existence of Komichi today might be traced to Harada Naō's shock at the transformation of Japanese society after August 15, 1945. That phenomenon was also experienced as historical hypocrisy by Yano Toshio:

> I am presently sixty-one years old and a physician. I do not belong to any political party, and I do not favor supporting a party simply on the basis of individual interests.
>
> As you will understand from my age, I grew up in a society colored entirely by militarism, where a boy was educated to believe that to sacrifice himself for his country and his emperor was to walk the noblest path of all. When I finished middle school, I volunteered for the navy. August 15 was to come only four months later.
>
> The world changed after that day, but what surprised me more than anything was that the emperor, who, in military

uniform, had declared to us, "I am thy commander-in-chief"
and issued rescripts—I can still recite them—upon which he
affixed his imperial seal, transformed himself overnight into a
suited and hatted figure pictured lovingly with white doves
symbolizing peace, attempting thereby to appeal to the people
and to the Occupation authorities.

I thought then, if that brilliant transformation from deity
to human were to be allowed, then every evil in this world
would be condoned.[15]

Mizusawa Makoto, age fifty-nine, who identifies himself as a
writer from Tokyo, challenges even the semblance of transformation:

It is frequently said that the emperor's "sacred decision" to
end the war saved the Japanese people from ruin, but we must
equally appraise the fact that it was his "sacred decision" to begin the war. It is said that only one-sided information was available to him, but that is surely incorrect. Whether through Konoe
Fumimaro [twice prime minister during the war years and a
close adviser who urged the emperor to surrender in February
1945] or a direct relation such as Prince Takamatsu [brother
to the emperor], he had access to an abundance of information.

I feel deep sorrow and anger over the fact that the emperor
is approaching the end of his life without proper recognition
of his own responsibility. It is said that in the postwar years,
he worked for the reconstruction of Japan and that he has been
useful as the symbol of Japanese unity. I acknowledge that this
may be true in a certain respect. Furthermore, he himself has
frequently declared his love for the Japanese people, and it is
said that the people extend to him a loving respect. This may
also be true in a certain sense. However, I will never forget
such words as the following uttered by the emperor in the years
following the war:

"I hope that the United States will continue its military occupation of Okinawa and the other Ryukyu Islands." (September 1947 message to MacArthur)

---

[15]*Letters*, p. 13. In almost all cases my selections are excerpts.

"I do not understand much about such rhetorical matters [the question of war guilt] since I have not pursued literary studies very deeply." (October 31, 1975, press conference)

"I find it regrettable that the atom bomb was dropped, but given the wartime circumstances, although I feel sorry for the citizens of Hiroshima, it could not have been helped." (same)

In considering these words, I cannot help finding the claim that the emperor loves the Japanese people to be utterly without substance.

Moreover, when Curtis LeMay, the U.S. commander of strategic bombing who exposed Japanese cities to massive, indiscriminate nighttime bombing—slaughter and destruction remarkable even in the pages of history—visited Japan after the war, the emperor bestowed upon him the First Order of Merit with the Grand Cordon of the Rising Sun. This is an incomprehensible act. To confer decorations is one of the few "state functions" left to him. Surely we should not presume that he performed it unselfconsciously. To judge from this instance, if the commander of the atom bomb missions had visited Japan, he probably would have decorated him as a matter of course, too. Therefore, when I consider the question of the emperor's war guilt, I cannot help seeing it not only in his acts during the war, but in his words and deeds thereafter as well. (p. 20)

The indiscriminate bombing of civilian targets by the United States began in 1945. Although the extent of casualties has never been precisely determined, approximately 80,000 people died in two and a half hours of bombing over Tokyo on March 10 alone. In Hiroshima and Nagasaki, 130,000 and 70,000 people, respectively, were dead three months after the bombs. Uncertainty and ignorance, both genuine and willful, have exacerbated the difficulties of determining the death toll from the atom bombs. Should second-generation victims (both those who were fetuses at the time of the bombing as well as those born years later to irradiated parents) be included? Even more basically, is there such a phenomenon? Counting is always motivated: who will pay for the health care of second-generation victims if they are recognized? Will there be renewed public anxiety about nuclear reactors? "Official figures" must therefore always be treated with care, but the combined death toll of Hiroshima and Nagasaki as of 1990 has been set at 295,956. The total number of mainland (always omitting Okinawa) casualties from conventional bombing is conservatively estimated at 256,000.[16]

Although Motoshima was not in Nagasaki at the time of the bombing, his being mayor of Nagasaki made the bomb a common point of reference. Judicious public figures found a way to express sympathy for his statement yet subtly and safely explain it away: because Motoshima is mayor of Nagasaki, he is driven to making such extreme statements. Others found the bomb the most compelling reason to support him. [A-bomb victim] Takagi Tomeo, who calls himself an "unemployed" seventy-year-old, also recalls the press conference at which the emperor was asked for his views on Hiroshima and Nagasaki:

> Nagasaki went unmentioned. The instant I heard his response, I shouted at the television screen: you idiot, who asked you to start a war, it was you bastards who started the fighting, feeding us that self-serving nonsense about a sacred war, His majesty's children, the Imperial Army, peace in Greater East Asia, the Greater East Asia Co-Prosperity Sphere—all that at a time when anyone who opposed the war or criticized it was ruthlessly thrown into jail, not to mention people who actually criticized the emperor. I hear there were a lot of people who were simply slaughtered.

---

[16]Figures on conventional bombing from the *Kadokawa Dictionary of Japanese History*, p. 885; on Hiroshima and Nagasaki, Iijimi Sōichi, *Hiroshima, Nagasaki de Nani ga Okotta no Ka: Genbaku no Jintai e no Eikyō* [What Took Place in Hiroshima and Nagasaki: The Effects of the Atom Bomb on the Human Body], Iwanami Booklet no. 8 (Tokyo: Iwanami Shoten, 1982), p. 25. 1990 figures from television and newspaper coverage of memorial ceremonies for that year.

Even though I describe myself as a soldier, I was an assistant trainer for privates and new recruits. Our first year we were beaten almost every night. And out on the front, we got malaria or dysentery, probably from the germs spread by Unit 731 [thought to have experimented with germ warfare and vivisection] and died. So-called field hospitals were crude affairs consisting of tables taken from the homes of the Chinese, with doors, rush-woven mats, and one blanket apiece piled on top. Bodies were lined up in rows day after day. I don't know if locks of hair were sent back to the families. It was Chinese laborers who had to dig the holes and bury them.

That fateful moment of 8:15 [in Hiroshima] is one that I can never forget. The weapon that annihilated grammar school students, middle school students, old and young, men and women without leaving behind even a handful of ashes or a fragment of bone. We say we will never permit such a wretched thing to happen again, but war in various forms continues to be waged and causes me the deepest grief.

That one who declared himself a human being continues to be revered as head of state is already a violation of the Constitution. As for your recent statement, I want to express my respect and hope that you will persist unyieldingly without changing your outlook.

I struggle to comprehend how people can sign [wishes for the emperor's recovery] without knowing the meaning of what they are doing. (pp. 38–39)

Sixty-five-year-old Ogawa Fusako from Tokyo writes that her husband, who died "four years and nine months ago," was sent to Sumatra and Burma immediately after their wedding. Though wrecked with malnutrition, he was one of the lucky ones who came home.

In May of 1983, I traveled to Nagasaki with my husband. When I saw the exhibit of artifacts from the bomb, it made me shiver to think of that moment, and I broke out in hives so badly that I did not know what to do. I find it only reasonable that the mayor of a city that suffered such terror would make the statement you did. No, it is not just reasonable. I want to send you my cheers for your courage.

I was so excited by the news on televison [on the mayor] that my hands began to shake, and I had to take up my pen to write to you. (pp. 58–59)

In contrast to most women supporters of the mayor belonging to the war generation, Uchida Sumiko, age sixty-nine, from Ibaragi Prefecture, writes not from the perspective of a wife left to struggle at home but as a direct witness of the price paid by Japanese soldiers and colonists for their country's imperial ambitions:

It seems to me that you must have known the repercussions that would follow from making such a statement at this moment [of the emperor's dying]. That you nevertheless did so made me cry out in joyous triumph. As an ordinary citizen I have neither the opportunity nor the courage to raise my voice, but that does not mean I have abandoned all critical spirit. Although my own scope of knowledge is limited, I have been all but consumed by doubts about the war and the emperor.

In my early twenties I roamed the mountains of northern Luzon [in the Philippines] through piles of starved bodies. At the end of the war, by sheer miracle I was able to return to Japan. To see the youth of my generation as well as breadwinners sacrificed to a pointless war, to witness those whitened skeletons still in uniform fallen by the wayside—this I cannot forget. In the red of the Rising Sun I see the blood spilled on battlefields. On the notes of "The Reign of Our Emperor" [the "national" anthem] float the boyish faces of the students of the Naval Aviation Academy struggling to relinquish their attachment to life.

While rejoicing in the prosperity of our nation so splendidly risen from ruins, I cannot suppress my anxiety over how long our current luxury-drowned existence can last. (p. 41)

Mori Tazuko, a fifty-five-year-old housewife from Aichi Prefecture, describes her young girl's credulity and subsequent skepticism:

> I was a sixth-grader when defeat came. Until then I had been taught that Japan was a divine land, that in times of peril a divine wind [*kamikaze*] would blow, that we should fight for the emperor, and rather than taste the shame of falling captive, we should dispatch our own lives.
>
> With the undoubting heart of a young girl, I prayed earnestly at shrines and struggled through the air raids. So when defeat came unexpectedly, I simply could not understand why the emperor and professional soldiers did not slit their bellies and die.
>
> Shouldn't the emperor have died by his own hand on the day of surrender? Or else, for the sake of the people who were sacrificed, if only he had abdicated of his own will on the day of Okinawan reversion, or when he turned fifty, or sixty, or on the sixtieth anniversary of his reign. These were the thoughts that settled in my heart to haunt me.
>
> But this year, when I saw him come out of the helicopter to walk to the hall for the annual end-of-the-war memorial service, I wondered if it were not he who, having missed the chance to say, "I'm sorry," were not treading the most difficult path of all.
>
> POSTSCRIPT
>
> The care that he has received since he vomited blood—transfusions solely for the sake of prolonging life—truly symbolizes the wastefulness of medical care directed at prolonging life in an aging society.
>
> The shamefully wasteful medical care provided the emperor: hasn't the Imperial Household Agency set a bad example once again? I cannot help thinking that the modesty of spirit that yields to nature, saying "We have done everything possible," has been forgotten. (p. 43)

The handling of the emperor's last illness is subjected to a different critique by tax accountant Hayashi Akira, age fifty-eight:

> Now it is Showa 63 [1988], and peculiar expressions are in the air. I am referring to Japanese of this kind: rectal bleeding that is "more than a slight amount but less than a considerable amount"; or "This falls within the normal range of fluctuation and cannot be deemed to represent a change in His Majesty's condition." How do such expressions differ from "The Imperial Navy sank one enemy battleship and inflicted great damage on two cruisers, but our losses were trifling"?
>
> When information is manipulated for the sake of one person, and only the results of the actions of the masses who believed that information are recorded as historical truth—that frightening situation seems to me not to have changed at all. (p. 44)

Many letters from the war generation attest to the difficulty, bordering on impossibility, of speaking critically even after August 1945. Toshima Chieko, who, at age seventy-five, in contrast to many elderly writers, identifies herself as a retired grade school teacher rather than as an "unemployed" person, is articulate about her own silence:

> I learned about your statement and your intent in the Chū-goku [Hiroshima] paper on December 10 and 11 and could not bear to put off writing to you.
>
> First I must tell you that I agree with you totally. Judging from today's paper there are some who oppose you. I pray their views will not spread and cause yours to wither away.
>
> I have held the same opinion as you since May of 1941. If someone were to reproach me by saying, "Why haven't you said anything during the many months and years since?" there is nothing I could offer in my defense. Upon repatriation [at the end of the war, from former Japanese colonies such as Korea or Manchuria], I was caught up in the struggles of daily

life and besides, even though men and women are supposed to be equal, that is something that is beginning to take root only now. Please think of me as an ordinary citizen who was unable to speak out in such a Japan.

Though lamenting the course of events in the world, being powerless and moreover unwell, I have arrived at the age of seventy-five without having managed to say anything, let alone translated it into action. Just as I was wondering if my thoughts were fated to disappear without ever being unearthed, I read your statement in the newspaper and could not refrain from writing you. (p. 15)

A younger woman (age fifty-seven), Nakamoto Kimiko, is pushed into new resolve:

Your public statement shocked me with the force of a blow on the head. I am fifty-seven years old. Until now, I have said plenty in private about what I think and feel, but I have managed to get away with niceties in public. What an irresponsible way of life.

I was born in Okinawa, and I love Okinawa more than anything. I abandoned that home in the fourth grade, moved to a temple in Ōita, then to Nagasaki. Forced to live like a rootless plant, I was physically and spiritually torn to shreds. And for whose sake?

We mustn't allow the generation of children who are growing up (all over the country) to be forced to experience the sadness and the abjection our generation has known. To that end, we must have responsibility made clear.

I wish you could give me a part of your courage. I think, from now on, however modestly, I will have to become a peace activist, also to prove that your statement was not made in vain. I must become brave. (pp. 27–28)

The phrasing "we must have responsibility made clear" is an attempt to render a common Japanese locution for having someone do something for one. If Hirohito missed his moment for saying "I'm sorry," then ordinary Japanese citizens also missed their chance to demand that apology and therefore to consider the possibility of their own responsibility—a responsibility different from that of public officials and the emperor, to be sure, but a responsibility whose continued denial has been translated into silent acquiescence to the harsh discipline required by economic success.

Still, the demand or yearning for apology is a persistent theme. Hatakeyama Eiichi, aged sixty-six, now working in the fishery business in Iwate Prefecture, and like Mayor Motoshima once an officer who urged his men to die for the emperor, puts it this way:

> I have long wanted to make the emperor say during his lifetime, "I [*chin*, analogous to the royal "we"] was wrong." His empty words at the memorial ceremony every August 15 are unbearable. If he can't bring himself to say "I was wrong," then "I, too, was wrong" would do. Then my dead comrades could sleep in peace. (p. 88)

That statement was never made. In its absence Tanimoto Michitarō, an eighty-two-year-old man from Kanagawa Prefecture, addresses a one-line message to the mayor:

> Your statement came as a shaft of light through dark clouds. (p. 87)

But Hashimoto Yoshisada, at seventy-three, is moved to appeal to the mayor from snowbound Aomori Prefecture:

> I read about your statement in the *Tōōnippō*, which has the largest circulation in the prefecture. I am just an old country man with no learning, but I would be grateful if those who find your statement about the emperor's responsibility disrespectful would read the following and judge accordingly.

Apparently Mr. Hashimoto's younger brother died in service in the Kurile Islands, which extend northward from Hokkaido toward Kamchatka Peninsula. Prefectural military records are scant, and Mr. Hashimoto has never been able to verify the site, let alone the circumstances of his brother's death. The flimsy, bureaucratic communication from the Health Ministry in response to his latest request for information only accentuates his unabated sorrow:

> For whose sake did he dedicate himself to his military duties? On the memorial marker it is carved, O spirit, rest in peace. But my brother, for whom official record and truth must differ so, my brother, who had no comrades-in-arms, my brother, who vanished in an unknown land, leaving behind only unspoken thoughts: how could he be sleeping peacefully?
>
> How can I say to him, sleep peacefully? Was life so paltry a thing? The cruelty, the misery, the coldness, the vanity of war. Where shall I cast them? Whose understanding would comfort me? Where shall I seek salvation?
>
> I want these thoughts to be heard. (p. 58)

Many of the letters critical of the mayor were sent anonymously, but the diction and punctuation often suggest the writer's age and sex. The following letter, gentle in tone and replete with polite circumlocutions, appears to be from an elderly woman:

> I am a person without social standing or any other qualifications granted a place on earth though lacking learning or training in faith. You who are in a position of leadership, who must go on loving and educating the citizens of Nagasaki: are the words of your statement so important that you cannot withdraw or correct them? The life of a politician should be one of righting wrongs. I think you would be better off withdrawing or correcting your statement sooner rather than later.
>
> It is because the military took over in those days that the people united in the face of danger and advanced into the

Greater East Asia War. It is the responsibility of all the people, and the peace we enjoy today is owing to the heroic spirits (soldiers) that each household sent forth in devotion.

From the age of the gods the imperial line has continued for 2,648 years, and it is thanks to the protection of our current majesty, 124th in the line, and of the Ise Shrine (the great guardian deity of Japan) that Japan will continue to live on.

Since the war, thanks to the unimaginable effort of all the people, the Japanese nation has become the greatest economic power in the world, just like the old proverb says: to lose is to win.

I have caught glimpses of your true feelings in the newspapers and on television. I know you are a man with a sense of veneration and sanctity, and I believe and trust that you are a Japanese after all in the depths of your heart.

As we move into the twenty-first century, there will only be young people who know nothing about either the prewar or the postwar periods. It is your duty as a leader to teach them accurately and in detail. Please recover the reverent heart of a beginner and express your thanks and apologies to the citizens.

I would like to beg of you, that through your repentance ("the richer its fruit, the lower it bows, stalk of rice"), you will learn absolutely to refrain from speaking disrespectfully of the gods, the buddhas, the royalty, the imperial family, His Majety the Emperor, and the princes and princesses. (p. 27)

This, too, seems to be from an elderly person, but probably a man:

Is Mayor Motoshima of Nagasaki a human. Or a beast. Or an idiot. You say that if we criticize the emperor, democracy will be born, but do you know what democracy is. Don't think that just because you bark, you've got democracy. It is more than three months since His Majesty the Emperor took to his sickbed. On this of all occasions, to all but say, hurry up and die—to whip him with words—is that what you call democracy? You've gone beyond stupidity, you can shed no human tears, you are not even a beast, you are a demon. Free speech might be important, but for human beings there is such a thing as common sense. There are things that should be said and things that shouldn't.

Let me say to you that democracy has no fixed definition. Every country has its own laws and its own national character, and democracy itself isn't uniform. After the Second World War, many independent countries were born in southeast Asia, Africa, Korea, North Korea, and the South Pacific, but the Soviet Union stole parts of Poland, Finland, and the Japanese Northern Territories. And with its vast military force it continues to suppress eastern Europe, or invade Afghanistan. Yet even a country like the Soviet Union calls itself a democracy.

Do you have any good sense. You're spoiling the image of Nagasaki as a tourist city. What are you thinking? The head of a local government ought to study harder. An American lady once told us what democracy was. She said it meant not causing trouble to others. Democracy is different in every country. People without any common sense are hopeless. (p. 23)

Not every letter of opposition reads like a version of the shrill blarings from right-wing sound trucks. (The reference to tourist benefits strikes an oddly pragmatic note.) Yamamoto Kenji, a forty-one-year-old Shinto priest from Shiga Prefecture, outlines the standard objections to the specific notion of imperial responsibility and to the application of Western values to Japanese practices:

Since you seem to be a sincere person, I hope you will try to read my views through to the end.

The emperor of Japan, who is not an absolute monarch, only issued proclamations according to the decisions of the nation's legally established institutions. To criticize him after the war is equivalent to saying "The emperor should have been an absolute monarch."

It is unclear what sort of responsibility you are referring to, but if it includes ethical responsibility, then how do you explain the journeys His Majesty made around the country right after the war, and how do you interpret his words every year on August 15, "Even now my heart aches"? Whenever His Majesty travels, he stops at the Defense-of-the-Nation Shrine of the region and bows his head; his feelings on such occasions exceed our capacities of comprehension. If you intend to press the matter of ethical responsibility any further, you would be behaving inappropriately as a Japanese.

It is said that you are a Christian. However, the fact that you are a Christian and that you are mayor of Nagasaki are two separate things. Whenever you speak in a public place such as the municipal assembly or in your capacity as mayor, you must absolutely avoid assertions based on your subjective views as a Christian. Even though the late Prime Minister Ōhira was privately a Christian, in his capacity as prime minister, he worshiped at Yasukuni Shrine and offered deeply felt consolation and gratitude to the martyred spirits.

There is an error that those with Western inclinations, including Christians and people who are called intellectuals, often fall into, namely, their failure to grasp that Western and Japanese societies are fundamanentally different in their religious concepts. Forgetting this premise, they attempt to place a Western superstructure on a Japanese base.

It cannot be helped if it is thought that you all too readily fell into the provocations of a Communist assemblyman. (p. 40)

The combination of calmly reasoning tone and shifting ground of argument suggests that it would be difficult to argue with this writer. His initial appeal to the emperor's having acted as a faithful constitutional monarch in declaring war—a thoroughly Western, modern notion—is quickly undermined by his subsequent points, which are governed by an unshakable sense of what it means to be Japanese. And yet this argument itself deploys the Marxist vocabulary of base and superstructure. As generations of Japanese thinkers have learned, the very effort to extricate Japan from Western modernity is inescapably contaminated by Western tools, notably philosophical concepts and the language in which they were formulated.

The opposing letters often raise controversial or repressed issues. An anonymous letter from Tokyo, written by a man, to judge from the verb endings, filled with angry platitudes ("The people of Nagasaki are unfortunate to have a *mayor who can neither judge people nor recognize the truth. That it was the emperor who wanted more than anyone to avert World War II and to end* it is a *truth proven* long ago in Japan and throughout the world") also includes such paragraphs as

> Don't you even know that it was the Americans who dropped the bomb, not the emperor? Moreover, it was Germans, Jews, and Americans who invented the bomb, not the emperor. And the bomb on Nagasaki wasn't the only damage suffered in the war. Tokyo and Osaka died [sic] from American air raids, and the soldiers at the front, the men in charge of transport, and the ones in Manchuria who were unlawfully detained in *Siberia* by the Soviet Union for so many years after the war— why don't you have the guts to call this an inhumane act on a par with Auschwitz?
>
> War is the final form of the unsightly ambition that drives stupid men who begin it with the full knowledge that they will kill each other. (p. 25)

A young man, Tanegashima Yasuo, age twenty-two and un-employed from Kagoshima Prefecture, also denies the emperor's war guilt:

> If directing the war effort was a crime, then why haven't Roosevelt, who began the war against Japan, and Truman, who approved the use of the atomic bombs leading to the slaughter of many civilians, been charged with crimes?
>
> I think it is because the Far East War Crimes Trials and the Nuremberg Trials were both one-sided victors' trials con-ducted in a spirit of revenge. (pp. 42–43)

There is one neglected topic that writers who oppose the mayor never bring up: the effects of Japanese aggression in Asia. A thirty-three-year-old anonymous writer, probably a woman, writes on the basis of her fondness for history books and anecdotes told by her father-in-law:

> My father-in-law says, "It was kill or be killed. I chopped off the heads of POWs with my Japanese sword. You absolutely had to obey orders. Postwar democracy came on top of countless sacrifices, and it makes me sick to watch television. Who do they think they're kidding with all this praise of the emperor?" He is angry.
>
> Many times the number of Japanese who died in the war died in China and Korea. Nobody says anything about that anywhere. And all this talk about Japan as the leader of Asia incurs the resentment of our neighbors. Isn't it sad? (p. 56)

The Motoshima statement obviously provoked dormant memories of the war for older Japanese, but it also provided an occasion for unusual intergenerational exchange. Sasaki Yūji identifies himself as a white-collar worker from Nagano Prefecture:

> I was born in 1959. My father was born in 1916 and was the same age at the time of surrender that I am today.
>
> My father was a career soldier. When I was a child, we used to go together to the public bath, where, without meaning to, I would see scars on his body from bullet wounds and ask him about them. Then, as we soaked in the tub, my father would begin his "tales of the army." However, perhaps because I was so young, he seemed to pull back from telling me why he had become a career soldier and why the war had begun.
>
> What was my father thinking in the year of surrender, when he was the age I am now? Why did he become a career soldier, why did he come to think in such a way as to support the war, why was a society created that produced conditions in which it was impossible to speak out. . . .

For my father, the shock of defeat must have been considerable, for he even tried shock therapy in an attempt to banish memories of extreme war experiences.

Through your statement and your actions, I feel that I have been given an assignment.

That is, to prepare an answer for the day when my child will voice his own simple doubts. I decided to write this letter as a first step in preparing an answer to the question, "Father, what were you thinking and doing in 1988–89?" I think I would like to go on to consider such issues as "What is the responsibility of those who contribute to creating conditions in which nothing can be said?" (p. 126)

Serizawa Kiyondo, a newspaper reporter living in Kanagawa Prefecture, describes the worries he felt when his sons were younger:

I was born in 1930. I am the father of two sons, aged 25 and 21. As they proceeded from middle school to high school to university, there were times when I was gripped with anxiety thinking, "Will there come a time when these children will have to get into military uniform?" to which I would say to myself, "I'll be damned if I allow that to come to pass."

When I think of the future of Japanese children, I can't help worrying about the "textbook issue" [censorship by the Education Ministry, especially pertaining to Japanese aggression in Asia], the "Rising Sun and 'The Reign of Our Emperor' " question. These days, especially as I watch the actions of the LDP cabinet—putting the lid on the Recruit [stock] scandal investigations, forcing passage of the sales tax—I cannot help thinking, "Japan is headed for danger."

As a reporter, I fear the emperor's death more than most people. This is because the pages for the day of his death have already been prepared, and I know they impose a spirit of "praise for the emperor" and "a nation united in mourning."

Within my newspaper company, many reporters as well as workers in the printing plant have doubts about the trends in our coverage and are pressing management to be faithful to the Constitution in which sovereignty is stated to rest with the people. As a journalist, I want to retain my conscience; I do not want to "engage in concealment of the truth, distortion of history."

I intend to make a conscious effort to bring up your words along with my own thoughts in conversation with acquaintances, friends, and especially my fellow reporters. We are resolved to do our best to prevent the coming of an age when we cannot speak out."

I am grateful that you have given many citizens the sense that Japan is not lost yet, and that there are still possibilities for democracy here. Thank you.

Suzuki Keisuke, a forty-seven-year-old schoolteacher from Saitama Prefecture, is also the son of a teacher:

My father has told me with bitter grief about how he, as a schoolteacher, "deceived" more than one hundred pupils about the "sacred war" and not only sent them to their deaths but caused them to murder numerous Chinese and other Asians. He is always talking to me about the importance of peace education. I am a high school teacher.

An ordinary schoolteacher admits to the enormity of his guilt. Where in the world would it be possible to assert with any credibility that the supreme commander bears no responsibility? I think it would be best for our descendants if that family were to move down to Ise Shrine; what do you think? (p. 117)

Mr. Suzuki is slyly suggesting that the imperial family be removed from even the hint of political involvement by relocation to the site of its divine ancestry.

Tanaka Sawako, age thirty-two, is a second-grade teacher in Fukuoka Prefecture.

Human life cannot be exchanged for anything. I am sure that the emperor wants to live a long life. His family must also want him to survive. And the people who were sent to war and died, the people who had their futures stolen by the A-bomb or air raids, and the children of Okinawa who were killed by Japanese soldiers, each of their lives is [worth] the same as the life of the emperor. And their families feel the same way as his family.

Today was the last day of the second quarter. The children seemed so excited about their long-awaited winter vacation; they rushed home cheerfully. No doubt they will spend a happy Christmas and New Year with their families. I wouldn't want any of these children to die in war.

POSTSCRIPT

I felt I had to write this letter for the sake of the thirty-six children in my charge and for the child who will be born to me in the coming year. (p. 86)

Tomiyama Keiko is a twenty-four-year-old teacher from Kagoshima Prefecture:

The other day, my pupils asked me, "If the emperor dies, we get a day off, right?" and "We're not supposed to send New Year's cards, right?" I answered without hesitation, "The emperor isn't a relative or anything of mine, so I'm coming to school and I'm sending lots of New Year's cards." (p. 24)

Ms. Tomiyama would have been appreciated by this anonymous seventh-grader, a girl, to judge from her "Wee, White & Warm-Hearted Li'l Chillun' " Sanrio stationery:

I don't think it makes sense for New Year's cards not to sell just because the emperor's going to die. It's one thing if you're related, but why shouldn't we be sending cards? My dad's been reading up on the emperor and the war. Even though he usually hates writing New Year's cards, this year he's sending them all over the place. (p. 48)

This is part of a three-page letter, reproduced in full in Komichi's book rather than transcribed into print. The hand is poor, the overall appearance is untidy, and on one of the pages the "Li'l Chillun' " heading is at the bottom (with scrawled apologies; how engrossed this writer must have been). No doubt this girl has been consistently harangued and marked down in school. There is a raw power to her thoughts and expression: "Since the emperor is a 'symbol,' I wonder why he gets to use our blood. I don't want blood to be used on such a thing." In conclusion she begins a sentence with "The emperor should taste the suffering of all the people he has killed up to now (including foreigners), then" but blacks out the rest. The violence of her thoughts, even though by "using blood" she is referring to transfusions, as well as the compulsion to cancel them, attests to a violence lurking in all discussions of Emperor Showa that even his decades as kindly-old-man-overseeing-peaceful-prosperity could not eradicate.

Ozaki Machiko, a thirty-seven-year-old mother of two in Ka-gawa Prefecture, like so many others begs the mayor not to with-draw or modify his statement: "Please do not give in. Please do not give in. Please do not give in." Then she avows,

> I do not belong to any organization, but at the end of the
> era known as Showa, I plan to wear a red sweater. It is the
> color of the blood of those who fell in battle. (p. 96)

To wear bright colors in times of mourning—in fact, with the intensified uniformity of the present, to wear anything but black—is wildly improper. Some radical organizations which, unfortunately for them, have nothing to do with housewives like Mrs. Ozaki, campaigned for colorful attire and balloons on the day of the funeral.

A disheartening letter comes from Nagakura Kumiko, who attempted one of the most difficult things of all—to organize in her children's school:

> I am a thirty-seven-year-old parent of a second-grader and
> a fifth-grader. Toward the end of the year, I drew up a statement

requesting that the school not impose expressions of mourning on the children on the occasion of X-day [the popular term for the day of the emperor's death], talked to people I knew, and managed to get eight people to be cosigners and submit it to the school.

But later, one person who had agreed said she was pulling out because the chances of success were nil and we would only be earning ourselves a reputation. She said we would be discriminated against by the school, and that it would be hard if any of us wanted to be active in the PTA.

Since she was someone who had worked hard in the PTA, I found her words persuasive. I myself had been resigned to the ineffectuality of the effort but had decided that unless we were willing to think simply and raise our voices when we objected to something, all action was impossible. But after that, when I heard another person who had originally agreed say, "Well, I might as well kiss good-bye to any chance of substitute teaching during a teacher's maternity leave," I decided I should be more cautious.

I lost heart and ended up doing nothing at the end of the quarter and put it off until the new year.

I greeted X-day listlessly and talked on the phone with a friend about at least going to the beginning-of-the-quarter ceremony at school the next day, but we ended up not even doing that. In the end, I was unable to do anything.

Every time I think about your statement, I am moved from the bottom of my heart. That you should have confronted a subject that is still taboo—if that isn't courage, what is?

I understand that you are a Christian, so I have also imagined that you gain strength from a faith that steadfastly sustains the soul.

In any case, it is amazing that you spoke out for us in your capacity as mayor.

I cannot deny my shame in not having been able to do anything. Still, there is the future.

I have decided to try to meet regularly with the people who agreed to sign. Our first meeting is four days from now. I don't know how it will turn out, but I would like the group to become strong enough to do its part in protecting freedom of expression, thought, and belief on the local level. (p. 133)

Hashimoto Nozomu from Hokkaido contributes this:

> Hello.
> I am a sixth-grader. In social studies we are studying the rights of citizens, and we learned that we are supposed to have freedom of speech and thought. According to my parents, though, "That's not the way things work these days." But I think that you, Mr. Mayor, are doing just as the textbook said, saying what you think. I want to become a person like you. (p. 20)

In fact, Mayor Motoshima was once a schoolteacher, and that is how Sano Moriichirō, a fifty-four-year-old "white-collar worker" from Aichi Prefecture, addresses him:

> I apologize for my rudeness in writing to you so suddenly. I never thought to be writing to you, my teacher, on such a matter as this.
> I read your views on the emperor in the newspaper and was deeply affected.
> I have moved to Nagoya. Not one of my acquaintances here disagrees with what you said.
> Lastly, as one of your pupils from thirty-odd years ago, I would like to say that it makes me deeply happy to witness your putting into practice in society what you taught us back then. Thinking back to your classes with affectionate longing, I find myself profoundly moved. (p. 139)

If the mayor's older supporters felt their sufferings vindicated by his statement, his postwar-generation supporters felt they had been given lessons for the future. Nomura Mizue, age forty-five, identifies herself as a greengrocer:

> When you appeared in the "People" column in the *Asahi*, I read it many times over with tears streaming. It was from the

joy of encountering a noble person for the first time in such a long while.

Since last year I have been studying "citizen responsibility for the war," and the more I study, the more evident not only citizen responsibility but imperial responsibility becomes. In an English movie called *Marilyn and Einstein*, Einstein's watch is permanently stopped at 8:15. And every time he looks at his watch, he imagines the wretched spectacle of Hiroshima and clings to Marilyn [Monroe], saying "I have killed many children." I have wondered for a long time why Japanese haven't developed that kind of a sensibility.

These days, as we talk about Recruit, taxes, and your statement, it is evident that we can no longer sit back as ordinary housewives.

"We have to do something to express our views," everyone is saying. One of my friends said, "I'm going to write Mr. Motoshima a fan letter." I promised myself that I would write one too, but it is hard to write a letter to someone you've never met (especially a fan letter).

The precious things you have taught us—we will translate them into action. Thank you. Truly, thank you. That you showed us what a mayor should be, what attitude human beings should adopt—for this I am profoundly grateful. (pp. 105–106)

For another woman in her forties, writing to the mayor becomes a challenge to communicate, a challenge she had failed to meet many years ago in love:

I was born in 1942. In my forty-six years I have never once written a "fan letter." In fact, I am such a bad correspondent that I lost my first love for failure to write a letter. But this time, I am determined to write.

Of course, what you, Mr. Motoshima (I don't know if I should address you like this, but I'm going to do it anyway), said about the "emperor bearing responsibility for the war" is a historical fact and *shouldn't* be something we fuss over as a "courageous statement." But that it should sweep over the

archipelago like a great shock wave, that it should have provoked irrational, oppressive, and hysterical responses, is a reflection of the situation in Japan today.

I have heard that on the anniversary of the end of the war
in Europe, President Weizsäcker of West Germany said in an
address to Parliament, "All Germans must take responsibility
for the past. It is neither possible to change the past nor to
deny it. Those who shut their eyes to the past are blind to the
present as well."

Our "peace" today is nothing firm. As you have aptly put
it, it is as if we were "drinking on top of a carpet with which
we've covered over an enormous stockpile of nuclear weapons."

State censorship has erased photographs of the bomb from
textbooks and articles describing the ravages of war because
"overly cruel events hurt children's feelings" or "[such writing]
will make them lose their pride in Japan." I believe this is one
reason that we have children like the ones referred to above
[who cannot identify August 6, 9, and 15 as the dates of Hiroshima, Nagasaki, and surrender, respectively].

And, if we inquire into the state of the media, it is as we
have seen since January 7.

I have neglected to introduce myself, but I work in a publishing firm. I am in no position to be criticizing the media
as if it had nothing to do with me. I am aware that I have to
take it on as my own problem and dig in my heels each day.
It's not as if I haven't felt that way before, but I have often
been overcome by despair that the opposite current is so strong
that no ordinary determination can withstand it.

As punishment for having failed to write when I should
have, I am, to my deep chagrin, lacking the words that would
be adequate on such an important occasion as this.

It is all too clichéd, but please take good care of yourself,
and please stand firm. In the January 30 issue of the weekly
magazine we publish, you are reported as looking exhausted
and saying, "I was too tired to sleep again last night." It makes
my heart ache.

I pray from the bottom of my heart that peaceful days will

come soon to you, Mayor Motoshima, and your family. And of course to City Hall and all the citizens as well! (pp. 130–31)

Tender concern also comes from a sixty-year-old "self-employed" man. Surprisingly, he is a supporter of the Liberal Democratic Party:

> During the past ten days, each time I read news reports of your declarations, I have been surprised by tears coming to my eyes and have found myself trembling. I send you my heartfelt respect.
>
> I will remember you forever as the person who most deeply moved me and whom I respect the most, and I will pass on your story to my grandchildren.
>
> Please take the utmost care of yourself, and continue to speak the truth. If members of your family are in danger, please use my house in Kyoto. Since we are entirely unconnected, I believe that you will be safe and the secret could be kept. We are an elderly couple, living behind the Arashiyama Mountains. We renovated our house last year and the upstairs is completely empty. My wife is also tearfully anxious about your and your family's safety. (pp. 64–65).

The last section of the Komichi book is reserved for letters from abroad and from foreigners residing in Japan. Included in the latter are so-called "resident Koreans," the children and grandchildren of Koreans who were driven to Japan by the harsh economic dislocation caused by Japanese annexation of their country in 1910, or who were literally rounded up and forced into slave labor to substitute for the manpower lost to the war effort. Resident Koreans have been fingerprinted, harassed, and treated as second-class citizens, the combined effect of government policy and ordinary prejudice. Mayor Motoshima has been a stalwart campaigner for their rights, though that was hardly known before his "statement." Byun Won Choong, age fifty-one, self-employed in Gifu Prefecture, writes,

> Nothing good can possibly come of human beings in the present neglecting the past. It cannot possibly be good for the future of human beings alive today, who must bear the burden of history, to have the citizens of an aggressor nation that had engaged in the crime called war feign ignorance before the world.
>
> Your recent statement in the municipal assembly on the emperor has moved me profoundly.
>
> When the war was over, civilians as well as soldiers returned form China and Korea. Have the people there forgotten how those who had ventured forth as citizens of an aggressor nation behaved toward them? I have not forgotten how mainland Japanese behaved toward us.
>
> I watched repatriated Japanese see that the emperor had escaped responsibility for the war, put down their rucksacks, and from that instant on, turn into benevolent Japanese. As for those Koreans who were rounded up to take part in a war of aggression, or the seven to eight thousand Koreans who were charged with protecting the emperor to the end in Matsudai in Shinshū [in north central Japan, away from the capital], where preparations were being made for mainland battle, they have been lost in the ignominy of history, and their souls wander homeless to this day. But it doesn't occur to any Japanese to refer to them, and when a person like you makes a confession of faith to God and a declaration of conscience to your fellow human beings, he is greeted with stones and whips.
>
> You stand alone among Japanese mayors. I am one who has received relief and encouragement today from witnessing a true human being.
>
> Do not lose heart. Stand firm. It is not a question of a mere two or three thousand who support you. I want to report to you that there is a great majority among us whose thoughts go unheard. (p. 145)

Two ways of assessing the wartime past emerge from these letters. One follows the fallacy of *post hoc, ergo propter hoc:* after Hiroshima and Nagasaki, therefore because of them. The horrors of the war are justified by current peace and prosperity. This is a view held by many veterans and bereaved families. It is easy to understand the appeal of such a redemptive narrative for those who sacrificed heavily, yet it is also exploited by such parties as right-wing militarists seeking the restoration of imperial sovereignty and the recovery of empire and by Education Ministry officials consolidating their powers of censorship. People of this persuasion never expected an apology from Emperor Showa. Yet there are also veterans, bereaved families, and other elderly people for whom present-day prosperity is tainted precisely because of the missing apology. There are still others, many of them younger people who did not experience the war, who adopt the latter view and extend it, suggesting conjunctions between wartime repression and the more subtle, apparently non-life-threatening forms of coercion that ensure the order and harmony crucial to postwar prosperity.

I can't help wishing that these letter writers could meet beyond the pages of the book. They need to have their hearts and minds quickened and consoled by each other's knowledge. What has happened to those who risked signing their names—especially the teachers, journalists, corporate employees, and mothers— those still active in the mainstream of contemporary Japanese society? Have they had to pay for what might have proven a reckless, solitary moment of resolve once they returned to the relentless sociality of routine? Have they found that other mothers are more polite than ever when they can't avoid them, or that colleagues maintain an awkward distance until they can drunkenly blurt out their disapproval? If only they could meet, for alone, it is too hard, especially in a society of abundance, to live up to the promise so many of them seem to have offered the mayor and themselves: from now on, I will speak out, before it is too late.

My aunt in Nagasaki, one of my favorite figures from childhood, is a woman of passionate but undirected intelligence who has never spoken out. Now I wonder if her intelligence is undirected because she never could speak out, and in her supreme isolation, it became autotoxic. I was her beloved niece from the years before she married until I left Japan. Knowing she is prepared to bestow the same unmeasured affection on my daughter as she did on me, I decide we should both go on the journey to Nagasaki.

To speak of this trip as a "journey" may seem excessive, but it suits the spiritual and historical geography, both private and public, invoked by the name of the prefecture and its capital city: Nagasaki, remote on the island of Kyushu, once the site of exotic trade and Christian persecution, now a city whose mayor is held captive through a single utterance, city also of my suffering aunt, exemplary wife of Japanese High Growth Economics.

When I was born, Aunt spent all of her first paycheck to buy me a rocking chair. She had a talent for excess, for injecting color into our always cautious, often marginal lives, which fluctuated with the fortunes of the foreign-movie market. Like my mother, her older sister, she is under five feet tall, and probably was not quite ninety pounds in those days. But if the spirit seized her, she would single-handedly move chests of drawers, tables, and bookcases, all in a day's work. The Japanese call her disproportionate sort of strength the "strength of idiots." After ruthlessly shifting the furniture, she would sew up muslin curtains with ruffles and white chair covers destined to be excruciatingly starched, try out new embroidery stitches on old fabric to cover up battered tables, and in a day, or at most two, have whipped up a new room. Before her wedding, she had no fewer than eight nightgowns and pajamas custom-made by a dressmaker. Several years later, when my mother and grandmother and I lay side by side haplessly flu-ridden at Christmastime, Aunt arrived unannounced bearing a cageful of finches.

She took charge of my education: she made beautifully drawn and written exercises not merely replicating but developing the smudgy purple mimeographed assignments I brought home each day from first grade. She knew that with but a handful of English words to grasp at I would surely drown, so she set herself the task of teaching me at least to read. She also supervised my deportment, turning me into a girl who could seem a reasonable facsimile of the well-brought-up child. The catch was that I would fail on sight, racial difference being precisely what registers immediately upon the senses. Now, nearly four decades later, I wonder if Aunt wasn't striving to achieve with my conduct exactly what she tried with my schoolwork: to compensate by cultivation where biology as interpreted by history had disadvantaged me.

She succeeded to the extent that I believed the neighborhood children avoided me only because I was superior to them and not because I was a half-breed whose father had taken up with another native woman while his wife lay in bed with tuberculosis. My grandmother's walled garden on a fine corner lot contributed to this illusion. There, and within the house, I was the center of attention: schooling and manners were supervised by my older aunt; drawing, music, and silliness by the younger; health and hygiene was the province of my mother, who boiled my drinking water and dishes until I was ten, as if my father's genetic input had left my digestive tract irreducibly different from her own. Mercifully holding it all together was my grandmother's inexhaustible readiness to soothe and to please.

Now, this fine world could be maintained reasonably well in the five rooms of a comfortably dilapidated house and an enchanted garden, but there were occasions when I had to leave, and not just via school bus for another walled world in the form of an American base. Usually, it was to go to the pediatrician or the ear, nose, and throat doctor or the dentist, and it was always my grandmother who led me forth. On such occasions she acted as if I were perfectly normal, and sometimes she even took me to visit her old landlady, or her sister until she moved away to a grander part of the city (this being the sister whose daughters became Catholic). When my grandmother was well into her seventies, she contracted a case of shingles. It happened during one of my prolonged returns, so I was able to walk her every day to the dermatologist and the ophthalmologist. It was blistering summer, but she concealed her face with a navy blue chiffon veil. She always apologized, assuming I would be embarrassed to be seen in such odd company, but the veil, together with the hesitant gait introduced by the unpleasant surprise of illness, only accentuated my grandmother's elegance; and besides, the ophthalmologist's office was in the direction of my old ear, nose, and throat doctor, and we could carry on as we had so many years earlier, stopping to admire other people's gardens where they persisted and bewail them where they had turned into parking lots.

It was early in my second-grade year that my father left the household. I am still unsure whether he forsook us or whether my grandfather was summoned to play the manly role and announce to him that he was no longer welcome as his daughter's husband. It was not much more than a month after my father's departure that my aunt's wedding took place, and she went off to Nagasaki. My mother and I stayed home. We went to neither sister's wedding, I suppose because our presence would have been inauspicious.

Luckily, my uncle didn't seem in any way a competition for my aunt's attention, for he was thoroughly attentive to me, too. He was a good storyteller, expert in Norse mythology, a polymath of sorts who taught me geometry and took me to my first art exhibit, a massive loan from the Louvre, serving in the early

1960s as yet another sign of Japan's new acceptability to the world community. There, his comments so engaged the university student behind us that he asked to follow along, even taking a lunch break with us.

From faraway Nagasaki Aunt continued to lavish her affection on me, most often in the form of letters carefully saved by my grandmother. There was always a letter when a commemorative stamp was issued, with a first-day-of-issue cancellation and an explanatory note on beautiful stationery, rice paper decorated with a traditional motif, for my aunt was unimpressed by the commercial culture of cuteness. The note explained the commemorated feature: International Children's Week, when I should be mindful of children studying in other countries and especially of those less fortunate than I; or antarctic exploration, in which Japanese scientists and a team of loyal Japanese dogs participated, establishing a base camp named, of course, Showa Base. Distance only made my aunt more exhortative: now that spring is coming and the days are longer, it will be easier for you to study and play. How lucky you are to have such a long summer vacation. I am studying German with the 6:30 radio program. You have to huff and puff to pronounce German correctly, and my heart gets tired out by the end of the program—isn't it silly of me to exaggerate like this? Why don't you ask your mother and start studying Japanese through the same series? You know there aren't many foreigners who can speak Japanese correctly, let alone read and write it. Still, Aunt never badgered or bored me with the usual injunctions to stand firm, persist, and refuse surrender at all cost—I suppose to the multiple temptations to go astray that presumably offered themselves to children like me.

Even more than exhortation, my aunt offered vivid accounts of her new life. How my uncle brought home a watermelon. They had no refrigerator, so they chilled it in water, ate the whole thing, and ended up collapsing ill-manneredly. A wind chime seller was passing under her window, pulling a laden wagon and calling out (and here my aunt would carefully reproduce the dialect), "Won't somebody buy a wind chime?" The most common form of Japanese wind chime in those days was a glass sphere painted with summer motifs, perhaps goldfish, with a slender glass rod suspended from the center, attached to a strip of paper often bearing the words of a familiar haiku, such as the one about the plopping frog. Aunt thought that one wind chime hanging from the eaves had a cooling effect, but a whole cartload actually made you feel hotter; what did I think? And always, there were invitations. Come visit Nagasaki, spend the whole summer, come with your mother, bring your friends (she always learned the names of my American school friends). Uncle will take us all for a yacht ride, the waves lapping against the sides of the boat make you feel so cool. Some day Uncle wants to build a sailboat and sail it around the world. I don't know when, but I hope the hydrogen bomb testing in the Pacific will be over soon.

There were other letters, addressed to my mother or to my grandmother. My aunt had (and still has) a beautiful, rounded hand, of which the best efforts seemed to have been reserved for her letters to me. (Moreover, unlike everyone else, she did not write my name in the script customarily used for foreign words and names.) Her writing to the adults is marred by the urgency of the subject matter. To my mother: please send a pair of your old shoes that you aren't wearing anymore, preferably black with medium heels. To my grandmother: please have three fresh ten-thousand-yen bills ready by the end of next week. My aunt was desperate to get her older son into the preschool attached to Nagasaki University, and she and my uncle were visiting anyone remotely connected with the process, bearing fresh notes and tins of English cookies, also procured by my grandmother. Between the requests and the apologies there was little room for news, but occasionally she sandwiched in observations such as, I stood in line to get forms for the lottery; other mothers were talking about failing; it made me terribly forlorn. On his first attempt to get into preschool, my cousin had passed the academic part—a putative test of ability—of the entrance exam but had failed in the lottery, a candidly arbitrary mechanism for elimination.

My aunt seldom writes any of us anymore. Nor is it possible for us to write her directly; we must address our correspondence to her oldest son, my cousin who did, in fact, successfully pass written and oral tests *and* the lottery on his second attempt to enter Nagasaki University preschool. He forwards our mail to Nagasaki via a special delivery service. Aunt does not want any letter carriers coming to her house. I cannot ask her to follow the local papers for news of Mayor Motoshima, because she does not want newspapers to be delivered to her house. Most of the time, we cannot reach her by telephone, either, for she fears harassment calls. Only recently, with my grandfather's greatly advanced age, has she agreed to a prearranged code, though she and my uncle would have preferred to install a fax machine in my grandmother's house. But even these codes are apt to be changed without notice; the dates of change are meticulously recorded in my uncle's notebook, but my mother and grandmother are not informed. Through my aunt's escalating refusals of contact with even her most intimate world, my uncle either acquiesced or in fact assisted in the implementation of barriers. Did he, does he, in fact approve? If not, did he have no choice? Was he so exhausted by the demands of his career that he lacked the wherewithal to resist, let alone to coax her back into a more social existence? Or was he yielding a compensatory form of affection?

My uncle, hero of my adolescence, had been a properly left-wing youth who, by the time I was finishing high school, would conceal his corporate lapel pin in the company of my grandmother and mother if they were wearing "blue sky" antipollution campaign buttons for independent progressive Governor Minobe

Ryūtarō. The governor's father, constitutional scholar Minobe Tatsukichi, is remembered for his theory of the emperor as "organ of the state," for which he was charged with lèse-majesté.) Those were the days, in the early 1960s, when Tokyo smog was so thick that pictures of policemen with gas masks appeared in the international media.

My uncle is a man whose life was dominated by High Growth Economics, those two decades beginning in the mid-1950s during which the world learned to use the word "miracle" whenever it referred to the Japanese economy. (Did anyone in those days think to juxtapose the miracle with the gas masks?) Uncle married Aunt in 1954. In 1955 the Japanese gross national product accounted for but 2 to 3 percent of the world economy. My aunt moved into the second-floor six-mat room that Uncle had rented as a bachelor. It had a western exposure, which meant that the afternoon sun of a southern land beat mercilessly into the tiny space for several long hours every day. Even a watermelon cooled by tap water would have been refreshing once the sun went down. There my aunt studied German, kept finches, wrote letters, sewed and mended, cooked multicourse meals featuring the cheap, abundant fish of the region on one burner, and suffered her series of failed pregnancies. And my uncle—worked. I didn't appreciate then what generosity of time and funds was represented by the outing to the Louvre exhibit, complete with lunch and postcards. My uncle worked, and worked, and worked. Highly skilled, the recipient of an elite education all the way through graduate training, he had entered one of the handful of corporations that had supervised and realized Japanese industrial and financial modernization from the beginning. It was no simple matter of profit, though it certainly was that, too. Uncle belonged to that generation of men—"one-digit Showa," they are called, meaning they were born in the first decade of Showa, beginning in the mid-twenties—who felt that nothing less than the resuscitation of Japan in the postwar world rested on their shoulders.

Eventually, Aunt and Uncle had their own house and two children and later, a dog, who became my aunt's sole companion when she entered her years of high isolation. The preschool entrance crises passed, but daily life itself became a dull, unending crisis. For a number of years Uncle left the house at seven and returned at two in the morning. If there were accidents at his work site, Aunt had to make hospital visits; as for deaths. . . . Periodically, Uncle brought home the men who worked under him for the requisite drinking and feasting, and there Aunt was again, valiantly, desperately catering while attending to her young sons, who were sickly. At election time the couple were expected to display on their fence posters of the candidate supported by the company. There, extraordinarily enough, Aunt put her foot down. Decades later, she says to me, "I thought I should at least be able to vote for whom I pleased!" So she took the posters allocated her to some of the shops she patronized and persuaded the properietors to display them instead.

This gesture, and her success, are emblematic. My aunt and uncle were colonials from Tokyo. At work, only people like Uncle, graduates of the University of Tokyo, would rise through the ranks. At home Aunt was surrounded by the wives of the men fated to be subordinate to her husband all their lives. She received, imagined, and absorbed their hostility with every fiber of her being. An ardent gardener like her mother, my grandmother, she became convinced, when her prized rose of Sharon bushes bloomed, that neighbors trespassed in order to make a subtle cut in a single petal on each flower. She took to keeping an enormous flashlight, with which she patrolled the nights in search of intruding neighbors. The oven fan and radio were on all day so that conversation—of which she had none, since she had forbidden telephone calls from her family—could not be overheard. In the days when mail was allowed, it had to be triple-sealed, with elaborate marks designed to betray the slightest attempt at opening. Naturally, the house was closed up even in the sultry summers. More bolts, and ever stronger bolts, had to be installed at all openings. Sushi, even when it was allowed in the earlier, more relaxed days, had to be microwaved to destroy the effects of maliciously unsanitary hands. (And she who had so loved the fresh fish of Nagasaki!) Her husband and sons dutifully observed every dictum. The older son was in fact persuaded of the validity of many of her concerns. He is a young man who keeps a basin of disinfectant at the entrance to his own apartment, hates Communists (applauds Reagan), and reveres the emperor. The younger one decided on his own while in middle school that his mother was afflicted with what he had heard referred to as "psychological problems"; he developed a dual strategy pursued in the solitude of his room: he read up on psychology and slept through the battles his mother waged with her neighbors. The menfolk did not come home without first calling (by code) from a public telephone fifteen yards away from the gate; regardless of the hour, Aunt would go out armed with broom and bucket to wash away the dirt and indignities she was convinced had been spitefully deposited since the family's morning exodus. She slept more and more lightly. Her body began to corrode, beginning with her teeth, since of course she would not see a dentist.

My beautiful, high-spirited aunt of many talents. I wept with anger the first time I confronted, in my mid-twenties, the ruin she had become. I'm afraid that then, it was mostly anger at her. Why had she submitted to her own destruction? I didn't know that I was asking, why had she consented to become a High Growth Economics bride? As if she could have known it, or as if, having recognized it, she could have imagined any other life from the thousands around her. Of course, the recognition came sooner to her than it did to me. Once during our long separation through my college years, she wrote to describe her recent devotion to crochet. She was probably in her early forties then, my age now. She didn't know how the years had passed, how she had become the age she was. It sent chills down her spine to think of it, and the only way she could numb that terror was to move the crochet needle so fast that she could think of nothing. We, her family, are the beneficiaries of that terror in the form of doilies, antimacassars, and magnificent tablecloths. They are intricate patterns of dry white threads, the residue of her once sinewy vitality.

She has never lost her lucidity, her capacity for acute insight. She was capable of observing, even in the years when Uncle's work was expanding apparently without limit, "What's the Japanese economic miracle worth? Look at him, worn to a rag. And when they're through with him, it'll be just that. They'll be through with him." And even now, after so many years of willful solipsism, there are moments when her spirit soars in exuberant generosity. She no longer comes unannounced with a cage of finches, but she will fly up to Tokyo just to stay with my grandfather so that my grandmother and mother can go together to see us off at the airport. She offers me family history more specific, more vivid, and no doubt more imaginative than anyone else's. It was she who told me about my great-grandmother sending off soldiers to the Russo-Japanese War; about my aunt next door crying over stories told by her grade school teacher of his soldier-brother's exploits, of playing with Chinese children, then tricking them into serving as live mine detectors ("we'll run a footrace"); or about how my father gassed the dog after it was diagnosed with distemper by unhooking the tube from the twin burners in my grandmother's postwar kitchen and sticking it into its mouth. At such moments I am tempted to think of Aunt as ravaged but undefeated. But that is the romanticizing of a wishful niece, and there is no condoning the wanton ruin of her prime and her maturity.

When I hear my Reaganite cousin, her older son, telling me that she has been a sheltered woman, as is her due, a fury rises in me against him—as if now, knowing it is pointless to rail against my aunt or even my uncle, I can only seize upon him to explain those damaged lives. Then I see his lonely young face proudly demanding chopsticks (wasn't this Japan, after all) with which to eat the escargots he has just ordered at a pretentious American restaurant in Tokyo; I hear him fastidiously but noisily gargling after every egress into the outside world; I recollect schoolboy letters chronicling a prematurely pedantic idolatry of the monuments of Western civilization—Versailles, Mozart, the British Museum—an idolatry spelled out in the unreformed script of the prewar, inexplicable for one of his generation except as the expression of nationalist sentiment. And I must acknowledge that he, too, is a victim, inasmuch as we can be victimized—though to vastly different degrees, depending upon the inequities of birth—through socialization as well as by physical coercion. I, no less willful than my cousin and his parents, believe they would, or certainly should, have wished their lives to be otherwise and have acted accordingly. This implies that such victimization is partly consensual, but from what age, and in what circumstances? For at any given moment in history, societies that are regarded as peaceful and orderly exact vastly different penalties from those who engage in nonviolent dissent, whether it takes the form of irregular dress or hunger strikes or, for that matter, writing letters to an elected official at the heart of a controversy.

The bullet train does not penetrate the island of Kyushu beyond the gateway city of Hakata, long famous for its earthenware dolls. The ride from Hakata to Nagasaki City follows the ragged coastline, with spectacular views of my uncle's beloved sea. Seventeen years have passed since my last visit, but it is not unrecognizably changed. Uncle meets us at the train station and sees us home in a taxi. He has retired only days before. Like so many Japanese couples, he and my aunt have been separated because of his job, and they are living together for the first time in four years.

Uncle makes the requisite telephone call, and Aunt greets us in the dark with broom and bucket. Our beds have been made with stiffly starched linen sheets, indescribably refreshing after the sultry day, and our pillowcases are embroidered—this the work of my uncle, who finished some of the tasks my aunt abandoned as she lost the will to beautify. We sleep comfortably enough with the air-conditioning to lull us through the night, since windows cannot be opened.

Early next morning when it is barely light, I hear Aunt rattling through her self-appointed tasks. By the time I come downstairs, she is already exhausted, settling into a sort of crouch on the floor to watch the news and drift into her first nap of the day. Still, she consents to join us on the outing I have planned, to the atomic bomb memorial park and exhibition hall. Uncle had taken me there when I was preparing to leave Japan for the first time, and I want to show it to my daughter.

Uncle calls a taxi for us. It arrives promptly enough, but as we climb in and drive off (leaving Uncle to guard the house), Aunt realizes that it is not noticeably cooler inside than the summer day outside. Several times, she asks the driver to turn up the air conditioner. I become anxious, having learned over the years that nothing is meaningless, that is, arbitrary, in my aunt's world. It is therefore crucial to establish meanings other than the ones she will assign, so I say coaxingly to the driver, "It must be hard on you to have to spend all your days in an air-conditioned car." It works. "It sure is. That's why I turn it off when I'm just cruising." Aunt settles back, discontented but no longer suspecting the driver of belonging to the omnipresent conspiracy bent on tormenting her every moment.

At the bomb exhibit I am surprised by the great preponderance of warped, melted artifacts over photographs and accounts of human suffering. When I had come here as a teenager, I could read only enough Japanese to detect a consistent gap between the Japanese and the English signs. The former were, perhaps understandably, more complete, but I could not understand why the most gruesome details should consistently be omitted from the latter. I had wanted to find out if those signs had been changed, or amplified, and I see that they have not. Midway through, Aunt asks me if I am feeling sick; she is, but she dutifully accompanies us all the way, for I am eager to see if there are any hints of the new impetus I have heard about, to situate the bombs in the context of a war of aggression waged by Japan. There are none. I tell myself I can understand, it would be difficult to incorporate such a perspective in a city that had suffered directly and massively. Vaguely disappointed, I leave my aunt in the air-conditioned lobby and move into the melting heat with my daughter to explore the peace park.

The park is ideally situated for taking in the hilly verdancy of Nagasaki City, but the scorching afternoon, a scant ten days before the anniversary of that day always described as hot and cloudless, dulls our senses. After a mechanical walk to the end of the park, we descend to the—souvenir?—shop. Unlike the Princess Lily shops in Okinawa, with pencil stands made of miniature bombs, there are no bronze replicas of the mushroom cloud for sale. There are items made by bomb victims, and a portion of the proceeds are to benefit them. There is a good selection of literature, including some in English. Still, it is awkward, this meeting of tragedy and entrepreneurialism. Though I have not visited Hiroshima, I have heard that commercialization of the bomb legacy has proceeded much more rapidly there. The logic seems inevitable. Hiroshima has been described by a city official as the "only nonreligious sacred site in the world."[17] The city is planning the construction of a Peace Tower to soar to the altitude at which the bomb exploded.

By the time we return to collect her, Aunt is all but convinced

---

[17]Quoted in Doi Toshikuni, "Sensō Kagai Keiken o Naze Katarenai no Ka" [Why Can't We Speak about the Experience of Wartime Aggression?], *Asahi Jānaru*, August 11, 1989, p. 24.

that we have been kidnapped. Variously relieved, we speed home in a taxi blasting cold air into the backseat.

The beginnings of the "Nagasaki Citizens' Committee to Seek Free Speech" can be traced to a drinking session the night after Mayor Motoshima's statement. The four who gathered were veteran activists of the anti–nuclear power and arms industry movements who were by no means favorably disposed toward their conservative mayor. Yet the statement had them excited, and after several rounds they dialed the mayor's official residence where, as he is often said to do, he picked up the phone himself. They invited him to join them. No, he couldn't; he was too heavily guarded to go out. Too bad; might they go to him instead? No, that wasn't possible either. Reluctantly, they gave up on the idea of drinking with the mayor. But the heady talk that night led to more talk, building to the recognition of a need to do something visible, something public, "not to let Motoshima stand alone."

When the citizens' group was coalescing, its members thought of themselves as like-minded people assembled to protect free speech; but soon it began to seem that in Nagasaki there was no free speech for them to defend, and that this was precisely what they had to fight for. To this end they drafted a statement for which they would seek supporting signatures. The document affirms the content of the mayor's statement as a reasonable assertion based on historical fact and deplores the threats and pressures against him as an attempt to crush freedom of speech and thought. It goes on to assert,

> As citizens of a nation that imposed immeasurable terror and misery upon the people of Asia in the last war, we believe, in order to gain the trust of the people of the world in international society, that we must reflect with humility on our history of

aggression and promote free and wide-ranging debate on the emperor system and the emperor's responsibility for the war. This is because a democratic society must not tolerate taboos of any kind. *(Citizens' Declaration on the "Motoshima Statement" and Free Speech)*

In one week, from the fifteenth of December (eight days after the Motoshima statement) to the twenty-second, the Citizens' Committee collected 13,783 signatures from around the country. The first response came by telephone from Okinawa. Indeed, citizens from Okinawa and Hiroshima responded vigorously throughout the campaign. Over the next few months, the numbers swelled to 370,000, accompanied by numerous letters and considerable sums of money. This provoked a countercampaign of signature collection against the mayor, but it was soon numerically overwhelmed. The sound trucks and threats continued unchecked.

Committee members turned first to good friends and colleagues for signatures rather than to neighbors or even peace-activist and labor groups—in other words, to trusted individuals. In spite of the enormous enthusiasm with which this effort was greeted, they did not take to collecting in the streets until February. They began in fear and trembling: first checking the location of the nearest public telephone (for dialing the emergency number, 110), carrying a fistful of ten-yen coins (forgetting they didn't need them to dial 110), and wearing sneakers in case they needed to make a quick getaway. Appealing from the street corners turned out to be deeply gratifying, giving the members a chance to experience immediate support and to sense that they were not, after all, such an isolated, peculiar (un-Japanese) minority as they had supposed. On the other hand, even in the process of private solicitation, they encountered hesitations. Unlike petition campaigns against nuclear power plants, for instance, signatories tended not to volunteer to pass the forms around to their own acquaintances. They also tended not to be from Nagasaki City itself. And it was easier to appeal on the grounds of "free speech" rather than "the emperor system" or "the emperor's war guilt."[18]

The members of the Citizens' Committee I was able to meet included schoolteachers, a truck driver and his wife, an economist, a modern French historian, a high school student, and a Burakumin (outcaste) liberation activist. All of them are normally critical of the Motoshima administration. They have tended to think of him as a run-of-the-mill politician who heads a town that is in the pocket of a major arms producer. They fault him for being slow in getting Nagasaki City declared a nuclear-free zone and in adopting the three nonnuclear principles of refusal to manufacture, possess, or introduce nuclear weapons. But it is also clear that since December 7, 1988, they have had to revise their views of him.

I want to know why they got involved. The truck driver's wife joined because she couldn't say no. It was after she took a vacation trip to Okinawa during high school—the teacher who guided the tour is also a member of the Citizens' Committee—that she began to take part in antiwar sit-ins. Her husband had grown up in Sasebo, site of a large U.S. naval base. He loved jazz, and he used to go to the clubs catering to American servicemen. One night during the Vietnam War, he happened to be at a club when the Japanese owner started yelling at the black GIs as they sat drinking: you fools, can't you see they're using you as fodder to save the white boys? That was the beginning of the truck driver's education. He is far better informed than I am about the history of the American civil rights movement. The high school student

---

[18]Genron no Jiyū o Motomeru Nagasaki Shimin no Kai [The Committee of Citizens of Nagasaki Seeking Freedom of Speech], eds., *Tabū e no Chōsen: Motoshima (Nagasaki Shichō) Hatsugen ni Shimin Wa* [Challenging Taboo: Citizens in the Face of Mayor Motoshima's Statement] (Nagasaki City: The Committee of Citizens of Nagasaki Seeking Freedom of Speech, 1989), pp. 30–31.

is there because he realized he wasn't learning anything about prewar education in his school and because there is generally no opportunity for students to express their views in the present-day school system. He finds school regulations stifling, but normally he doesn't think much about the emperor. His parents, on the other hand, regard him as someone to be respected. The modern French historian thinks that Japanese capitalism continues to require the emperor system, that there is no concept of citizenship in Japan, and that therefore it is essential to dig in one's heels on basic, almost childlike positions and defend elementary freedoms. The economist is an A-bomb survivor and a pioneer advocate of the position that bomb victims must incorporate the history of Japanese aggression in their worldview, where they figure preeminently as victims. He is an exception in the group in his longtime acquaintance with and glowing admiration for the mayor.

Members come in and out of a room they share with other citizens' groups. They chat as they go about their respective tasks, keeping the books, answering correspondence, shipping out copies of the booklet they have just published. I ask about a controversy I have just heard about, generated by one letter in the Komichi book. The letter was from a former schoolteacher, affiliated with the Communist Party, about how his right to free speech had been violated by the Buraku Liberation League. This mass organization is one of several that militate on behalf of a group of Japanese (perhaps 1 to 3 percent of the population) considered outcastes because their ancestors' occupations, often involving animal flesh (butchering, tanning) or death (execution, cleaning corpses), were considered defiling—the usual explanation being that they violated the Buddhist prohibition against taking life. Many of these people still live in virtual ghettos; there are always anxious moments for those seeking housing elsewhere or intermarriage with other Japanese, even though there is no racial or ethnic distinction. The persistence of pernicious discrimination has led liberation activists to develop a tactic known as denunciation, which has included such extreme forms as kidnapping alleged offenders and detaining them for prolonged verbal confrontation. The mainstream media and even the scholarly world rarely deal with Buraku activities, out of fear that mere mention might be regarded as discriminatory and invite denunciation. This taboo on discussion of the outcaste world has often been compared to the chrysanthemum taboo on critical discussion of the imperial family—which makes Harada Naō's controversial decision to include the teacher's letter sharply appropriate. In his letter, the former schoolteacher attributed his support for Mayor Motoshima to his own experience of undergoing Buraku denunciation. Now, one of the leaders of the Citizens' Committee to Seek Free Speech is explaining to me why it was wrong for Komichi to publish this letter. I seem to have stumbled to the brink of another abyss of festering wrongs and conflicting remedies. For now, I can only sip the barley tea produced from a refrigerator just big enough to keep a supply of that perennially refreshing Japanese summer drink.

My aunt and uncle's reception of us has exceeded all expectation. When I originally wrote to say I would be visiting Nagasaki because I wanted to meet the mayor, I planned to stay at a hotel so as not to burden them. Aunt wrote back immediately, ordering me to report to her house since there were "unknown elements" wandering in Kyushu who might kidnap and ship me off to North Korea. The timing of our visit is far from ideal. My aunt, like my grandmother, has never been much good in the heat, although she refuses to compromise in performing such tasks as cutting off every bloom from ten or so huge rose of Sharon bushes at the end of the day so that there will be nothing but fresh blooms the next morning. Moreover, I know both she and Uncle are tired from his recent move back to Nagasaki. Yet they are

gracious and accommodating, and in more than the normal
hostly ways. I am allowed to make, and even receive, calls at the
house. I venture to give Aunt an extra copy of the Citizens'
Committee booklet.

For the first time in years, I listen to Uncle talk at length. His
mode was and continues to be one of assertion, sustained by
abundant information flavored with the insights of experience.
And just as I have remembered it, the flow of knowledge is
punctuated with hearty laughter. Still, and as usual, I find myself
rebelling, against his assumptions more than his conclusions, but
as usual say nothing. I don't know how to challenge in any seemly
way the lifelong philosophy of an intelligent man who has been
devoted to me since I was seven. Uncle has just entered his sixties.
It is absurd for him to be retired, and yet I detect signs of an
unreluctant settling into retrospection.

But maybe I've always misapprehended him. In his late thirties
he was already speaking with the confidence of age and status—
of retrospection. Uncle's career was historically timed so that he
was not only able to contribute to the glorious crescendo of High
Growth Economics in Nagasaki, but also forced to orchestrate
its decrescendo—in other words, to manage the sad effects of
declining prosperity. On this visit he doesn't comment on what
I am trying to do, though once he breaks into pleasantly aimless
conversation with, "It's a good thing, what he did, after all." I
know that the course the mayor has set out upon is anathema to
the forces that governed my uncle's career. So again, I only nod
in assent. Or, peering out from his veranda at the houses perching
from the surrounding hillsides, so heedlessly carved out in spite
of perennial typhoons and mudslides, he observes, "I've been
asking myself if humankind isn't bent on destroying itself some
time, and sooner rather than later." I begin to wonder if the
confident, anticipatory retrospection I detected years ago wasn't
an antidote for early disappointment and alienation. Here, too,
the war had played a role. My uncle and his family stayed in

Tokyo through the inferno of the March 1945 fire bombings and on to surrender. He experienced the sudden intimacies that chaos brings and their equally swift dissolution at the first hint of normalcy. And most unforgettably, as the son of a community leader, he was constantly called on to help—as by burning, in a single day, forty-one corpses and distributing the ashes as best he could to family members. "You've no idea how long it takes to burn one human body," he has said to me. "It changes your view of life to burn forty-one bodies when you're seventeen."

In the meanwhile, Aunt produces an artifact representing the consistencies in her life: the iron my granduncle (across the street from my grandmother's house) gave her as a wedding gift thirty-five years ago. She expects me to use it to press the dress I will wear to see the mayor. The iron weighs at least five pounds. It is excruciating to use, and sparks fly from the connector, depending on the angle of the cord. I suggest retiring it, partly to give my aunt the pleasure of rebuttal. Nonsense, she says, just as I had hoped. It works precisely because it's so heavy. My sadly shrunken aunt still has spectacularly sinewy arms. The strength of a fool. She doesn't like the dress I'm wearing; she thinks it is too old and faded. Don't I have anything more reasonable? No; besides I'm comfortable in it. Well, at least soak it in starch. (As far as I can tell, neither my mother nor my aunt has accepted spray starch. A nightgown Aunt gave me retained its stiffness through three summers of American machine washing and drying.)

Nagasaki City Hall in late July of 1989 is a considerably more relaxed place than it has been in nearly eight months. The reason is that the director of a local hospital has just been arrested under suspicion of sending the mayor bullets along with notes threatening to kill him if he attended the emperor's funeral or refused to resign. This man is personally known to the mayor. Still, there are two plainclothesmen immediately outside the mayor's office. They will be there for some time.

The antechamber is full of Nagasaki artifacts. In the great Japanese leap onto the bandwagon of internationalism, Nagasaki at least has a claim to historical priority, for when the rest of the country was closed to foreigners for three centuries, a restricted group of Portuguese and Dutch traders maintained a continuous presence here. Indeed, Portuguese Jesuits were instrumental in the creation of a port and therefore the city itself in the late sixteenth century. Nagasaki was quickly enlivened by the comings and goings of Chinese as well as Portuguese and Dutch traders and missionaries. It became cosmopolitan, or exotic, long before Madame Butterfly watched Pinkerton sail off. Its exoticism derives some of its allure from the dark shadows of suffering, for the favorable policy toward Christians changed to one of ruthless suppression by the early seventeenth century. In Nagasaki many of those who neither recanted nor embraced martyrdom withdrew their faith from the public view and nurtured and transmitted it from generation to generation, accruing idiosyncrasies along the way. They are known as "Hidden Christians," and Mayor Motoshima comes from a family of such believers. It is also worth noting, as the mayor did on the occasion of the fortieth anniversary of the bomb, that outcaste villagers (Burakumin) were driven to undesirable, barren lands and charged with the task of spying on the Christians.[19] Thus have minorities been prevented from making common cause. I see that the mayor is adept at yoking issues of discrimination and militarism; his 1988 statement seems less and less accidental.

Motoshima Hitoshi turns out to be a small man with a shuffling gait and a prepossessing mumble. He opens our conversation

---

[19] Motoshima Hitoshi, "Hibaku 40nen, Sensō to Sabetsu no Teppai o Negatte" [Forty Years after the Bomb: In Hopes of Abolishing War and Discrimination], *Buraku Kaihō Nishi Nihon Kōza, Kōenshū* [Western Japan Buraku Liberation Lecture Series], vol. 10, edited and published by Buraku Kaihō Kenkyūsho (Osaka, 1985), p. 41.

with a reference to *The Mandarins*—you know, he says, that passage where the Sartre and De Beauvoir characters have just learned about the bomb. The headlines exude shrill triumph, but De Beauvoir's protagonists are horrified by the casualties: "Would they have dared to do this on a German city, on white people? But yellow people! They hate yellow people!"[20] I wish I could have shared with the mayor what I learned subsequently from conversation with an African-American friend, of how similarly she and her friends had reacted when they read the headlines in a New York subway. I appreciate the pointed subtlety of his choosing *The Mandarins* as a way to introduce the topic of the bomb with me, an American of the postwar generation whose alliances he has no reason to know. I know that in other contexts, when he wants to underscore Japanese aggression, he reminds his audiences that "there were people around the world who clapped when they heard about the bomb."

The other subject he raises at the outset is Prime Minsister Uno's sex scandals. He wants to know what I think bothers Japanese women the most about it. As I embark upon a multi-claused discussion, he cuts me short with the air of a man accustomed to making his points in a dozen words or less. "It's the money," he says. "If Uno hadn't paid her, as well as the others, women wouldn't be so furious." He is convinced that the woman question, generally speaking, represents a severe test for the Liberal Democratic Party. One month earlier, in response to a question from an assemblywoman, the mayor had agreed that a muncipal beauty contest degraded women by discriminating on the basis of age and marital status.

He stands and leads us—me and an assistant—into his office. The coffee table and the surrounding floor space are covered with piles of his current reading. Many of the books are about the emperor system. I have read that he resents having to devote

---

[20]Simone de Beauvoir, *Les Mandarins* (Paris: Gallimard, 1956), p. 221.

himself to this subject when he has been engaged in a different reading program concentrating on death.[21] I can finally broach the topic at hand.

I suggest that he must be relieved, referring to the recent arrest.

> *I'm sick and tired of this. Kids have to study so they'll know what to do when they grow up. What I need to be studying now is how to die.*

How long have you been concerned with death?

> *A while.*

A while?

> *Well, I was born in 1922. It's about time I thought about it.*

He rattles off the names of writers he has been reading, specifying that one of them is a Protestant. His schoolboy habit of memorization has evidently left him with innumerable catalogs covering subjects of interest, as well as thousands of lines of poetry, Chinese-era names, and of course, biblical passages.

> *American medicine seems to be very advanced along these lines. Isn't the ultimate question for medicine—well, not so much medicine, maybe, but for the twenty-first century, whether people will be able to die with hope?*

What do you mean, hope?

> *Oh, when it comes to that, I'm a Catholic through and through. I just saw the Auschwitz exhibit. Why do human beings engage in war? Why do they kill each other more cruelly than beasts? Why must young lives be lost, and what kind of responsibility must they bear who steal those lives? Those young ones were granted the gift of life, but they couldn't live out their span. What are we to make of that? It's impossible*

---

[21]Kamata, "Mr. Motoshima Hitoshi," *Aera*, July 18, 1989, p. 56.

for me to think about these questions without referring to God who rules heaven and earth and who will judge all human beings. And remembering that we are commanded to love and respect strangers.

Such faith has sustained your thinking for a long time?

I suppose so. I was born on February 1 and baptized on that day. But nobody thought about registering me at the village office until February 20. That's my official birthday. So I like to say I was baptized before I was born.

Let's go back to death for a moment. I've been thinking about the still-common Japanese practice of not telling cancer patients the nature of their illness. Do you remember the court case in Nagoya earlier this year, where the bereaved daughter and husband of a woman who had not pursued any treatment because she hadn't been told of her cancer brought suit against the physician and the hospital, and the court held that it was the physician's prerogative to withhold such information? Not to mention Emperor Showa's cancer. I've begun to think that this practice is another form of the emperor system, so to speak. The reason everybody gives is that Japanese are too fainthearted to be told such distressing news, that patients would die needlessly of shock. I don't believe that anymore. I think it makes it easier for doctors to manage cancer patients if they don't have to tell them. They don't have to address their fears and anxieties. Cancer patients tend to suspect their condition anyway, and it's common enough for people who don't have cancer to worry that they do. Current Japanese practice precludes, forbids, the airing of these feelings even between the dying and their families.

Yes, you've got something there. Every book I read talks about how kind doctors and nurses are in America, how warm they are at the bedside compared to Japanese doctors. I suppose, because they're not going to be honest with you, Japanese doctors can't afford to get close to you. The same with nurses. They're afraid they might be asked for the truth. So even if they want to be kind, they end up holding back. Doctors here don't tell you much about the nature of your illness anyway, right? But when it comes to whether this practice should be changed, I don't know. I don't know if I'd want to be told myself if I had cancer, or whether I'd prefer just to have my wife and children know, and for me to be able to hang on to the hope of making a comeback till the end.

Do you recognize any benefits to this period of enforced confinement from society?

Well, this is July. It's getting long. But let's say, from the seventh of December to about the end of the month, I remember thinking, this is better. I'm glad to be living this protected life. I was so busy until then. My days were measured out to the last minute. And at night, there would be one, two, or even three parties I'd have to show up at. And I did it because I thought that was what mayors were supposed to do. All that came to an end. No more invitations. I was free to leave the office at five o'clock. I had time to think, and I could read. Well, there's never enough time for all the reading you want to do. It's been better for my health. You know, I'm rather fond of drinking. And if I get started, I'm apt to go over my limit even though I know it's not good for my health. And imagine, getting home before dark. I've never done that in my life. Japanese are said to spend less time at home than anybody in the world. I'd get home while there was still daylight, and I'd say to myself, look, it isn't dark yet. April 19 was my fortieth wedding anniversary. I've been able to talk to my wife of forty years.

Does your wife see merits to your confinement?

Haven't asked her. But it's got to be better to have somebody to eat with than to eat by yourself all the time. At least she's got somebody around now to complain to. She's got three complaints for every one of mine. But that's all right.

But still! If I want to go somewhere, I can't. It's knowing that I can't that's oppressive. I might not even want to go there, wherever it is, if I were free to go.

Don't you hope to preserve some of the benefits of this period even when you're freed?

I've gotten to the age when I really want time to think about what I'm doing. I want a new life, a renaissance! When I'm finally free, I expect I'll look back at this period and remember feeling constantly, vaguely oppressed, and that will accentuate my new freedom, make it palpable.

I ask you these questions because I've been thinking that we can't understand the usefulness of the emperor system today without connecting it to the reality of Japan as the premier economic power of the world and the requirements for staying in first place. How do you keep people convinced of the worth of working so hard throughout life? And especially for children, it's such uninteresting hard work. (The worst of it is, they don't even seem to mind anymore because all their friends are doing it, too.) Sometimes I think that Japanese education enslaves citizens by making them competent, whereas American education enslaves them by leaving them, probably making them, incompetent. In Japan the whole population's kept busy and out of mischief, even the kids. No doubt the capacity for sustained hard work has been fostered by older—some people would say traditional—methods of social control, in which the emperor system has played a crucial role. But most of the time the visible demands and rewards of economic success are so compelling that people don't need to refer to earlier values in order to be motivated. I'm not suggesting any of this ever becomes explicit. But if there's some sort of stress, brought on either by internal or external factors, so that people start looking for deeper meaning, then the emperor system can be very helpful by suggesting a whole set of values that seem worth sacrificing for. Crude tactics like the Education Ministry's new flag and anthem directives prepare the ground, so that when the time comes for the emperor system to be activated, it will have the desired effect. It guarantees enforcement of the state's needs, to a great extent coinciding with corporate needs, from war at one end of the spectrum to studying nineteen hours a day at the other, depending on the historical moment. The emperor system is useful even when it's in the background, as a reminder. How can you have a democracy in a system like this, when everyone's so tied in, when there's no possibility—literally, no time—for developing a critical spirit?

Democracy here isn't the democracy of America or the democracy of France, the democracy that developed under the banner of freedom and equality. It isn't the real thing. All right, if you're not going to let me say that, I'll just say it's not American-style or French-style democracy.

The way I've been thinking about this issue over the past several months is this: why wasn't it possible to avoid war? We all assume today that it wasn't possible. And I think that's true. Of course I was right in the middle of it, though I was among the youngest. There was something called Taishō democracy, during that brief period early in the century when liberal practices seemed to be gaining ground. I ask myself what that was about. There wasn't much development of horizontal, rather than vertical, hierarchical, relationships. Even if a great scholar said something important, it didn't reach a lot of people. And our intellectuals were too German, they were too exclusively interested in the abstract and the theoretical and didn't come up with much work that could help in concrete situations. So even though there were people

who were aware of the problems and who tried to act consci-
entiously, their efforts didn't spread or take root. I wonder if
that isn't what contributed to the state of affairs in which
everybody began to think of war as inevitable. We all thought
that going to war was the right thing to do.

You yourself felt no sense of resistance?

No.

Not even on account of your Christian background?

Of course they asked me who was greater, the emperor or
Christ. And of course, I didn't think the emperor was any
god. Where I grew up, on the Gotō Islands, religious education
was much more important than schoolwork. I really studied
the Bible. In that sense I probably have as much religious
training as European Christians. So I naturally wondered to
myself, how can anybody think of the emperor as a god? Right?
But everybody else did, so I wasn't going to deny it.

You had no intention of becoming a martyr.

Oh, I was young. No, of course I wasn't going to go around
saying, we don't need an emperor, he should be killed, etc.
And remember, by the time I got to high school—well, all
those books on Marx, for example, had disappeared.

So you didn't read Marx until you entered university.

Right. After I came back from the war and started school in
Kyoto. But don't forget. I'd been in the army. I'd forgotten
everything—German, English, math.

Your official degree is in engineering.

Yes. You know what I did, I just showed up at the office
window with a rucksack and asked—nervously—if I was en-
rolled, and they said I was, so I stayed.

What did you do in university?

I got involved in the student movement. I went around to the economics department or the literature department, picking and choosing, doing what I wanted. Never went to classes, really. Just made sure I knew what the professor looked like so I'd show up for the right exam.

Did you become a Marxist?

Yes, but I couldn't stick with it.

You never joined the party?

No. I'll tell you why. Apart from historical materialism, what sustains Marxism is a notion of justice having to do with the relations between oppressor and oppressed. I'm reading a book about how Christianity spread throughout the Roman Empire. Christians braved terrible persecution with the conviction that justice and morality were values bestowed by God, that they were the highest values governing human life. For someone like me, justice was essentially a Christian concept, to which Marxism seemed secondary. In the student movement at the university, I was the representative of the engineering department. I started an organization called Catholic Students of Kyoto University, which eventually spread all the way from Hokkaido to Kagoshima. It became the League of Catholic Students in Japan. It's still going.

That's quite an undertaking.

Well, I wasn't doing any studying. Even when I started school, there were hardly any books around. I read whatever I could get my hands on. Became a master of miscellany.

Hasn't that been useful?

Especially these days. Here, look at this issue [July 23] of the Weekly Yomiuri. It's the beauty contest business. I told them about the history of women's dress. There're two characteris-

tics, East or West, it doesn't matter. First of all, it's men who determine women's fashion. They want to make sure that they can grab women, which is why you get high heels and bound feet. Women can be stripped at a moment's notice. The straight, tight skirt was invented in 1601. Before that there was the corset. Women's clothes have always been designed to reveal the lines of their bodies. That's the work of men, too.

I admired your comment on the municipal beauty contest.

Oh, that. I think I have a sensitivity to discrimination because as a Christian I experienced it myself, growing up.

I'm impressed that you haven't forgotten your youthful difficulties, and that you remember them in the way you do.

You know I've talked a lot about the generation that came of age in the war. At the end of All Quiet on the Western Front, *Remarque writes about how, for the older generation, the people who were already grown when they went to war, who had homes and lives to return to, the war would seem like a bad dream in ten years' time. But for those who went in as adolescents, who sacrificed their youth to the war—they wouldn't be free of the war as long as they lived. That describes me. I'm still living the war. So there's that. Then there's the prejudice I experienced as a kid. Remember, I didn't really have a mother or father, and there was my grandfather with his problems.*

The mayor's grandfather was one of those unfortunate Christians persecuted in the early years of the Meiji era. As a boy of ten he was subjected to torture by "stone-hugging," in which the victim was made to sit on a stone slab, with legs folded under and kindling wood inserted between calf and thigh, and stone pestles were piled on the lap until the bones were crushed and the skin full of splinters. The young Motoshima Hitoshi remembers his grandfather hobbling around his blacksmithing shop.

This was in a hamlet of thirty households, all of Hidden Christian descent, on the Gotō Islands off the coast of Nagasaki. His mother, the grandfather's daughter, was a woman who was being educated to become "one who teaches," or an assistant to the priest, at parish expense. One of the conditions was that she not marry for five to six years. The mayor's father had his own boat and sold fish and watermelons at the big market in Sasebo. He already had a wife and children in a big hamlet the next village over, but he used to come over to the hamlet where the Moto-shima family lived (the mayor uses his mother's maiden name) because the catch was better. Motoshima Hitoshi's parents met but once. The baby who resulted was baptized as Ignatio Loyola. His father was driven from the village, and his mother had to give up her vocation. Still, she was relatively lucky since she was able to marry into another family before her baby was a year old.[22] Motoshima Hitoshi was left to grow up with his grand-parents and, later, an aunt.

Did you ever live with your mother?

Yes, after grade school.

You stayed on with her?

Only a year. I don't know if it would be the same in America. It was a special situation, you see, not like a regular parent-child relationship. My mother had other children by her husband. I left.

After leaving Gotō, the mayor worked as a newspaper boy, an office boy, an apprentice typesetter, a box crusher and disposer at a fish market, an apprentice smith, and a dentist's houseboy, going to school at night when he could and finally completing high school. This pattern of changing jobs continued even after graduation and marriage. First he taught high school in Nagasaki.

---

[22]Ibid., p. 54.

His subjects were English, Japanese, math, and science. Then, in the mid-fifties, he went to Tokyo as the secretary of a distant relation, Shirahama Nikichi, when he was elected to the parliament. (Shirahama rose to become minister of posts and telecommunications.) When he returned after four years, he taught at the night school he himself had graduated from, became a lecturer at a beauticians' academy and then at a junior college for naval construction.[23]

What was so great about moving from job to job?

> *Think about it. Nothing to tie you down. If they start making too many demands on you, you just say good-bye. Pack up and leave. Of course I never had much to pack. Two or three things to stuff in a rucksack. It doesn't add up, logically. Once, when I was working on a boat, I fell overboard and went drifting into the sea. And I'm still here. I had an uncle who wrote a will and attached it to a fishing weight. He was still young, but he had a wife and kids. He died in the war. I didn't have anyone to write a will for.*

Let me ask you something entirely different. Since the Japanese shipbuilding industry collapsed some years ago, you have arms production as the major industry of the city. For a peace activist, that puts you in a difficult spot. Even among your supporters there is criticism that you really haven't made much headway at home. How do you view this yourself?

> *In the census of 1925, Nagasaki was the largest city in Kyushu. By 1930 it was overtaken by Fukuoka. Today, Nagasaki ranks fifth in Kyushu, twenty-fifth nationally. Are politicians ultimately responsible for the economy, as is commonly thought? I don't think so. You can't force economic growth to take place. There have to be favorable circumstances. My figures are old, but ten years ago, 80 percent of available resources*

---

[23]Ibid., pp. 54–55.

were concentrated in financial institutions in fourteen pre-
fectures. What can one politican hope to do?

It's become increasingly apparent to me that peace activists or
ecology activists have to study economics. You always run up
against economic questions or objections, and without being able
to propose alternatives, it's impossible to be persuasive.

Of course. That's the greatest issue for peace movements today,
to confront economic questions. Everybody in the world wants
peace. But Japan is building up its weapons stockpile. So is
the United States. Excuse me, but in your country, even
university professors can make a living off the arms race, isn't
that right? It's worse than in Japan. Capitalist enterprises
always have to provide for self-perpetuation and expansion.
They've got to have bigger numbers to show this year than
last year. We've got the horror of the industrial-academic-
bureaucratic complex to contend with. Arms production, such
as the nuclear weapons industry, often becomes the center of
the economy. That's the hardest part. No one's figured out
how to change that dynamic.

Or how to shift the logic of expansion.

That's right. So it doesn't get you anywhere to call Mitterand
an idiot, for instance. You know the old phrase, merchants
of death. Well, what we've got today are governments of death.

Including the government of Japan?

Japan? It's everybody. France is the worst. Then there's West
Germany, the United States. People even making chemical
weapons. The minute the economy starts flagging, it's what
people turn to—the sure thing you can make a profit off.
When two enemies meet on the battlefield, the one with the
better weapons wins, right? So the frantic race goes on.

Japan's got to slow down, don't you think? Take wooden
chopsticks. Japan alone uses 540 million pair a year. I don't

need to be telling you this, but one of the biggest problems today is the gap between the developed and developing nations. Here's my favorite book [Susan George's How the Other Half Dies: The Real Reasons for World Hunger]. [24] *I've read it eight or ten times. Ninety percent of the population in developing countries are farmers, and one-third of them don't own any land. The population of Africa is 350 million, of whom 150 million are starving. The food eaten and thrown away in Japanese homes and restaurants would be more than enough to take care of such people.*

It's difficult to be aware of such facts in Japan. Can we go back a bit? Tell me about the Rising Sun organization that you headed until you were fired.

If you're going to be involved in peace movements, you have to decide whether you're going to go for breadth or quality. If you go for quality, you're going to spend time thinking about who the enemies of peace are. In Japan, for example, there is the peace envisioned by those who support the U.S.–Japan Security Treaty, and the peace of those who oppose it. My position is that both kinds of people must join hands and work together. The pace becomes very slow, but we have to work together. This may sound presumptuous, but people in positions such as mayor or governor have to try to educate the public. That's why I tell everybody I'd still like to head the Rising Sun Association. Why? I only see those folks once a year, on Foundation Day [February 11; the 1966 revival of a holiday established by the Meiji state to commemorate the installation of the legendary Jimmu as the first emperor]. Four or five thousand of them come together, and I give a speech. It's impressive, you know, big platform and all. I talk to them about patriotism. How it's about loving our homes, our par-

[24](Totowa, New Jersey: Roman & Allanheld, 1983).

ents, our history, and our traditions. Then I tell them it's
something our neighbors in Korea feel as well. The thing that
went wrong with Japan was that nationalism made us feel as
if we were a unique, chosen people. That's what led us down
the path of aggression. What I emphasize to them is that we
should love our own homes so that we can respect the homes
of others.

I wanted to stake my life on staying the course of rightist
tendencies. I wanted to turn the Rising Sun Association into
an organization that wouldn't engage in emperor worship,
that wouldn't fall for claims of Japanese superiority. I didn't
care what people said, or even if it was actually in my power,
but I wanted to do everything I could to make it into an
organization that would never again support war.

Any chances of your being reinstated?

None. But I haven't repented. I'd risk my life to turn the
Rising Sun flag into something acceptable to the world. The
reason I dwelled on Korea and China in my speeches is that
up to now the Japanese have only been interested in dealing
with rich people and scholars from the United States and
Europe. It's southeast Asia that should matter to Japan.

There's an economic Co-Prosperity Sphere in place today.

It's terrible. Where we used to conquer them with bullets we
now do it with the yen.

I wanted to ask you about situating the A-bombs in the context
of Japanese aggression.

I've been working on that for a while. The bomb has its roots
in problems going back to the Meiji era. I mean the problems
of Japanese aggression, especially the annexation of Korea in
1910. I'm trying to learn as much as possible about those
issues. What we can't lose sight of is that there were people
around the world who rejoiced when the bomb was dropped

on Hiroshima. So when I go to America, I say we did wrong in Pearl Harbor, you did wrong in Hiroshima and Nagasaki.

The statement you made last December was perfectly reasonable, even ordinary, and look what it brought about!

I still think it was unexceptional. I didn't want to be a hero, I didn't want to become the center of conversation.

Circumstances made a hero out of you quite independently of your will.

But I want to be done with it!

Of course, it's not up to you.

Sure it is. I can just quit.

No you can't. Being a hero isn't like other jobs.

I just won't stand for re-election. I'll go into hiding. I want to go traveling.

With a rucksack?

No, this time with a Samsonite suitcase on wheels. And hiking boots inside. You know, it's good to live in a place where you know everybody. But it would also be interesting to live in a place where you know no one.

Having spent this year in Japan, which I haven't done in a long time, I've been reminded of what a profoundly difficult place it is to live in.

Sure it is. You're always worried about embarrassing yourself, you spend your whole life worrying about what other people think.

And the act that takes the most courage is to say something awkward.

That's it.

In that sense you said the most awkward thing possible at an awkward moment.

> *I just said what I was thinking. Then there was that response, all those shocking reactions. But I wasn't stranded. But look, there's something that's annoying me. Here's a new book on the emperor system and the Showa era. It takes the position that people from around the country rose in my defense because they wanted to defend free speech. But that wasn't it. I talked about the emperor's responsibility for the war. The newspaper editorials, whenever they wrote about it, only talked about free speech.*

It's easier for people to handle if it's abstracted as a free speech issue. And by turning you into a hero, everybody, especially the media, expect you to do their work—fighting for free speech—for them.

> *But think of how it looks one step outside Japan. "Hirohito, 20 million; Hitler, 6 million." You know, back in the days of the war crimes trial, the* New York Times *wrote that one war criminal's seat was unoccupied, and that seat was the emperor's, but that only history would tell whether that was the right decision or the wrong one. So when a* Times *reporter came to interview me, I asked if that was what he'd come to talk to me about.*

I've been thinking that Americans haven't confronted their own war guilt.

> *True. Americans think about their own convenience. Though about the bomb, you can't argue with the reasoning that it was supposed to save a million American lives.*

But I wonder if it was really a question of a million American lives, or anticipation of the Cold War.

> *That can't be helped either. Look, I'm reading a new book*

about Magellan. Christians were so brutal, too. I can't be proud. If someone were to say to me, you Christians have been a barbarous lot, I couldn't deny it.

I'm trying to write the Peace Declaration for this year's anniversary. I usually try to write it myself. I have to pay attention to the sounds of the Japanese language. But eventually the words begin to smell like me. It's the smell of age.

Don't you refer to the 2.5 nonnuclear principles instead of the 3 of not manufacturing, possessing, or introducing nuclear weapons? What's the .5? Is it because the principle of refusing the introduction of nuclear weapons has been shown to be a lie?

Yes.

In 1981 former U.S. ambassador Edwin O. Reischauer created a furor by referring publicly to a discussion he had had eighteen years earlier with then-prime minister Ōhira on nuclear weapons aboard American vessels in Japanese waters. According to the terms of the U.S.–Japan Mutual Security Treaty, the United States government is supposed to "consult" the Japanese government before introducing nuclear weapons into Japanese territory, and since there have never been any consultations, the Japanese government has maintained that nuclear weapons have not been introduced. Official United States policy is to neither confirm nor deny the presence of nuclear weapons on vessels calling on Japanese ports. The policy continues, even though as recently as June of 1989, it was disclosed that in 1965 a fighter carrying a hydrogen bomb had rolled off the deck of the U.S. aircraft carrier *Ticonderoga* and sunk into the coastal waters of Okinawa.

The conservative members of the Nagasaki City Assembly had long resisted passage of a municipal "peace charter," which was finally passed in March of 1989—well after more than 1,350 municipalities nationwide had declared themselves to be nuclear-free zones. This tardiness is another indication of the ironies characterizing Motoshima's city: A-bomb victim and host, or perhaps parasite, to the arms industry. It is revealing that even such symbolic measures—the three nonnuclear principles have no legal standing—should encounter tenacious resistance. In Nagasaki's case, provisions for supplementing current government assistance for survivors were eliminated. And in mid-July, shortly before I met the mayor, the assembly refused to budget funds for seventy-seven signs to be placed throughout the city to explain the meaning of the new charter. The number was reduced to three.[25.]

The mayor reads out passages from his draft. Referring to the belief of many Japanese citizens that nuclear weapons have been introduced into Japan, he speculates, " 'Does the Japanese government fear that if it were to refuse entry to vessels it knows to be carrying nuclear warheads, the U.S.–Japan alliance would cease to function?' " To make sure I understand, he adds, "I'm being sarcastic." By referring to the "2.5 principles," the mayor is calling for an end to the fictional treatment of the nuclear issue.

Those blunt words about Japanese government hypocrisy were to be excised at the recommendation of the drafting committee. Instead, on August 9, 1989, the mayor would urge that the government (a) confer legal status upon the three nonnuclear principles of not manufacturing, possessing, or allowing the introduction of nuclear weapons; (b) pass the (supplementary) assistance bill; (c) provide comparable benefits to Japanese survivors living abroad and foreign survivors (such as POWs, missionaries, and Koreans): and (d) establish an international medical center for those exposed to nuclear tests and nuclear-reactor accidents in addition to the victims of Hiroshima and Nagasaki. By incorporating his modest phrase, "from Pearl Harbor to Nagasaki," the mayor, for the first time in a memorial peace declaration, would touch upon the issue of Japanese responsibility.

---

[25]*Yūkan Ehime*, August 1, 1989.

During the turmoil caused by your statement last December, the people who rose in your support tended to be ordinary citizens. Very few politicians had that sort of courage. Still, I think many of us were waiting to see if the head of the other A-bombed city would say something in solidarity. Why did the mayor of Hiroshima so expertly avoid supporting you?

Yes. Yes. If only he had said, "It's just as Motoshima says," then Japan might have turned into a different place. Don't you think so?

It's only recently that I've become alert to the differences between Hiroshima and Nagasaki. Of course, there's the memory of Christian repression in Nagasaki. I don't know if that's too remote to play a part today. But I also wonder if there isn't a second-city phenomenon, if it isn't that the citizens of Nagasaki have had a chance to develop a more critical instinct than the people of Hiroshima just because they've always been relegated to a secondary status.

Well, of course. The two bombs had a completely different meaning to begin with. It's possible to explain the Hiroshima bomb rather simply as a maneuver to speed up the end of the war. There're many factors you have to take into consideration in thinking about Nagasaki—not wasting money already expended on the Manhattan Project, anti-USSR strategy, interest in experimentation itself.

Maybe there's something else, too, at least about the mayoral relationship. A bit of an inferiority complex.

On Mayor Araki's part?

No. On mine. You see, Hiroshima and Nagasaki are in somewhat different situations. Two years ago we had a conference in Como, Italy—the World Conference of Mayors for Peace through Inter-City Solidarity. The mayor of Hiroshima is the president and the rest of us—from Hanover, Sacramento,

Volgograd, East Berlin, and Nagasaki—are all vice presidents. The mayor of Hiroshima was adamant about restricting discussion to nuclear disarmament. But you've got to remember, European cities were devastated in the last war. They wanted to talk broadly about antiwar activities. Seventy to eighty percent of the world's population live in cities today. It's natural for mayors to think about what we should be doing to protect our citizens. Of course, as the mayor of Nagasaki, I wanted to talk about nuclear disarmament, too. But we had to resolve this conflict, so I said okay, Nagasaki would take on the antiwar plank. You see, the mayor of Hiroshima and I were supposed to go before the U.N. General Assembly. He wasn't going to talk about anything besides nuclear disarmament. So I suggested a division of labor. People begin to wonder, does Hiroshima exist only for Hiroshima?

Although the young Motoshima Hitoshi was not in Nagasaki at the time of the bomb, he returned soon enough to witness the ravages.

You know, he always wants international conferences to be held in Hiroshima, to gather world executives there. Maybe that's a good thing. But I say, even if Hiroshima and Nagasaki stand on their heads, we haven't preserved one one-thousandth of the horror. There's nothing left of the atmosphere, even. So I never talk in those terms. I just say, please go ahead and have the meeting in Hiroshima. But it wouldn't be good for Hiroshima and Nagasaki to get into a fight.

My time's almost up, but let me ask you this: why did you join the LDP? Was it a pragmatic decision?

No, no. After I served as Shirahama Nikichi's secretary, I came back to Nagasaki. I didn't want to go into politics then. As you know, I became a schoolteacher. And joined the Socialist Party. Well, eventually, I got involved in local politics, got elected as an independent to the prefectural assembly. I'd been in for three years when a gubernatorial election came up, and Shirahama asked if I wouldn't join the LDP for his sake. So I thought then, there're socialists who remain socialists all their lives; then there're others who veer off. I decided I was one of the latter.

I thank him and wish him well.

I won't be talking about the emperor anymore.

Why not?

Don't want to be attacked. Besides, as long as I'm an elected official, I'm pledged to uphold the Constitution. And that means the symbolic emperor.

As I prepare to leave, he asks me to look at something in the antechamber. It is a large wall map resting on the floor. He asks me where it was made. I have to get down on the floor to decipher the fine print. It is a West German map.

There, that's enough, get up. You see how Japan isn't in the center of the map. Every Japanese world map has Japan in the middle, so I ask all my visitors to take a look at this one.

I think of how every American world map I have seen, like this German one, has Japan stuck at the right-hand edge.

Outside, the last severe rays of the afternoon sun fall on my back as I walk to the station. There, I look through the shops for gifts to take home. Everywhere there are samples of Nagasaki glass, perhaps the prettiest legacy of the Dutch presence. Fluted plates, vases, and best of all—for what is more intriguing than a transparent container?—shell-shaped dishes with matching lids in light pinks, blues, purples, greens, oranges. So irresistible, so utterly affordable, these enchantingly breakable, un-vulgar baubles afford a kind of pleasure that's now vanishing before the onslaught of Lucite, harsh colors, and licensed character imprints which raise prices threefold. I recall that one of Mayor Moto-shima's economic revitalization schemes is craft production—maybe Venetian glass. Why, I said, you already have glass here. But he wanted the real thing, complete with master glassblowers from Venice.

I struggle back laden with packages, including elaborate box lunches for dinner, purchased at an Aunt-approved store. She will be angry with me for walking from the streetcar stop instead of calling first and taking a taxi, but this is the last night of our visit, so I hope for clemency. Besides, I have a souvenir anecdote just for her.

"Do you know what the mayor did as I was leaving?"

"What?"

"Well, he looked me up and down, apologized, and asked if I had enough money to get home."

"What did I tell you? You should never have worn that dress."

"It's okay. I laughed—he was so apologetic—and told him I was fine."

Aunt burst out laughing, too, for the first time this visit.

The next day, Uncle calls a cab to send us to the station. Again he will guard the house while Aunt sees us off. She is in a frenzy to buy us the best box lunches before they are sold out. Having succeeded, she prepares to collapse into a chair in the air-conditioned waiting room. My aunt is not a woman who does anything casually in public. She scrutinizes the available seats. It is just two days before the upper house elections, and she finds a stack of fliers on the seat in front of her. Not having her glasses, she summons me to read the message, which turns out to be a vicious, possibly slanderous attack upon a local progressive woman candidate. Aunt orders me to take the entire stack and dispose of it in the garbage bin.

Once the train comes, she accompanies us into our car so she can be sure my thirteen-year-old daughter will be safe as well as comfortable. Back out on the platform, she waves, even running after the train, until we can no longer see her.

As the memorial month of August begins, Mayor Motoshima is almost never out of sight. His is the only politician's name to appear on a statement calling for official apologies by the Japanese government to Korea and the Korean people.[26] His promise of reticence notwithstanding, he expresses regret that the new emperor failed to touch on the war during his first press conference. I hear that the mayor has told the police he doesn't care anymore, he would rather they suspend their protection, but that the police tell him it isn't for him to decide. Every time he makes a statement, there is always the possibility of an attack. His own campaign committee has lost patience with him. He is a politician with a thirty-year career whose constituency has been unrecognizably transformed in eight months.

In late August, as the flurry of anniversaries passes, boat people from Vietnam crowd into Nagasaki. The official reception center in neighboring Ōmura City overflows, and Mayor Motoshima opens up Nagasaki City facilities. In the meanwhile, the national government has determined that a number of the purported Vietnamese are actually Chinese coming not for political asylum but for economic opportunity. Again, the mayor speaks out: given the recent situation in China, as well as the unemployment figures throughout southeast Asia, Japan as an economic power has a humanitarian obligation to at least try to accommodate such people. Such statements are of course unwelcome, as the chief cabinet secretary promptly makes clear by asserting that "national policy is different."[27]

---

[26]Paid advertisement, *Asahi Jānaru*, August 11, 1989, p. 75.
[27]*Asahi Shimbun*, International edition, December 5, 1989.

In mid-September the mayor is confronted with an unusual set of events. Since 1974, the city has maintained a policy of not allowing warships from countries deploying nuclear weapons to call on its ports, and none in fact has, until a U.S. naval frigate arrives on September 15 for purposes of "friendship" and rest-and-recreation for the crew. Prefectural police prevent demonstrators, representatives of bomb survivors' organizations, from approaching the ship. When the ship's commander, Peter Roberts, pays his courtesy call on the Mayor, the latter asks for evidence that the *Rodney M. Davis* is not carrying nuclear weapons. Citing U.S. policy, Commmander Roberts refuses to reply, adding, however, that the terms of the Mutual Security Treaty are being faithfully adhered to and that he "understands the feelings of the citizens."[28] To demonstrate as much, he proceeds to the Peace Park to lay a wreath, even though Mayor Motoshima declines to escort him. There, as soon as he leaves, the wreath is trampled to pieces by a group of survivors and families, some of them carrying portraits of their dead. The mayor calls this act a breach of courtesy and apologizes to the U.S. naval command in Japan while stating that he also sympathizes with the survivors. The latter turn their fury on him, demanding to know who committed the graver discourtesy. (Their organization had sent word in advance to the U.S. consulate in Fukuoka requesting that Commander Roberts refrain from visiting the Peace Park.) The prefectural police consider charging the tramplers with vandalism. The mayor makes clear he will not join. Commander Roberts, in the meanwhile, finds the situation regrettable, but declares that his "feeling of friendship" for the people of Nagasaki City has not been damaged.[29]

---

[28]*Tokyo Shimbun*, September 16, 1989.
[29]*Tokyo Shimbun*, September 17, 1989.

The *Rodney M. Davis* episode reads like an event from my girlhood. It stirs an atavistic anti-Americanism in me, the kind I felt as I rode the chocolate-colored buses to the base school and tried madly to eliminate all traces of Japaneseness from my person and my tongue. I suppose Commander Roberts is too old and too senior to chew gum, but his avowals of friendship for the people of Nagasaki (I can even hear the accent) remind me of all the American boys in uniform in 1950s Tokyo. Like everybody else around the world, I loved American dresses and bobby socks and fruit cocktail. But my sympathies were indubitably, passionately with the short Japanese men in ill-fitting trousers, the women in made-over coats if they were lucky, the scrawny cats with bobbed tails. I don't understand the *Rodney M. Davis* incident—who planned it, and to what end. The clumsy American arrogance stirs up a tenderness for the unluxurious Japanese past that I can't repress, but knowing what it led to strips it of its innocence and makes nostalgia grotesque. As I sit in the glacial cold of Chicago this winter of 1989, watching the Panamanian venture unfold, a kaleidoscope forms in my mind, of the camera-toting boys of my childhood Tokyo, of the boys arriving in Okinawa from Vietnam in black plastic bags, of the newly dead ones going into Arlington.

"We're hearing nothing but news about Panama and Rumania," my grandmother says. Fighting anywhere in the world makes her anxious. You never know when it'll stop, whom you'll end up hurting, she thinks. And besides, having the Pacific Ocean between us, at her age, means that all talk about the "next time" we see each other includes an unvoiced question mark anyway, without the added uncertainties of war.

Now, at this waning of the year, my grandmother will be busy cooking for the New Year. Every one of her four burners will hold a simmering pot for my aunt next door and her family.

These burners are usually kept scrubbed as clean as possible, with allowances for failing eyesight and, this past year, the desire to produce—yet again—enticing feasts for granddaughter, grandson-in-law, great-granddaughter, and great-grandson. Behind them, there's a precarious, somewhat disorderly array of pots and pans arranged for swift, unseeing access. In this season, with the tamarind vines bare against the windows, the sun floods the room in the mornings. An old-fashioned, stiff-bristled scrubber and triangular garbage catcher are settled neatly in the sink corner. A suction-pump Thermos justifies its hugeness with the promise of water hot enough for tea at all hours. The cabinet doors underneath conceal items such as the steamer purchased just in time as the metal-greedy Pacific War snatched all kitchen implements from store shelves; and stately jars of fruit wines, dated and labeled "plum," "mandarin orange," or even "Chinese quince" in an unexpectedly masculine hand, opened only when we descend from across continent and Pacific. My grandmother's house is animate with her energy, her always-radiating kindness. Early in the morning, before it was quite light, it would vibrate through the floorboards to the room I occupied for a year with my husband. No science lesson could demonstrate so convincingly for me that sound travels in waves: my grandmother's exchanges with my mother, perhaps weighing this or that choice for our children's lunch, would lose all syllabic distinction and brush my flesh as sensation.

I can't taste her New Year's feast this year. She would laugh and protest, earnestly too, if she heard me calling it a feast. I can't make anything, just the same old things, she would say, standing at the stove, stirring, stirring, whether tired, sick, or as happens most often, worry-filled—over fading business, distant grandchild, worm-eaten tree, slandered Socialists, ailing goldfish, leaking roof, barbarous husband, wrong-sized beans: so much care cooked into a pot, rising in the steam and into our nostrils, infecting us in turn with attachment to the world.

EPILOGUE

SUMMER 1990. Tokyo. The two items in the news are the death of a high school student caused by a teacher enforcing rules against tardiness and the wedding of Emperor Akihito's second son to a "commoner." The girl was just three months into her first year of high school, about to be tardy for the first time. The teacher was preoccupied with his countdown as he pulled the heavy steel gate across its tracks and didn't notice or couldn't stop as he crushed the girl's skull between the gate and post. The school washed out the blood and didn't call the police. In an assembly the next day, the principal suggested to the students that if they were more mindful of school rules, their teachers wouldn't have to be so preoccupied. One of those teachers urged the students to study even harder for the upcoming tests so that they could make up for the points their dead classmate wouldn't be earning.

The case did provoke a degree of discussion and even reflection

on the probability that it represented but the proverbial tip of the
iceberg. Still, most of the citizenry preferred to be entertained
by the wedding. The new princess is an alumna and the daughter
of a professor at Gakushūin University, the former Peers' School
once open only to members of the imperial family and the ar-
istocracy. She is a great smiler; it is said that her father, the
professor, presciently trained her to smile to the camera from her
earliest days. Having spent some part of her childhood abroad,
moreover, she usefully conveys the image of the International
Person. The ceremony has been marketed by the media as the
"royal wedding," the product as the "royal couple." The foreign
phrasing adds thrill to the putatively ancient and therefore exotic
traditional rites. It also puts the Japanese monarchy on at least
equal footing with European royalty, possibly higher, since it
possesses the paraphernalia of both Western pomp and circumstance and Oriental mystery.

In any case, the distraction of the wedding has been more than
sufficient to dispose of such residual skepticism as there was from
the imperial funeral. The public was primed to relish young
romance (the young prince couldn't wait for his older brother,
the crown prince, to be properly married first, or even to sit out
the year of mourning for his grandfather before having his be-
trothal recognized) and to absorb the image of an ever more
democratized and appealing imperial family. The Imperial
Household Agency's displeasure over a photograph showing the
young princess brushing a stray lock from the prince's forehead,
a displeasure that led to the photographer's dismissal from the
ranks of the officially approved, has only contributed to the couple's popularity. Each day brings new accounts of provincial
journeys through cheering throngs; inspection tours of museums
with the prince in the lead, peering into display cases, and the
princess following, looking exhausted; or back at their residence,
a regimen of jogging for the princess with her husband following
on bicycle.

The new princess is reproduced many times over as young women on Tokyo subways adopt pastel dresses and shoulder-length hair flowing from beribboned hats. They are doing their part to make it absurd to bewail the plight of the Constitution as preparations are made, with taxpayer money, for an astronomically costly drama in two acts, secular and religious: namely, the consecration of Akihito as emperor. In retrospect, the funeral was a rehearsal for this supreme imperial ritual, strategically located at harvest time, potent reminder to Japanese of their roots in rice rather than electronics even if the financial burden of the rite falls more heavily on the culture of electronics than of rice. Both funeral and ascension exemplify that fraught moment when the contradictory elements of modern statehood—the dreary requirements of rationality and the dangerous allure of myth—threaten to erupt and produce a chasm in the insouciant surface of routine. The Japanese government has expediently sought to reconcile the irreconcilable by juxtaposing the secular and the religious, placating demands for fidelity to an irretrievable past on the one hand and insistence on observance of constitutional rights on the other, all the while avoiding sacrifice of economic interests.

Even if this strategy serves to postpone—perhaps forever—sustained reflection on questions that engulf us all at the end of the twentieth century, it is insufficient to prevent those who seek other, more immediate remedies to the discomfort of modern uncertainty from inflicting harm upon others. Lulled by the wedding, harried by oppressive routine, people hardly remember the assassination attempt on Mayor Motoshima in January of 1990, even though at the time it filled the pages of the newspapers and dominated TV screens. The whole country was in favor of safeguarding free speech then, even those conservative legislators who had busied themselves with criticizing the mayor at the time of his statement. (The young ladies in pastel don't worry about what it means to have the media engineer one of their own into a different species through honorific language deployed with more

relentless uniformity than thirty years ago, when another "commoner," the current empress, married into the imperial family.)

The Motoshima shooting took place approximately one month
after police protection for the mayor had been lifted, partially in
response to conservative assemblymen's complaints about taxpayer expense. It was also shortly after the end of the year of
mourning for Emperor Showa. A member of a rightist organization took close aim from behind as the mayor prepared to leave
City Hall for a dentist's appointment. The bullet passed through
his lungs. The mayor vomited blood, then sat quietly in the
backseat of the car to wait for the ambulance. When it came,
he laid himself down on the stretcher. In springtime, in a letter
of thanks to those who had supported him through this trial, he
attributed his relative calm while awaiting death to the faith
inherited from his Hidden Christian ancestors.

In July of 1990, I traveled to Nagasaki once more to visit the
mayor. I had read that he had fully recovered from his wound.
His gait seemed slower, but what startled me was an aura of frailty
utterly absent one year ago. I realized with chagrin how the
public, political aspects of assassination had made me forget that
it was also a murder attempt upon a vulnerable, irreducible individual. My own response had been analogous to the media's;
I hadn't thought of how shattering it would be to experience a
hatred sufficient to rob you of life.

The mayor's old drollness was still detectible in such decla-
rations as, "Well, some days I tell myself I can't give in, I've got
to stand firm, but most of the time I go around scared." He was
spending more time in prayer: perhaps, he told himself, the attack
was meant as a reminder of the preciousness of life. He had
dearly reclaimed such simple words from the realm of cliché.
His renewed appreciation of life wasn't all somber, for that ir-
repressible pleasure in listing resurfaced as he enumerated boyhood activities he was recounting in a book: knocking off a crow's
nest from the tallest tree in the mountain, catching fish with his

bare hands, rescuing a still-living worm from ants trying to haul it off. Yet, at the end, his voice trailed into a question, and he looked up with earnest hesitation: "Writing this stuff isn't going to do the world any good, is it?"

Even so, in his peace declaration of August 9, 1990, Mayor Motoshima made his most forceful demand yet for both apologies and financial assistance by the Japanese government to foreign victims of the bombs. His words carried the weight of a consistent position now held at risk. By contrast, Mayor Araki of Hiroshima's appeal to human rights in his anniversary message rang hollow: a memorial to Korean victims of the bomb was still kept outside the Hiroshima Peace Park, leaving Koreans brought over as slave laborers as segregated in death as in life. This year the stone marker almost crossed the boundary into the park, except that a municipal commission appointed to facilitate the process insisted on the removal of all reference to the forced displacement and corvée from the inscriptions. Evidently the Hiroshima Peace Park is to be kept pure in its dedication to the suffering of Hiroshima.

On August 9, Mayor Motoshima appeared to have shed his fatigue and to have recovered his characteristic public tone, firm, without a trace of bombast. Friends tell me that since then, he has once again seemed to be strained and subdued. Nevertheless, following intense deliberation, he announced plans to run for a fourth term in 1991. He is now sixty-eight. He has lost his conservative support base. He may gain the official recognition of Socialists and independent progressives, but that remains to be seen.*

Mayor Motoshima's quest for a renaissance began with the dying emperor, and all but inevitably brought him to the brink

---

*On April 21, 1991, Mayor Motoshima won a difficult victory in his bid for a fourth term.

of his own death. So it will continue into the foreseeable future, as there is no prognosis for his freedom. It is a lonely renaissance, spurred by the recognition that he can do very little, but that perhaps only he can do it.

The fact of death makes possible daring reflection, imagination, and action in life. Surely Emperor Showa made his great, unwilling contribution in the form of his slow dying. I, too, am a beneficiary, inasmuch as these essays began from a chance encounter with a poem prompted by that dying, the poem which opens this book. Chong Chuwol, a Korean-Japanese woman, borrowed the words "thou needst not die" from a pacifist poem composed in 1904 on the eve of the Russo-Japanese War by Yosano Akiko, a celebrated Japanese woman poet, and twists them slyly to urge the emperor to prolong his dying so that he might achieve the humanity denied by his identity either as pre-war deity or as postwar symbol. The sadistic demand has a utopian dimension. As he sinks into death, Chong implies, the Japanese emperor may yet attain an incipient humanity acknowledging mutuality with the dead Korean laborer, whose own humanity was denied by the imposition of a Japanese identity masquerading as the privilege of becoming the emperor's own babe, just like other Japanese. It was, however, an invitation to slave labor and death, and those who survived found that only those born as the emperor's children could become citizens in the new Japan; the adopted colonial subjects were promptly abandoned.

Now, the world pitches in uncertainty before the Persian Gulf crisis. We live intimately with the possibility of death; indeed, thanks to the electronic media, too familiarly to be properly fearful. Trivializing death makes us devalue life, especially that of fellow humans we refuse to acknowledge.

The discussion across the Pacific has been reduced to American irritation with Japanese contributions to its willful arabian extravaganza. America's leaders display a self-interested blitheness about a life-sustaining constitutional fiction. For its part, the

Japanese government, successful in its own cynical management of Article 20 forbidding state participation in religious activities, has also been moved to reconsider the fiction of Article 9, which prohibits the deployment of military forces. That the "no-war" clause has proved instrumental to Japanese prosperity (to the annoyance of Americans who must curse themselves for the existence of that clause) does not diminish its worth as a modest resource for renouncing war as a solution to human problems. The fictionality of fiction veers in two directions, toward imaginative reconfiguration of the world on the one hand and shameful fraudulence on the other: fiction as dream and fiction as deception. Article 9 today is the source both of dreams for a world without violence and of deception about massive "Self-Defense" Forces. A perilous debate has emerged in Japan over whether it isn't time, finally, to jettison this fiction. It is perilous because those who would rectify the absurd deception of "undeployable military forces" by disbanding them will most certainly be outnumbered by those who would simply replace it with the reality of a powerful army, navy, and air force.

We can't afford to abandon our dreams of a world arranged otherwise in the name of a mature realism that can only prove deadly. At this hour it is more pressing than ever to pay heed to the words, "Thou needst not die—just yet," and to dedicate ourselves to a renaissance we can neither attain nor relinquish.

October 1990

A POSTSCRIPT ON JAPAN BASHING

PASSPORTED FROM BIRTH at the embassy of the United States of America (a country where I had yet to set foot), finger-printed from childhood for the Alien Registration card required by the government of Japan (the only country I knew), I developed early on a certain skepticism about the appeals of that entity known as the nation-state. When I was taunted by American kids at school and Japanese kids at home for being whatever they were not, my mother would say consolingly, "When you grow up, you'll find that people won't care whether you're American or Japanese." Sometimes she would say defiantly, "What's so important about citizenship?" She was worried to death about a regulation that stipulated five years of continuous residency on American soil for children of U.S. citizens born overseas. It would be another decade before the Supreme Court struck that down for discriminating against a certain class of U.S. citizens; still longer before Japanese women who, like her, had married foreign nationals, could transmit the privileges of Japanese citizenship to their children. (Needless to say, Japanese men marrying foreigners have always been able to sire legally Japanese children.)

My mother was both right and wrong. She was mostly right about people living in cosmopolitan societies in peaceful, prosperous times. For them, citizenship—or as it's more immediately experienced, nationality (blurring easily and dangerously into ethnicity and finally, inevitably, race)—doesn't much matter. But civilization is a thing of luxury. When times get hard, most of us grow impatient with abstract explanations and need tangible people to blame.

It's easy to confuse attachment to a place and people, and more subtly, to a language, with patriotism. They may overlap, but they're not the same, contrary to what flag-wavers the world over would have us believe. There are institutions that, intentionally or not, promote such confusion. International athletic competitions are enormously effective. In the 1970s I happened to be in Central Park when the leading runners for the New York City Marathon came in. To my surprise, I found myself moved, nearly to tears, to recognize a Japanese runner in the pack. Some people had rising sun flags. I had nothing to wave. Tardily and inaudibly, I cheered the runner in Japanese. Nearly a decade had passed since the Tokyo Olympics, and I was still thinking of Japanese as underdogs in the world arena. Besides, I missed speaking the language, achingly. For such a miscellany of sensations, the flag is always a convenient, and too often a deadly, simplifier.

One summer ago, I was in a Tokyo department store with American friends awaiting the opening of a special exhibit in which they were involved. The husband wore a rising sun pin in his lapel. In the eerie setting of the still-closed store, the clerks began to perform mandatory exercises to a recording of instructions aired for decades by the national broadcasting corporation. My friend joined in. I knew he was a firm believer in "buying

American" with his automobiles, but there was no questioning the sincerity of these gestures of friendship. I wanted to explain to him how his choice of symbols was making me squirm, how oppressive the rising sun was for some Japanese for reasons he would care about. But the symmetry of his expressions, and their apparent harmlessness—loyalty to his own nation and good will to another, a former enemy at that—discouraged me from trying.

This spring, at an international conference in Europe, I delivered a paper on Japanese children in which I cited Japanese statistics about the high incidence of elevated levels of cholesterol in the blood of grammar-school-aged children. A Japanese expert, in an obviously choleric state, rose to attack my presentation. He wanted, for instance, to suggest that high blood cholesterol was caused by broiler chickens from America. He finished off by warning that no one who had spent less than three years in Japan should be talking about it.

My friends said indignantly, "Why didn't you tell him you grew up there, that you're half Japanese?" Because, I would say, I don't want to legitimate my arguments with such claims. And practically speaking, if that gentleman had realized I was half Japanese, he would have been even more dismissive.

Here, the practical and the substantive had more in common than might be apparent. The Japanese expert's demand, that one have some firsthand knowledge of one's subject, is unexceptionable. But his fury suggested more. It issued from the fact that my presentation was critical. Of what? I was concerned with certain aspects of Japanese society today, with certain practices, mainly in the educational sphere, and I was interested in thinking about how these exemplified tendencies in advanced capitalist societies generally. I am reasonably confident that my interlocuter did not hear me in this way; rather, he took me to be attacking "Japan," and specifically, "the" Japanese. If only I were more familiar with "Japan," I would not be so critical. Better yet, if I were so familiar as to actually *be* Japanese, I would understand everything and not be critical at all—these are the presumptions I heard behind his anger.

To such a charged identification of legal, genetic, and spiritual nationality, an appeal of half-authenticity is worse than useless. It is, moreover, precisely that interlocking of the legal, the genetic, and the spiritual—being Japanese means having Japanese blood means being a citizen of the nation-state called Japan means feeling Japanese—that creates a vise on the many different kinds of people inhabiting the archipelago. But let me also add unequivocally: this set of equations can be found anywhere in the world, to more and less unpleasant effect, depending on the status and nature of the state sustaining it.

Who has the right to criticize a society? Only its own citizens, supposing they are not caught in the vise such that they are blinded to or silenced from expressing their oppression? But prior to that, what are the principles justifying criticism? Both the phenomenon called Japan bashing and its critical discussion are often motivated by economic interest. Those who, with little or no security, have suffered the effects of American economic decline, particularly in areas with a Japanese presence, have understandably been most visible in the activity of bashing. They have been abetted by politicians who purport to be their leaders and by corporations competing badly with Japanese enterprises, some of which have in notable instances abandoned their own American bases for cheaper offshore production. On the other hand, many who criticize bashing are also those with an economic interest in maintaining friendly ties with Japan. Civility has often, if not usually, depended on the mutuality of economic interest. It is too late in the day to begin complaining about that.

What is more complicated is the position of those who, with indisputable sincerity and considerable legitimacy, consider the United States to be a society bent on dominating the world and prone to racism while so doing, who deem any criticism of Japan to be tantamount to bashing. Racism indubitably continues to poison American life, but not all criticism of Japan is racist. To maintain that is to fall in line with a racialized Japanese nationalism. Surely we need a place to stand, beyond the boundaries of the nation-state and the close horizon of economic interest, where we can ask, what are the conditions conducive to just and meaningful lives for human beings at the end of the twentieth century? In posing that question, we must necessarily delineate the obstacles confronting us both in specific societies and in their relationship to each other.

Ironically enough, my first reaction to the remark on "broiler chickens from America" was one of shame—on behalf of "Japan." Here's another Japanese male behaving insensitively on an international stage, I thought, regretting it for all my friends, for all the tenderness, the erudition, the stern self-examination that I had encountered in my own history of that society. Perhaps my regret stemmed from a confusion analogous to that experienced nearly twenty years ago in Central Park. But I realize that I have been neglecting quite a traditional motivation for criticism, namely, attachment. In writing this book, I was sustained by my admiration for and sympathy with people who found themselves at odds with Japanese society as they were experiencing it. I was attached to them and to the idea of a society different from the one currently silencing them. Attachment can come from birth and literal kinship, shared experience, intellectual empathy, or sheer fantasy. It doesn't guarantee the quality of the criticism, its rightness, but it can explain why one bothers to criticize a structure, a set of practices, in the first place. Bothers, that is, for reasons other than or in addition to economic concerns, which I do not mean to dismiss inasmuch as economic well-being is essential to our capacity to think, to give and take pleasure, to live humanly.

To reduce all criticism of Japan to bashing is to congeal a complex of people, places, food, cars, movies, gestures, longings into a rigid singularity, "Japan," populated by "the" Japanese. Ditto for America. It kills the possibility of declaring a complicated love.

June 1992